D1376322

Organizational Behaviour

Edited by:
Raisa Arvinen-Muondo and
Stephen Perkins

ANDOVER COLLEGE
STUDY CENTRE
658·3
ANDOVER COLLEGE

KoganPage

LONDON PHILADELPHIA NEW DELHI

Publisher's note

Every possible effort has been made to ensure that the information contained in this book is accurate at the time of going to press, and the publishers and authors cannot accept responsibility for any errors or omissions, however caused. No responsibility for loss or damage occasioned to any person acting, or refraining from action, as a result of the material in this publication can be accepted by the editor, the publisher or either of the authors.

First published in Great Britain and the United States in 2013 by Kogan Page Limited

Apart from any fair dealing for the purposes of research or private study, or criticism or review, as permitted under the Copyright, Designs and Patents Act 1988, this publication may only be reproduced, stored or transmitted, in any form or by any means, with the prior permission in writing of the publishers, or in the case of reprographic reproduction in accordance with the terms and licences issued by the CLA. Enquiries concerning reproduction outside these terms should be sent to the publishers at the undermentioned addresses:

120 Pentonville Road	1518 Walnut Street, Suite 1100	4737/23 Ansari Road
London N1 9JN	Philadelphia PA 19102	Daryaganj
United Kingdom	USA	New Delhi 110002
www.koganpage.com		India

© Raisa Arvinen-Muondo and Stephen Perkins, 2013

The right of Raisa Arvinen-Muondo and Stephen Perkins to be identified as the authors of this work has been asserted by them in accordance with the Copyright, Designs and Patents Act 1988.

ISBN   978 0 7494 6360 1
E-ISBN   978 0 7494 6361 8

British Library Cataloguing-in-Publication Data

A CIP record for this book is available from the British Library.

Library of Congress Cataloging-in-Publication Data

Perkins, Stephen J.
   Organizational behaviour : people, process, work and human resource management / Stephen Perkins and Raisa Arvinen-Muondo.
      p. cm.
   Includes bibliographical references.
   ISBN 978-0-7494-6360-1 – ISBN 978-0-7494-6361-8   1. Organizational behavior.
2. Personnel management.   I. Arvinen-Muondo, Raisa.   II. Title.
   HD58.7.P4626 2012
   658.3–dc23
                                                                                    2012037106

Typeset by Graphicraft Limited, Hong Kong
Printed and bound in India by Replika Press Pvt Ltd

CONTENTS

05   Leadership, communication and organizational effectiveness   127

Linda Holbeche

06   Talent management   155

Raisa Arvinen-Muondo and Qi Wei

PART FOUR Shifting contexts for organizational behaviour 181

**10   Creativity, innovation and the management of
knowledge**   265

Pauline Loewenberger

PART FIVE Summation and reflection   293

11   Coda: HRM and OB – accenting the social   295

Stephen Perkins and Raisa Arvinen-Muondo

LIST OF FIGURES AND TABLES

Figures

Tables

CONTRIBUTORS

Raisa Arvinen-Muondo works in the area of office administration and HR management in Luanda, Angola. Raisa has undertaken doctoral research at the University of Bedfordshire and is an experienced intercultural resource consultant. Her expertise lies in human resource development in Africa. She has co-authored event reports and conference papers and is an experienced presenter at practitioner and academic conferences. She has also taught OB and HRM at postgraduate level and works with clients in the oil industry consulting on Angolan history, politics, economy and culture.

Faten Baddar Al-Husan is a senior lecturer in HRM at the University of Bedfordshire with a PhD for a study of the processes of human resource reform introduced by French multinationals in privatized Jordanian companies. Her principal research interests are in multinationals' strategies and policies; cross-border mergers and acquisitions; change management, cross-cultural and international management, and key account management. Dr Baddar's work has appeared in a number of journals including the *International Journal of Human Resource Management* and *Thunderbird International Business Review*.

Caroline Bolam is a senior lecturer in human resource management (HRM) at the University of Bedfordshire. She has over 10 years experience working in HRM, up to Business Partner level. In January 2011 Caroline started a PhD, a qualitative study of how academic 'performance' is influenced by 'managerialism' in higher education in the UK.

Philip Davies is a former senior lecturer in strategy and general management at undergraduate and postgraduate level at the University of Bedfordshire. He is an experienced teacher and has run programmes throughout Europe and the Middle East for companies and for postgraduates. He consults for private and public sector organizations up to board level. Prior to joining the University of Bedfordshire Phil taught strategic management at Cranfield School of Management and was a senior manager in the NHS. His first career was as an officer in the

Intelligence Corps with service in Hong Kong, Germany and Northern Ireland. His current research interests are on how strategy happens in practice. He has also published articles on the link between social networks and innovation as well as how business strategy relates to military strategy.

Linda Holbeche is an established author, commentator, consultant, developer and a thought and practice leader in the fields of leadership, HRM and organization development. Linda has previously been Director of Research and Policy at the CIPD, of Leadership and Consultancy at the Work Foundation and Research and Strategy at Roffey Park. Currently Visiting Professor at Cass, Bedfordshire and Imperial College Business Schools, Linda is also Fellow at Roffey Park, and the UK Commission for Employment and Skills, Associate at Ashridge and Erasmus Business School. Recent books include *HR Leadership* (2009), *Aligning HR and Business Strategy* (2009) and *Organisation Development: A practitioner's guide for OD and HR* (with M-Y Cheung-Judge, 2011) and *Engaged* (with G Matthews, 2012).

Janice Johnson is a senior lecturer in HRM at the University of Bedfordshire, teaching on undergraduate and post-graduate programmes. She has been involved in teacher training as subject strand leader on the PGCE (14–19) Applied Business Programme for a number of years. She is a fellow of the Chartered Institute of Personnel and Development as well as a Fellow of the Higher Education Academy. Research, conference papers and publications have been in the areas of Western HRM practices in developing countries and diversity and professionalism in UK higher education institutions.

Sarah Jones is a senior lecturer at the University of Bedfordshire as well as an experienced human resource consultant. Her specialist area of research is employee reward and she has co-authored a number of publications in this field as presented at international conferences.

Konstantinos Kakavelakis is a lecturer in organizational behaviour at the University of Bedfordshire. His research interests to date have included organizational change, knowledge management and workplace learning. Dr Kakavelakis' work has appeared in journals such as *Personnel Review, Journal of Education and Work, British Educational Research Journal* and *Management Learning*.

Eliot Lloyd is a senior lecturer and the undergraduate field chair in strategy at the University of Bedfordshire. He has been responsible for delivering core undergraduate modules in strategy and also delivers a module on the CMI programme. His research interests include using the balanced scorecard to improve the delivery of taught modules and development of short-course programmes in designing balanced scorecards for small businesses.

Pauline Loewenberger is a highly experienced lecturer and a fellow of the Higher Education Academy with a PhD in facilitating organizational creativity. Dr Loewenberger's research has been presented at international conferences. Her contribution for this book is an extension of this work through synthesis with knowledge creation, management and organizational learning.

Stephen Perkins is Dean of the London Metropolitan Business School and Professor of Corporate Governance and Leadership. He is also a visiting professor at City University, London. His career has combined roles in both the academic and business worlds, driven by a mission to keep both communities in reciprocal dialogue. He holds a doctorate from the University of Oxford. He was a member of the UK power generation privatization team and first HR director for National Power International. He has consulted with a range of organizations in both private and public sectors internationally. With approximately 100 publications, including 'Strategic International HRM' published by Kogan Page, he has completed a number of research and reporting commissions for the Chartered Institute of Personnel and Development. He is a member of a transcontinental research team funded by the Australian Research Council analysing the problem of alignment between corporate strategy and reward management, using data assembled in Australia, Canada, the UK and the United States. He serves on the Chartered Management Institute's Academic Advisory Council and is current Chair of the British Academy of Management Corporate Governance Special Interest Group.

Nahid Rozalin is a PhD researcher at the University of Bedfordshire, and also teaches courses in international HRM. She has an MBA and an MA in international HRM. Formerly she worked as a visiting lecturer in a London college and as a lecturer in a leading university in Bangladesh. Nahid has published articles in several academic journals in Bangladesh and has presented a number of papers at academic conferences in the UK.

Christina Schwabenland taught diversity management at London Metropolitan University for seven years prior to taking up a readership in public and voluntary sector management at the University of Bedfordshire. Dr Schwabenland continues to research into diversity management in the voluntary sector and her second book *Metaphor and Dialectic in Managing Diversity* will be published by Palgrave in 2012. Her previous experience includes over 20 years in management positions in voluntary organizations in the UK including 14 years as CEO.

Rod Smith is a highly experienced HR professional and works with organizations to help them achieve their business objectives through their people. In parallel with his consultancy, Rod also shares his experience with business students worldwide on the University of Bedfordshire international MBA programmes.

Qi Wei has been a HR practitioner and academic researcher for several years in both the UK and China. Dr Wei's research interests include reward management, cross-cultural management and Asia Pacific management and business. Her recent publications are in the *Asia Pacific Business Review*, and *Human Resource Management: The key concepts*.

PART ONE
Introduction

Introduction

STEPHEN PERKINS and
RAISA ARVINEN-MUONDO

LEARNING OBJECTIVES

- Identify what we mean throughout this book when talking about management – as a 'thing' managers do and as a process they are involved in.

- Establish a sense of where the body of knowledge referred to as 'organizational behaviour' (OB) has come from and how it interacts with management and managing – specifically people management.

- Present an overview of debates that the human resources management (HRM) community has been engaged in and how that surfaces a need for some means by which to frame analysis and interpretation of the claims and issues.

- Present an overview of what is on offer over the course of the remaining chapters making up this book.

Managing others to a purpose

Many volumes written under the title of 'organizational behaviour' (OB) are positioned to inform readers at the most introductory level of management studies. We have written this text specifically to appeal to those who have already been exposed to 'basic' commentary and are ready to engage with argument and evidence that is at once more sophisticated and more critical – ie not only introducing but evaluating ideas and research findings. We hope that if you are a final year undergraduate honours student or beginning a master's course you will find the book both relevant and stimulating as a study aid. And we hope your tutors will too. Our intention is to put before you and assess knowledge interacting between the boundaries of OB and HRM as we consider that each can benefit from this, in the sense that HRM can ground socio-psychological and other social science theory grouped under the OB banner while a fuller understanding of HRM will be informed by social science knowledge that moves consideration of 'people management' in organizations beyond a preoccupation with recipes and techniques. Whether your management studies course is generalist or specialist, we believe you will find the material in the chapters that follow useful.

Management in its simplest definition is 'getting things done through other people'. That's, in turn, what 'managers' do: their task is to organize the work capacity of others to achieve purposeful outcomes. There are all sorts of questions we might ask about the nature of that purpose, and its likely impact on people involved in setting and trying to achieve it. These questions will be discussed in this book – with a view to understanding how such matters have an impact on the task we're discussing here: getting things done involving a group of people playing various roles.

As you can see, we've already extended our simple 'management' definition: now we're signalling that groups of people are involved in activities covered by management – that's the managers and those who managers are trying to organize to a purpose, interacting with one another. Each of these players is undertaking roles – roles that have been set for them by people influencing the purpose of organization, and roles that as self-determining human beings they choose for themselves. In turn, as we've begun expanding on the opening statements, we're using words such as 'interaction', 'organization', 'self-determination' and 'groups' as distinct from although made up of individual 'actors'.

You'll have noticed the way these descriptions are increasingly formed using metaphors – a figure of speech to represent something, used frequently in management and organizational writing – metaphors that use the language of theatre. A well-known line from a play by William Shakespeare, 'All the world's a stage, And all the men and women merely players' says it all. The text (from the play *As You Like It*) continues: 'They have their exits and their entrances; And one man [or woman] in his time plays many parts.' Even in this section, another word to convey an idea of a human activity has been introduced – perception. That idea – perceiving, and then interpreting to make sense of the environment in which people are acting out their roles – also has an important place in the kinds of things we're going to discuss in this book.

We hope this volume will help not only students of management, but also practising managers. There is plenty of debate about what 'practising' implies for management. Is management all about a series of practices – things that can be separated from the people and places and times in which they occur? Do managers need to learn about these practices – practices on their own and in bundles – as 'things' or 'objects' to be applied to others when trying to get them to do things to achieve some purpose? Alternatively, rather than objects that can be understood independent of the context (people, place, time) in which they may occur, should we view what goes on under the label 'management' as a process, or series of processes – hence (in British English) signalling something different by using an 's' not a second 'c' to complete the word, in the sense that management is something practised (a verb not a noun or object). It's something dynamic not static, that unfolds in a particular setting, and so is a creation of the people and the place and time in which they are interacting (another word we need to pay attention to).

If it's a creation of 'social interaction' then the practice resulting, let alone the outcome, could have been different, something difficult to predict in any generalized way. And if the practice has been constructed by a group of human beings – managers and other organizational actors – there's also the potential for it to be reconstructed. And in some variants of management study, analysts would call for the practices to be *deconstructed* to reveal aspects that while maybe unstated, 'below the surface' of an *observable* organizational setting, have had an important influence on what becomes visibly apparent. As we'll see later in the book, concepts for articulating and interpreting those implicit influences have been identified and specified in academic writing on management and the social sciences; eg cultures, conflicted interests between groups, and differences in the levels of authority, power and/or influence they may bring to legitimize their actions. There are plenty more.

Why is all this important and worthy of inclusion in a course of study on management – with the goal of preparing people to become 'professional' managers? ('Professionalization' – as a process and an implied state of being, itself dynamic – is yet another concept we'll encounter along the way working through the discussions to follow.) One answer is that if management is a social construct concerned with achieving purposeful action where groups of people interact, then people who want to lay a claim to competence in 'doing management' are likely to enhance their credibility if they have mastered a body of knowledge and how this is debated brought together as a 'social science'.

The notion of 'science' is used here in the sense of offering a way of systematically specifying assumptions and ideas about organizing people managerially, so that the issues in play, including the contextual conditions, the choices to be made, and some ideas around the likely consequences from what's done and how it's translated from idea to action can be more readily grasped. In the general field of organization studies and management, the body of social science knowledge has come to be grouped under the heading of OB. OB can include inputs from a variety of social science disciplines specializing in their own right in the search for meaning and understanding in how humans individually and collectively function: anthropology, occupational and social psychology, political science, organizational and work sociology, labour economics or 'personnel' economics, transaction cost economics and industrial relations.

The summary argument here, then, is that getting a grasp of a body of knowledge that can help us in approaching our task as professional managers can be seen as a prerequisite to success in completing that task. It's a very complex activity – as is human life in general, as we know from a moment's reflection on all the things we experience in the society we inhabit. And, of course, given that the body of knowledge is subject to debate, as students of management we're likely also to benefit from learning about the ways in which to sift and evaluate the competing ideas making up that body of knowledge.

Given the emphasis on management as getting things done through other people, as what management in general is about, we're not proposing to embark on a detailed study of discrete areas in management literature such as accounting and finance, marketing, or logistics to name but a few specialist directions. Here we're focusing in particular on a body of knowledge that's been grouped under the general heading HRM. This can of course be read as a management specialism too – able to offer long lists of techniques developed within its disciplinary boundaries: for recruiting, developing, engaging, rewarding and discharging employees, and so on. But advocates of HRM as a distinctive way of getting people to do things to a purpose specified managerially would suggest that beyond separate and bundled techniques the ideas that it brings together as a holistic view of organizing people and other organizational 'resources' are at the core of what managers can do to fulfil their core accountability – what they're employed to achieve (see the case study below). We'll see that using the word 'resources' to include people is itself controversial – with the implication that just as a resource such as money or land or machinery (inanimate, or lifeless, objects) can be put to work, so too can people (in the course of living a life), perhaps setting aside their own priorities as human beings in the world to serve an organizational goal.

CASE STUDY   Shifting from piecemeal to holistic HRM

Cathie Wright-Smith, Head of HR in Nampak, the UK's 'market leader' in plastic milk bottle manufacturing, was reported reflecting on the shift in thinking about how to organize to get things done through a workforce since she was hired in 2007 (Churchard, 2011): Nampak didn't really have people management procedures. When Nampak's Managing Director interviewed Wright-Smith for the job he 'basically said: "We've hired and fired people, we've disciplined people, we do day-to-day HR, but now I want an engaged culture in the business – how do we start?" [concluding] I think it was the challenge I was looking for.'

(For more on Nampak, see Smedley, 2011.)

In this book, we've set out to bring together ways of thinking about getting things done through individuals and groups of people in organizational settings, drawing on published writings collected under the general heading of HRM. Our goal has been to examine this body of knowledge using what social scientists tell us about the ways in which to specify and weigh up alternative choices around getting people to do things and to behave in certain ways in the course of these actions (collected together as OB commentary). Achieving a *critical* grasp of this is likely to help managers in practising their craft, with an awareness of the issues they will encounter and how to decide what to do – in all the variety of settings in which their organizational stagecraft may occur. So we see another interaction taking place: between ideas about getting things done through other people, these ideas themselves remember the product of social construction. We see the diversity of issues managers are likely to encounter when interacting with other organizational actors and see that OB commentary can show how these managers can make interpretations to inform what they decide to do. In other words, using another well-known metaphor, they will be able to 'look before leaping' into management activity.

How did OB get onto the management curriculum?

Taking a brief look at how – and where – OB as a discipline in its own right emerged will help us understand what's involved and how we can make critical use of the ideas and evidence bundled together under the OB banner. We'll follow this with a complementary section discussing the HRM paradigm (a way of thinking proactively about managing people), motivated by the same reason – to make sure we have a solid foundation for ongoing discussion.

Definition of OB

A simple definition of OB is offered by Stanford University in the United States. OB is 'the study of human behavior in organizational settings'. In its micro variant, generally informed by psychology, OB investigates 'how individuals and groups affect and are affected by organizations'. And in its macro form, incorporating organizational theory and economic sociology, OB studies 'organizations as social systems; the dynamics of change in organizations, industries and markets; and the relationships between organizations and their environments'.

In one article, George Strauss traces the origins of organizational behaviour as an academic discipline back to controversies around what became known as the human relations school of industrial psychology (Strauss, 2001). This school had emerged from attempts among employers in the United States to manage the people (or labour) they employed as corporations became increasingly large in the early part of the 20th century.

One of the first management consultants, Fredrick Winslow Taylor (writing one hundred years ago) took the view that labour is a commodity like any other available to be purchased in economic markets and on the face of it sought to dehumanize the labour process (see Braverman, 1974, and the critical literature that followed this seminal work). A 'scientific' approach to management emphasized the economic exchange inherent in the employment relationship and sought to introduce a strict labour–management division: expert managers were to do the planning; those hired to work under managerial supervision were simply to apply their muscle just in the way that mechanized equipment powered production processes in the industrial era.

A combination of disappointing productivity levels across US industry and severe conflict between managements and strong labour unions capable of disrupting production (Kochan, Katz and McKersie, 1994) led to some voices questioning the focus on the economic and the macro, organizational level of analysis and managerial action. Instead, attention was placed on individual workers and how they felt as human beings in the alienating surroundings constituted by large industrial complexes. Demands for cooperation over conflict in workplaces charged with producing necessities to serve the military effort in Europe during the Great War of 1914–18 added to the perceived imperative for an industrial truce. During the 1920s a series of experiments was conducted by industrial psychologists, shifting the focus from macro to micro sub-units of the organization and the individuals populating them that came to be known as the Hawthorne series, named after the lead investigator. Although beginning with an emphasis on experimenting to capture the effects of varying the physical 'shop-floor' working environment, what emerged from the studies was the sense that the pathway to increase labour productivity was by paying attention to workers as complex human beings, interested in a range of workplace motivators, not simply an economic wage for reporting to work.

But this line of reasoning too soon attracted controversy. On the political left, in the words of Braverman (1974) the so-called human relations movement represented no more than an 'ambulance service' offering palliative care to those 'wounded' by the ravages of large-scale industrial capitalism, that perpetuated a division of labour between brain power and labour power. On the right, as Strauss (2001) puts it, the results of this kind of industrial psychology were judged merely 'nambypamby marshmallow management'. For this school of thought, productivity would not be served by managers resting solely as they saw it on 'good intentions', rather than rational economic workplace controls.

On the other hand, in the era following the Second World War and with an emphasis on assuring a strong Western military-industrial complex (Mills and Wolfe, 1999) to meet the demands of the Cold War with the Eastern Bloc countries, the US academy was receptive to a new orientation to equipping managers with a basis to understand the people side of organizational affairs. Strauss (2001) points out this was prompted by criticism in the influential 1959 Ford Foundation report that lambasted US business schools for their lack of theoretical rigour and research base. In particular they were criticized for ignoring the behavioural sciences; a reflection of the then constitution of educators in much of the US business academy as in effect management practitioners-turned-teachers, rather than researchers and theorists, as in other areas of higher education.

To break away from the all-round criticism human relations had attracted, a new name – OB – came to represent this contribution to business school teaching. That notwithstanding, there remained separate strands offered by US educators, with then still strongly influential schools of industrial relations, grounded for the most part in economic and quantitatively informed analysis retaining the focus on macro level policy issues.

And a lowly ranked personnel or human resources field that was oriented less to rigorous analysis informed by social science ideas and methodologies and more to describing and training people in the administrative functions around hiring and firing lower level workforce members. For its part, Strauss (2001) argues that OB asserted its new-found confidence by distancing itself not only from the name of human relations, but also from the normative orientation that that movement had adopted. OB was to be a science too – quantitative analysis techniques underpinning the 'scientific method' and an effort to distil social science theories deemed appropriate to deliver objectively verifiable accounts of the nature of behaviour observable within and between individuals and groups at work.

What this brief history indicates is that the fields of HRM and OB have been to a greater or lesser extent intertwined for some considerable time. And when in the late 1980s scholars such as David E Guest, who wrote a much cited piece in 1987 and then offered an update on 'the workers' verdict' on this individual-facing approach to people and organization management a decade later (Guest, 1999), the transplantation of more action-oriented HRM to the UK employment scene got underway with gusto. Embraced by the professional body (CIPD), seeking its own rationale to one trading in the United States under the headline of 'high performance work systems' (Huselid, 1995), Guest, an OB professor, embarked on a series of empirical studies exploring what has become known as the 'psychological contract' at work (eg Guest and Conway, 2002, 2004). Reflecting the industrial or occupational psychology foundation in contrast to labour economics – but equally grounded in the scientific method and quantitative analysis – the promise offered by HRM in its UK variant was to lift the discipline (and its practitioners) above the lowly administrator status of the traditional personnel or employee welfare officer. The aim was to counter-balance the role of the IR specialist seen as too embedded with organized labour (ie the trade unions), putting emphasis on management and its core task: getting things done through others – in this case, dealing directly with the individual or managerially configured work team in ways that engaged in implicit (psychological) rather than overt (economic) relations between people and the organizations in which they are employed. Under Guest's preliminary (1987) specification, HRM was a new approach distinct from industrial relations, founded on:

- a managerially led, holistic approach to workforce relations intended to assure commitment to:
  - management plans and ways of achieving them;
  - in-built quality of work processes;
  - not being reliant on a third-party quality control mechanism;
- a willingness of individuals and work teams to be flexible in cooperating with managerial requirements to resource operations to match ever-changing customer demands;
- the need for efficiencies.

HRM and OB

One of the inspirations for writing this book was reading the article some years ago by George Strauss (a distinguished professor based in the United States). In summary, Strauss's argument concerned a question: HRM-OB comparing British and US perspectives – what's all the fuss about? (Strauss, 2001).

Definition of HRM

A classic definition of HRM appears in the opening section of one of the seminal texts written by Harvard Business School academics, published in the mid-1980s. This reads: 'Human Resource Management (HRM) involves all management decisions and actions that affect the nature of the relationship between the organization and its employees – its human resources' (Beer *et al*, 1984). The same authors promote the idea of HRM as a system – something that has inputs, throughputs and outcomes – that is the primary responsibility of general managers. At the time labelled 'groundbreaking' the approach was promoted as involving nothing less than a rethinking of the traditional relationship between managers and other organizational members.

As discussed in the previous section, the two areas – in particular when they come to be studied by management scholars – can be seen to blur, depending on the perspective adopted. However, for this volume we've deliberately set out to use the variant of HRM referred to as a normative approach. This is a set of ideas that as a student of management you're likely to encounter as saying 'this is how you *ought* to do HRM'. The normative HRM approach has had plenty of criticism – again from those with a critical orientation (perceiving the ideas as little different from the human relations school's palliative – as a 'developmental' but still exploitative approach to economic organization). Other scholars have criticized the a-theoretical nature of HRM, although there have been efforts over the past several decades to address this weakness – see Hendry and Pettigrew (1990); Guest (2001). The aim in this book is to use the scope for OB to provide the reader with access to frameworks from social science to enable a more informed assessment of the kinds of ideas (and the practical choices they face the manager with) an encounter with HRM arguments and research findings will give rise to.

While interrogating normative HRM primarily here, it's important to note that different approaches are discussed in the literature. Delery and Doty (1996) provide an overview of ways of theorizing, summarized as follows. The **universalistic (normative)** view is premised on the notion that for every 'best practice' applied, benefits will follow in terms of 'high performance work system' outcomes – note the idea of a system here, something holistic and integrated. A **contingent approach** (see the case study below) argues that the impact of applying best practices in HRM will depend on the context – people, history, stage of organizational development etc. A **configurational approach** argues that what is important is not simply to apply isolated practices – however 'good' they may be; the key is to configure bundles of practices that provide organizations with an edge over others (MacDuffie, 1995; Purcell, 1999).

CASE STUDY   Next generation HR

In the UK, the Chartered Institute of Personnel and Development (CIPD) have been exploring in consultation with a group of domestic and multinational employers ideas informing people management practices. A recent report on progress (Sears, 2011) describes findings that illustrate the way HR functions in organizations whom we might interpret as adopting a contingent view of HRM:

> They start with a very sophisticated understanding of the business and the unique context it operates in, and work from there, rather than starting with a systematic notion of the people processes and levers that have to be pulled first. Here, for example, HR may see its primary function as being to wake up an organization that has gone to sleep, and so to form unholy alliances with whoever is necessary to support that agenda. Equally, HR may try to take the "testosterone" out of an organization's strategy if they feel this best serves the interests of future stakeholders. In this world, HR starts with no set formula.

There is a logical linkage between views of strategy – one that implies that strategic planning comes first, with resources a bolt-on, choosing best practices for generalized benefits without paying attention to the nature of the resources or contexts. A contingency theory form of strategy does what contingent HRM suggests. And the resource-based view of strategy and organization argues that attention needs to be focused on the unique combinations of people and attendant systemic features of an organization that will enable sustainable competitive advantage to be gained. Thus, rather than policy interventions it is what emerges from releasing the potential of a configuration of resources that are valuable, rare, non-substitutable and inimitable that will result in organizational success relative to competitors that will sustain over time (Barney, Wright and Ketchen, 2001).

It's interesting to place alongside these ideas those that come from studies of international business organization: a universalist view that argues that with industrialization ways of organizing including HRM will increasingly converge on a single form. This is contrasted with con-vergence theories that argue that the settings are so different and deep rooted that although ideas and practices may be transplanted between places over time, differences in interpretation and thus outcomes will prevail. A 'crossvergence' perspective (Ralston, 2008) argues that it is likely that due to international mobility of elite groups and those from whom they gain education and advice on managing organizations a blending will take place. Ideas will be relocated, but there will still be a sense in which users will see the issues and course of action to implement solutions through lenses that result from their socialization across multiple settings (east, west, north and south hemispheres). The complementary view has been expressed that what may be observed is a 'directional' convergence in HRM practices, although 'final' convergence may be some way off (Tregaskis and Brewster, 2006). Different theoretical lenses may be applied to explain what is seen – from the universalistic to the comparative institutional to the cultural ways of viewing business systems and the interactions of people wherein managers seek to achieve purposeful action through others (Brewster, 2007).

Child's (1997) strategic choice theory adds another dimension in that while accepting the way institutional structures may set the initial boundaries for managerial action (or 'agency'), these agents interpret the world they seek to act on. The scope for a social reconstitution of those structures arises through the combinations of choices to act in this way or that over time among the multiplicity of organizational decision makers. And 'isomorphic' pressures (the impetus to imitate) as multinational corporations (MNCs) dominate the affairs of business and by extension state policy activity around the globe, with decision makers feeling compelled to do as others do to secure their legitimacy, mean again that at least directional convergence may be witnessed affecting what corporate managements do.

Institutional isomorphism has been divided into three broad types: coercive, memetic and normative (DiMaggio and Powell, 1983). If a foreign-owned company enters a developing business system and acquires others – or if, for example, a supranational body such as the IMF engages in funding development – then requirements may be stipulated to conform to the parent's or funders' ideas of how organization should be done. Legal and corporate governance (financial compliance) requirements may be a source of coercive isomorphism – for example, the corporate governance codes companies are now required to adhere to. Memetic isomorphism is a product of uncertainty: as companies compete with one another in unfamiliar circumstances they may find themselves drawn say through seeking advice from management consultants, and through employee migration, to following what turn out to be similar organizational paths as other organizations in the market place. In the case of normative isomorphism this may be the result of drawing on resources from professional groups that have certain norms and values their members have been socialized into. These then are carried into the organizations that recruit them. The same may apply from inter-hiring between firms and hiring people from similar educational backgrounds. Cathie Wright-Smith was described in a *People Management* magazine report as bringing to her new employer Nampak 'a blue-chip background including Asda, Nestlé and Volkswagen' from which the report concluded: 'she was used to HR best practice' (Churchard, 2011).

OB as a source of frameworks for clarifying and interpreting the practice of management may thus help when trying to understand what the continually emerging body of HRM knowledge has to say – as a normative approach or set in specific contexts or as a bundle of activities. It can further assist when trying to grasp the possible choices managers face, and the strategic opportunities and threats arising, accounting for the settings for managerial action in different employment systems worldwide, and the pressures to 'fit in' while at the same time seeking to leverage resources in ways that secure sustainable competitive advantage for the organization and its stakeholders.

Overview of the chapters to follow

If we're to help you to understand HRM using ideas and evidence that's been collected together under the OB field of study, we need to organize the volume in a systematic way. The chapters that follow bring together in an accessible form a significant chunk of what passes for the OB body of knowledge.

We start with the basic building blocks: individual social actors (people) and groups of them, classified in diverse ways, including occupational groups, hierarchical layers (supervisors, managers and others), not forgetting demographic classifications including ethnicity, gender and other differentiators that may have an impact on how people think about themselves and their sense of identity in their relations with other social actors and the organizational settings in which they work. We can then look at things that affect those individuals and collections of them, informed by the tools social scientists have given us to ask more focused questions about these 'social things' in search of understanding. Janice Johnson and Christina Schwabenland take a principled approach in Chapter 1, explaining why it is relevant managerially to value diversity and reduce inequality in organizations. Assessing the merits of UK and US thinking and practice in 'managing diversity' when this extends to other national settings, they explain how contexts and processes in organizational systems influence an individual's sense of his or her own and others' identities.

Another core question that organizational managers need answers to is how do individuals perceive themselves and their social environment? What is perception as a psychological process; does it have a social dimension? Given that while individuals' physiology may enable or inhibit use of the physical senses in observing and processing the environment in which they are situated, how they interpret those phenomena may be more than instinctual. They may be further enabled or constrained by the way people have been socialized – giving them a greater or lesser vocabulary with which to articulate to themselves as well as others what they sense going on around them. Does this imply that perception may be a collective as well as a purely individual action? In Chapter 2 Raisa Arvinen-Muondo discusses these and other issues, to help develop your capabilities in grasping how decision making is affected by human perceptions, and the implications for HRM.

A logical next step for managers of people in organizations is to think about what it is that does, or has the potential to, mobilize individuals and teams to act. There is a vast literature grouped under the heading of 'motivation' that, in Chapter 3, Nahid Rozalin examines with a view to addressing what and who and how people, as individuals and groups, with needs and interests vested in the relationships they negotiate with and inside and between organizations, get motivated to act in ways that they otherwise might not. Are people intrinsically motivated to do certain things? Do they respond to actions by others (managers) intended to motivate them to do what the manager is tasked with achieving through the actions of others? Is there a sense in which groups become motivated and so mobilized to act, perhaps in ways that are a product of the team interrelationships they encounter and actively forge, that as individuals might not occur? Is there, for example, something that a sense of common purpose – positively or negatively oriented – injects into a collection of otherwise disparate people employed in an organization?

Debates OB analysts are engaged in provide frameworks as well as indicators of likely outcomes to guide assessment of the range of actions managers might take to secure purposeful action through the people working under their direction and supervision. For example, when presenting an organization in the search for candidates to fulfil occupational and work roles, thinking about the way individuals perceive information available to them can help managers, in turn, to weigh up communications strategies for making the desired impression and managing expectations raised in doing so. When organization managers are seeking to increase the competencies among workforce members, an understanding of how individuals learn and the potential for codifying knowledge so that it may be transferred among individuals and groups is likely to prove beneficial. In Chapter 4 Caroline Bolam and Sarah Jones explore the literature grouped under the term 'performance management' to help build understanding around ideas of systematic performance management and how this may be viewed critically using the lens of managerial 'control', related to purposefully organizing the work of both individuals and teams of employees.

Getting individuals and groups motivated and organized to do things intended to serve a managerial purpose brings, in turn, the need for attention to questions about how that action and the process it relies on is lead. Do teams lead and manage themselves unprompted? Or is there a necessary role for someone either emerging from within the team, perhaps varying depending on the task being focused on, or supplied by the corporate organization as a formal leader and/or manager to do things that motivate others to follow the lead given in a particular direction? Is there a sense in which leadership and management are the same or different? Is leadership something that can be pre-specified using certain social codes that can unlock social action among groups and the organizations they populate – a form of objective, 'scientific' management? Or is the leader and/or manager something that has a spontaneous character, emerging as a function of the group of people involved in particular circumstances? From the leader's perspective, is this a subjective or objective state? Linda Holbeche explores the multifaceted and contested literature on leadership, in Chapter 5, explaining too why new approaches to leadership are called for in the second decade of the 21st century.

Organizational effectiveness depends on harnessing the talents of people identified and employed to resource activities. While it may be viewed as an omnibus term for processes embedded in HRM – selecting, socializing, developing and motivating – the notion of 'talent management' has been receiving attention. Indeed there has been a line of discourse among management practitioners and those who advise them dramatized using the phrase 'war for talent', carrying the implication that, as the source of intangible value at the core of competitive success, employers must regard this as a strategic imperative. In Chapter 6, Raisa Arvinen-Muondo and Qi Wei offer a critical appraisal of the still emerging talent management literature, to help tie down what is meant by the term, identify what challenges organizations need to overcome if they are to secure and engage talented people, and build understanding of the role the concept and practice may play as a strategic tool in developing human resources.

In thinking about groups of individuals, their motivation and leadership, we encounter debates in the literature that call for answers to questions of whether or not we should expect socially harmonious relations to be the norm, between group members accounting for demographics, occupation, hierarchy and so on. Or would the expectation be that individuals will be pre-formed by their socialization and economic background such that it would be naive to assume that even if they accept employment in an organization knowing it is subject to management, their interests and those of other stakeholders will coincide? Should we prepare for conflict in organizational encounters and if so how should we begin to make sense of this and perhaps as managers find ways of channelling and so resolving conflicts arising?

Similarly, power has long been debated among social scientists in terms of the ways in which it may be deployed to influence the outcome of relations between different individuals and social groupings. In management–employee relations we may assume that the fact that it is managers that do the hiring gives them the upper hand. For this reason, especially in large stable organizations, employees have banded together into unions to intermediate between the parties to the industrial relationship. However, not only has thinking about HRM changed the perspectives on giving employees a voice, and with moves over the past several decades to limit politically oriented regulation in favour of markets. The increasing shift from a manufacturing dominated to a so-called 'knowledge society' has given rise to arguments that power has shifted in favour of key workers on whom managers depend to get things done. In Chapter 7, Philip Davies and Rod Smith explore debates around conflict and politics in organizations and the relationship with the dynamic dispersion of power.

Managers may benefit from getting to grips with a significant literature on another area. It is one that relates to the issue of what influences individuals and groups in their approach to organizations and others encountered. And it raises questions about what managers may be able to do themselves to influence orientations to work and managerially specified purposeful activity. Eliot Lloyd will look at these phenomena in Chapter 8. A common term in the literature for thinking about this aspect of the contexts in which management takes place is 'culture' – in popular language expressed as 'the way things get done around here', or 'how a group of people solve problems'. Culture – as a series of underlying values and traditional ways of thinking and judging and acting in the light of such assessment of social situations – sets the basis on which people through their socialization into a particular culture may be pre-motivated positively or negatively towards the organization and its management. And it is an avenue that management writers have travelled along to offer ideas and suggestions about how managers might be able to construct (and change) a culture to be consistent with their goal of achieving purposeful action through others. An area of debate is whether culture is spontaneous or whether it can be actively managed, and in turn whether culture is a static or dynamic phenomenon. Does culture – as a form of social structure – determine people and how they're likely to behave in organizations? Or do people, generally or through the actions of particular groups, create the culture and ways in which it is legitimated?

Reflecting the turbulence in markets as the world has become more interrelated and interdependent – albeit with arguably divergent benefits between the countries and regions – and the need for organizations to be ready to adapt in the face of such developments, change and its management have become an increasingly prominent concern among OB commentators. In Chapter 9, Faten Baddar Al-Husan and Konstantinos Kakavelakis look at the growing literature in this area and its inter-relationship with policies and practices the normative HRM literature has generated. These policies and practices are intended to enable managements to take workforce members with them, with views bifurcating between transactional change on the one hand (founded on instrumental relations between employees and their employers) and transformational change (that, in turn, calls for attention to sustainable rather than extrinsically oriented short-term relations).

When introducing change to the organization and its practices, managers can expect to be able to choose pathways for action with greater confidence, equipped with rules of thumb for assessing the likely response among other managers and the workforce generally. Ideas and evidence about how people in organizations behave offers a foundation on which to test assumptions about the extent to which an organization as a cultural phenomenon is fixed and objectively verifiable or an evolving social construction, combining the dynamic interplay of multiple subjective orientations, needs and interests that 'change agents' will need to account for.

Such knowledge is likely to assist in more systematically assessing the extent to which giving employees a voice in the transformation process is likely to build engagement with what managers are trying to do. And such knowledge can provide a rationale for approaching this with the focus on communicating directly with individuals or involving third parties representing collective employee interests through formal and informal channels. Allowances may be made here for assumptions about the level and nature of power available to the various organizational stakeholders to set the terms for ongoing organizational activity distributed among managers and other individuals and groups on the payroll. And of course managers who decide that an active effort is required to motivate employees to cooperate with their planned performance goals, using various explicit and implicit 'reward management' techniques, may avoid naive assumptions about cause and effect if informed by what is known about what motivates people individually and in team groupings, positively and negatively.

In recent debates among academics and practitioner audiences alike the concept of 'knowledge management' has come to the fore, interrelated with ideas around creativity and innovation. This has been coupled with the longstanding preoccupation OB theorists have had with learning – which in turn has matured into examining not only how individuals learn and the effects that result, but also to ask about the possibility and extent to which there can be 'learning organizations'. In Chapter 10, Pauline Loewenberger examines literature discussing the scope for managerial action to encourage and reinforce creativity and innovation that may form into uniquely configured activity among a group of people or an entire organization (a firm such as Apple comes to mind here) that enables the firm to attain and sustain market leadership over competitors. The chapter examines attention placed comparatively between organizational learning and knowledge management, with the aim of achieving a synthesis between phenomena at the leading edge of managerial thinking and practice.

In a final chapter we briefly reflect on what the narratives developed throughout this volume tell us about the ways in which HRM and OB can usefully be considered, and what issues emerge for ongoing attention by management academics and practitioners alike.

Conclusion

In this chapter we've introduced ideas about management, understood in terms of getting things done through others, paying particular attention to ideas about people management grouped into a specifically HRM literature. We've indicated the rationale underlying this book for engaging with these ideas offering you as an aspiring or existing professional manager access to the knowledge that social scientists have collected together, leading to debates about the merits of ideas and the actions implementing them may result in.

We've discussed the idea of treating organizations and the interaction of various individuals and groups within them as static and open to objective observation, resources to be acted on managerially. And we've also considered arguments suggesting that instead people and organizations as sentient, indeterminate beings are in a constant state of becoming, or renewal, between apparently settled states of being. As such, with a more subjective sense in which to observe and then interpret what is perceived, influenced in turn by the socialization of the observer, we've noted that socially constructed states are open to reconstruction to suit the needs and wants of the members of the organization and its stakeholders.

The 'social history' of OB in and beyond the classroom has been briefly recounted, as well as reflecting on ideas that have come together over the evolution of ideas in the United States and then the UK branded as HRM – active, purposeful approaches to managing people. These ideas and particularly the normative practices advocated by some HRM commentators have come in for criticism, whether as inadequately theorized or more politically in terms of the assumptions about people and employment and organizational relationships underpinning HRM commentary, and the interests seen as being served to the detriment of others. On the other hand, in a similar way that the 'Hawthorne experiments' produced positive responses from the employees observed by virtue of the fact that managers appeared to be showing an interest in them, the 'workers' verdict' on HRM according to Guest (1999) has been to give it 'the thumbs up'. At a British Academy of Management HRM special interest group conference in April 2009, the consensus was that HRM's underlying problem as an academic discipline was the over-reliance on managerial accounts so that the 'employee voice' (Gollan and Perkins, 2010) was being overlooked.

Bringing this introductory chapter to a close, we've offered you in brief summary conceptual lenses for making sense of HRM ideas and practices that OB writers have developed. And we've sketched the various broad topic areas to be examined in detail by contributors to the volume over the chapters that follow.

Key learning points and conclusions

- Management is concerned with getting work done through mobilizing others.

- HRM can be understood as a collection of ideas to assist in this task.

- Organizational arrangements can be viewed as static or dynamic – as objective or as the product of social construction and reconstruction; and they can be deconstructed for sense-making purposes.

- OB forms a collection of ideas derived from longstanding social science analysis: it needs to be viewed and used mindful of its provenance, emerging initially for fairly instrumental reasons in business schools in the United States.

- HRM has had its own trajectory of development, and is the subject of debate that challenges its underlying basis for reasoning and even its legitimacy located within political-economic relations.

- OB can be applied to address the various approaches HRM commentary covers intended to guide managerial action to achieve purposeful action by others. OB uses ideas and evidence for evaluating the choices open to managers, the contexts in which these may be interpreted as a basis for action and the logical consequences to be aware of. OB flows from the managerial strategies embarked on in forming and reshaping their relations with those on whom managers rely to get things done in diverse organizational settings.

Discussion questions

- What examples can be generated from group reflections on experiences in the workplace, or from stories you've heard told by friends and relatives of what managers do? Use these personal experiences and stories to inform discussion to address the question: what's the main task a business manager performs? Does the nature of this task vary depending on whether the setting is a private business, a public service, or a voluntary association, or whether the organization is large, medium-sized or small?

- Who are the people managers rely on most in performing their core functions? Why?

- What are the ideas discussed in this Introduction with which you are familiar either from prior study, from practice or from publications in the general media?

- What would you list as the key components of HRM? What assumptions are necessary to implement policies to address each of the ones you identify?

- What would you do to help a manager taking on a new work team in preparing to do this?

PART TWO
Individuals at work under an employment relationship

01
Managing diverse identities at work

JANICE JOHNSON and CHRISTINA SCHWABENLAND

LEARNING OBJECTIVES

- Explain the relevance of valuing diversity and reducing inequality in a particular organizational setting.
- Understand how organizational processes and dynamics help to shape our sense of how we see ourselves and each other.
- Assess the relevance of US and UK approaches to diversity to managers working in other countries and cultures.

Introduction

'Managing diversity' is a term that refers to a bewilderingly wide range of policies and practices designed to respond to the increasingly hetero-geneous nature of the workplace. In this chapter we aim to demystify some of the key debates and dilemmas surrounding diversity manage-ment while maintaining a clear focus on the needs and interests of generic managers and management students, who are themselves in-creasingly likely to comprise a very diverse group with internationally determined interests, commitments and affiliations. We will start by presenting a brief overview of the origins of diversity management and some of the key debates. We will then go on to explore the key dilemma at the heart of diversity management, which was elegantly summarized by John Edwards: 'which of a multitude of differences between people justify us in treating them differently and which similarities justify similar treatment?' (Edwards, 1987).

Although many writers regard diversity management as coming within the domain of HRM we suggest that a wider approach is needed and so we will go on to explore some of the ways in which people writing from an interest in organizational behaviour have contributed to our understanding of the ways in which ideas about similarity and difference are constructed and make up our sense of individual and group identity. These characteristics serve to create and maintain a sense of similarity with those who share comparable characteristics and a sense of distance or separation from those who do not. In the final section of the chapter we briefly explore some of the cross-cultural dilemmas that arise in applying the diversity approach internationally. Examples and cases will be used to illustrate these different debates and approaches in organizations.

Key concepts and debates in diversity management

Diversity management refers to the various actions organizations can take to ensure that they are treating all employees (and potential employees) fairly and that they are not discriminating. Usually regarded as having emerged from the United States as a successor to, or development from the discourse of equal opportunities (Kirton and Green, 2005; Wrench, 2005; Kandola and Fullerton, 2003), the term is generally used to refer to the practices that have evolved in response to the need to accommodate a workforce in which individuals are increasingly likely to come from communities differentiated by geography and nationality and also by ethnicity, gender, religious affiliation, disability and many more aspects of identity. This is where the idea of 'diversity' comes from. However, because diversity management as a concept has evolved from what used to be called 'equal opportunities' it also implies a need to challenge discrimination that disadvantages people because of these aspects of difference.

However, there are many more reasons why diversity is important. All organizations need to attract the most talented recruits and then make sure that their talents are well used and the staff want to stay. This means creating a culture in the organization that is supportive and welcoming of people from many different cultures and backgrounds. This is not as easy as it sounds. Organizations create ways of doing things that may reflect unconscious assumptions about who can do what. For example, most organizations expect senior managers to be prepared to work very long hours, to demonstrate their commitment by being willing to fly off to an urgent meeting at short notice, and to adhere to a particular dress code that reflects contemporary ideas about how professional men and women should dress. These requirements, though, which are often unwritten and may even be unconscious, may make it more difficult for women, people with disabilities, and people who want to wear clothes that reflect their cultural or religious affiliations, to feel welcome. If we are to create a welcoming culture we need to think about how the things we are doing at the moment might be creating barriers.

Syed and Ozbilgin (2009) suggest that in understanding what organizations can do to promote diversity there are three different levels to consider:

- the *macro* level, which is the attitudes and characteristics of the wider society in which the organization is located;
- the *mezzo* level, which is the organization itself;
- the *micro* level, which is the attitudes and commitment of the individual workers.

Different strategies may be needed at each of these levels but in this chapter we are primarily concerned with the *mezzo*, or organizational level.

Law, policy and practice

An organization's responsibility for managing diversity

In order to manage diversity a manager needs to be familiar with the legislative framework and how to create and implement good policies and practices. In most countries there are laws that require employers to have certain measures in place to ensure that people are not discriminated against at work for reasons such as their gender, race or disability. In some countries, such as the UK, the legislation also covers sexual orientation, religion and age.

The first responsibility of all employers and employees is that they know what the law requires them to do, so that they can make sure they are not breaking the law and, even if unintentionally, making the organization liable to legal proceedings. Many of the settlements in discrimination cases are very expensive. For example, in 2010 one organization was ordered to pay £125,000 for a claim brought under the Disability Discrimination Act (*Personnel Today*, 22 April 2010).

Second, the organization needs to have good policies in place. These must ensure that all employees, applicants for jobs, and, in many countries, customers, service users and members are treated fairly. This means ensuring that systems and practices do not discriminate, either directly or indirectly; consciously or unconsciously, because of their race, gender, religion or any other protected characteristic. In practice, most organizations concentrate specifically on the HR functions of recruitment and selection, training and promotion and increasingly reward practices.

Third, managers should ensure that there is an atmosphere of mutual respect throughout the organization and that all people feel welcomed and valued for their contributions. Managers should also ensure that rude, disrespectful language, jokes, traditions and rituals are not allowed.

We all contribute to the culture of the organization. We all play a role in making people feel welcome and accepted, or just tolerated. Diversity is everyone's responsibility. But of course, different functions and departments have different roles to play. The HR department will be responsible for making sure that the organization has the right policies and procedures in place. Senior managers are responsible for the organization's overall strategic direction, including a commitment to creating products or services that are appropriate to an increasingly multicultural society. Line managers will be responsible for making sure that these are all translated into action on a day-to-day basis.

But what does it actually mean to 'manage' diversity? In the UK, Kandola and Fullerton are two writers who suggest that managing diversity goes beyond ensuring that the organization is not unfairly discriminating against people. Their definition of managing diversity is one that is very popular. They write: 'The basic concept of managing diversity accepts that the workforce consists of visible and non-visible differences that will include sex, age, background, race, disability, personality and work style. It is founded on the premise that harnessing these differences will create a productive environment in which everyone feels valued, where their talents are being fully utilised and in which organizational goals are met' (Kandola and Fullerton, 2003).

Case study and discussion questions

CASE STUDY   People Together

People Together is a registered charity that runs residential projects for people with mental health problems. Five years ago there was a staff vacancy for a residential care worker. There were only a few applicants and three people were interviewed by the selection panel. The choice came down to two candidates, both of whom did well in the interviews, but for different reasons. Jacob (who is white) had more relevant work experience and his answers were more detailed but the panel thought they were a bit formulaic, as if he knew what was expected to get through an interview, without necessarily believing in what he was saying. Serena had much less relevant work experience and was taking an Access to Work course, She had few academic qualifications but her answers seemed to be intuitively more in keeping with the charity's ethos and values. Although no-one said it in the discussion afterwards, the fact that Serena was black was seen by the panel as positive because they wanted to increase the number of black staff working for the organization. Serena was offered the job.

Serena was very pleased to be offered the job. She was committed and hard working. There were some problems, arising mostly from her lack of experience and understanding about social services provision, the roles of social workers etc. She was sent on several training courses and although her probationary period was extended, she was confirmed in post. She built good relationships with the residents, although these relationships tended to be slightly too informal, and not too professional. But she was very popular with the residents. Although there were some concerns, her work was seen to be 'good enough' to get through the probationary period.

She continued in post for a number of years. During that time a lot of other staff came and went, including the manager. The new manager tended to recruit graduates who had ambitious career aspirations within social work. Although there was no hierarchy among the team, some of the newer staff gradually took on more and more responsibility. Serena resented this because she was the most experienced by that stage and had been there the longest. But the quality of her work didn't seem to have improved beyond her first year – it was still only 'just about' good enough. Serena was happy with the job, she had commitments outside work that were important to her and she wasn't particularly ambitious.

The relationship between Serena and her new manager deteriorated. The new manager held a performance review meeting with Serena and made it clear that she thought Serena's work needed to improve in various areas. The manager was quite blunt about these. Serena got very angry and swore at her manager. Her manager was very upset and told Serena that swearing was unacceptable and that there would be a disciplinary hearing about it that might result in Serena being given a warning.

At the disciplinary panel three senior managers heard both sides. Serena admitted she had sworn at her manager but said in mitigation that her manager was victimizing her. Serena said that she had worked in the same way for five years and nobody had been so critical before. If her work was good enough for other managers why not for his one? She said that perhaps her new manager was acting in a racist way towards her.

Discussion questions

- What should the panel do?
- What issues does this case study raise?
- How could this situation have been avoided?

Kandola and Fullerton would argue that over the last 40 years we have gone through different stages in our responses to individual differences at work. Liff (1997) described these as moving from an approach designed to eradicate differences (the assimilationist approach, perhaps best pictured through the US metaphor of society as a 'melting pot'), ignoring differences (by treating everyone the same), accepting differences (and accommodating them to an extent through such measures as flexible working patterns for women with children, the provision of food for people with special diets as a result of a disability or a religious conviction) through to *valuing* differences, which is the approach that Kandola and Fullerton are describing above.

The 'business case' for diversity

The 'business case' for diversity argues that good diversity policies are 'good for business' and profitability. It is based on four key points:

- recruitment and retention of good staff;
- better products and services;
- better decision making;
- better reputation.

Recruitment and retention

The argument in favour of recruitment and retention is primarily based on demographics – organizations need to trawl as widely as possible to attract good staff and have good policies in place to keep them. As many parts of the world are becoming increasingly more diverse, due to migration, changing job opportunities and the impact of political and economic changes, organizations cannot afford to ignore the talent residing in women, people with disabilities and older people.

Better products and services

The argument in favour of better products and services is that organizations need to ensure that their products are desirable by people who come from a wide variety of groups and so the more diverse their workforce is the more likely they are to produce goods that people want.

CASE STUDY   Window on practice: recruiting Polish speaking staff to recruit Polish speaking customers

Managers at a building society in Peterborough realized early enough that it was ignoring a large percentage of its Polish residents, many of whom had been relocated from cities into the area. Many were sending money back home but were finding it difficult to do this on a regular basis with a reputable company. The building society's managers also realized that not having staff members who could speak Polish was another barrier to business. They started by creating positive recruitment and selection policies to attract qualified Polish workers, which in turn led to an increase in Polish customers who now felt as if their differences were being accommodated and an appropriate remittance service put in place to serve their needs as well as those of the business.

Better decision making

Better goods and services are the product of better decision making. Homogeneous staff groups are more likely to 'think alike'. This can make for poor decision making because alternatives are not given sufficient consideration and the dangers of 'groupthink' may become more emergent. A more diverse workforce can lead to a wider range of views being expressed and thus to better decision making.

Better reputation

The argument that having good diversity policies can improve a company's reputation is probably best demonstrated by companies such as the HSBC bank, 'the world's largest local bank', which has incorporated ideas of diversity into its branding. Another UK example is B&Q, a do-it-yourself chain that actively promotes the employment of older workers. The argument is also supported in reverse when companies find their brand image damaged by gaining a reputation for sexist or racist policies.

The arguments in favour of the business case look good, but are there any problems with it? One problem is that the evidence to support it is mixed. There is little research that has been able to track companies' performance over a period of time to investigate whether having good diversity policies has demonstrably led to improved overall performance (Wise and Tschirhart, 2000). There are some individual studies that do show a clear connection but others where no such connection can be made.

Berg and Hopnes (2001; in Wrench, 2005) studied two Norwegian companies. In one, the diversity of the workforce did lead to increased profitability, in the other it did not. They concluded:

'In one company ethnic diversity was seen to be directly relevant to profits and in another completely irrelevant. The former was a bakery experimenting with product development and innovation, and immigrant workers were being drawn on for their knowledge of various baking traditions... the latter was an industrial printing company where there was no use for employees with different linguistic skills... as the whole production was automated to such a degree that it made it difficult to see how ethnic differences could be drawn on and profitably exploited either in the production process or in the organization of work' (Berg and Hopnes, cited in Wrench, 2005).

Does diversity lead to better decision making? Again, in some cases it does. Milliken and Martins (1996) also point out that differences can lead to *conflict* that impedes decision making.

So, one of the problems with relying too much on the business case is that if 'diversity' isn't demonstrably good for profits will a company want to invest time and resources in it? And if so, why? Tomlinson and Schwabenland (2010) looked at diversity policies in not-for-profit organizations because for many of them (organizations such as Save the Children, Disability Rights, Age UK) the 'business' of the organization is social justice, but even here they found out that there can be conflicts between the requirements of their diversity policies and the needs of the people they were working with.

The 'social justice' case for diversity

The idea behind equal opportunities was the importance of social justice. If certain groups in society faced disadvantages, in the labour market and beyond, then it was the responsibility of the state to take action to redress these imbalances in opportunity, through legislation that required employers to have measures in place to ensure that they were treating every applicant, employee and customer fairly. Recent research indicates that the UK is now on course to become the most stratified country in the Western hemisphere because of recent developments in the political and economical environment. For example, The Resolution Foundation's Commission on Living Standards found that 'in 1977 of every £100 of values generated by the UK economy £16 went to the bottom half of workers in wages; by 2010 that figure had fallen to £12; a 26% decline' (Resolution Foundation, 2011).

Another important aspect of this debate is whether the measures that organizations take to promote diversity actually challenge inequality. Kandola and Fullerton (2003) argue that they do, and that '... the skills necessary to manage diversity are essentially a restatement of an old theme, namely good interpersonal or communication skills' (Kandola and Fullerton, 2003). This supports our initial claim, that the methods commonly promoted to manage diversity still reflect its origins in HR while its aspirations are much broader. However, Nkomo asks: 'is diversity management really just about talking about respecting all individual differences? If so, this is problematic and cannot in its present form lead to inclusive organizations. There is a real danger in seeing differences as benign variation among people. It overlooks the role of conflict, power, dominance and the history of how organizations are fundamentally structured by race, gender and class' (Nkomo, cited by Wrench, 2005).

Who is right? It depends on what evidence you look at. Some statistical surveys seem to demonstrate that the proportions of people in or out of employment from different ethnic groups in the UK have barely shifted in 35 years. The gender pay gap remains stubbornly wide. People with disabilities are still extremely disadvantaged in the workplace (statistics from the Labour Force Survey are available at **www.statistics.gov.uk**). However, more anecdotal evidence suggests significant shifts in workplace cultures, with many organizations becoming profoundly more welcoming and inclusive and individuals demonstrating significantly less tolerance of racist, sexist and homophobic attitudes.

Much of the practice of diversity management is concerned with the 'technology' of management; monitoring the workforce, establishing benchmarks and targets, and assessing policies for possible impact on equality initiatives. It is not clear how effective these approaches are. Anecdotally there is some support for more 'soft' approaches, such as creating a culture of respect throughout the organization, developing flexible approaches to designing work and the liberal use of encouragement; these last examples are practices that benefit everybody but may have a disproportionately positive effect on workers from marginalized groups. Kandola and Fullerton's (2003) survey of 2,500 organizations (57 per cent private sector, 41 per cent public sector) found that the initiatives that were regarded as most successful were universal benefits and flexible working, while the *least* successful were setting targets for the composition of the workforce and using positive action in recruitment.

Activities

Individually, can you list three ways in which diversity gives your organization a competitive edge?

In small groups discuss whether you think that a diverse workforce is good, bad or just irrelevant for business.

Points to ponder

Does valuing diverse identities lead to a reduction in inequality between different groups in society?

What evidence would you look for to decide? And what does existing evidence say?

Key concepts and debates – summary

We have seen that every organization must ensure that its policies and practices meet the legislative requirements that protect people from discrimination. This legislation emerged from the social movements of the 1960s and 1970s in the United States, the UK and beyond and their aim is to ensure that there is equal opportunity for all regardless of race, gender, disability or any other unfair cause of disadvantage. Nevertheless, the best way of challenging such deep-rooted causes of disadvantage is contested. Proponents of the business case for diversity maintain that a diverse workforce confers competitive advantage and is good for business. Advocates of the social justice case point out that inequality between rich and poor is increasing, rather than decreasing, and that the diversity approach, which, especially in the United States, is based on maximizing individual potential for the good of the firm, has lost sight of structural inequalities such as class and poverty – issues that are shared among a group.

Wrench writes: 'diversity management is too simplistic. It presents a model that is relational rather than structural in nature: its emphasis on aspects such as training, communication, mentoring and team-work excludes the more fundamental issues of structural equity and accountability. Even after diversity management programmes have been implemented real problems of exclusion, conflict, harassment and marginalization continue to exist in organizations' (Wrench 2005).

Wrench (and others) argue that the emphasis on diversity has actually worked against the realization of equality. They say that this is because, by ignoring the existence of structural inequalities, an emphasis on diversity implies that if an individual doesn't 'make it' it is that person's fault.

Furthermore, although one of the key differences between the social justice approach and the business case approach is that of repositioning diversity management as the responsibility of the entire workforce rather than reposing in the HR department. This is primarily because of its links to the business case and its emphasis on the relevance of diversity to other specialist functions such as marketing, strategy and product development. However, despite these claims the *methods* generally proposed to manage diversity still seem to be those of HRM.

The key dilemma seems to be the one that Edwards (1987) posed: how can we know when we should treat people similarly because of their similarities, and when is it more fair to treat people differently because of their differences? Our ideas about similarity and difference are at the heart of how we perceive our identity. Therefore, in the next section we go on to explore how contributions to understanding processes of identity formation, drawn from people studying organizational behaviour and processes more widely, can help us in developing a deeper understanding of the dynamics at play in diversity management.

Processes of identity formation at work

Many explanations of identity are based in psychology or anthropology. However, in this chapter we are primarily interested in how we see ourselves and others in an organizational (social) context and how organizational processes and dynamics influence this process of determining and reshaping our social selves. In this section we will explore some contrasting theories about how we develop a sense of personal identity and their implications for managing diversity at work. We will explore the intersection between the individual and the organization; exploring how the organization manages employees' identities, looking at those aspects it believes offer competitive advantage; those it finds problematic; those it regards as irrelevant, and how these differ in different cultures, sectors and occupational groups. We will ask whether the ways in which organizations and individuals influence each other's identity formation are benign, coercive or even discriminatory.

What is identity?

Identity captures those characteristics, friendliness or professionalism for example, that contribute to our sense of how we see ourselves and how others see us. But where does our sense of identity come from? The 'nature/nurture' debate refers to two contrasting positions; that the characteristics that make up our sense of identity are biologically determined (nature) versus the view that they are socially constructed (nurture). Theories developed from the biological determinism approach include those of Darwin, who explored the ways in which different species evolve over time to ensure survival, and the more recent work on the human genome project that aims to identify the ways in which personality is determined by our genes.

In contrast, there are theories that start from the assumption that identity is socially constructed by: a combination of individual and collective histories and experiences and our responses to them; and through the roles we take on (such as the role of a 'good mother' or 'professional manager') and how we carry them out. Individuals may feel most at ease with themselves when they perceive themselves as having a clear role to play that is recognized and confirmed in their relationships with others (Billington, Hockey and Strawbridge, 1998). Watson describes this two-way development of identity well. He writes: '"Identity" is a notion of who a particular person is – in relation to others. It defines in what ways the individual is like other people and in what ways they differ from other people. It has a *self-identity* component (the individual's own notion of self) and a *social identity* component (the notion others have of who the person is)' (Watson, 2002).

Watson's suggestion is that we actually have multiple identities that are comprised of our own notions about ourselves along with the ways in which we are perceived by others. These, of course, will include our membership of various groups, such as those defined by gender, race or ethnicity, religion or age, among others. So, the choices we make about our attitudes and behaviour shape our personalities, but then we are also recognized, chosen, defended or even accused by others, based on their perception and estimation of these different characteristics, as shown in Figure 1.1.

FIGURE 1.1   Factors that have an impact on diversity management

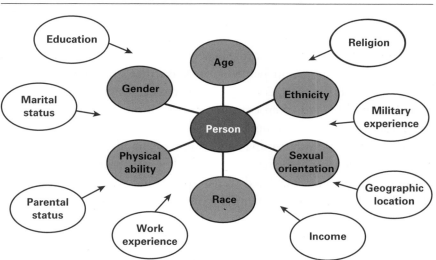

Dynamics of identity formation at work

Jenkins (1996) describes identity as process that is developed over time through constant negotiation with those around us. Identity then emerges as an ever-changing consequence of agreements and disagreements. Individuals make judgements on how to behave depending on their exposures to different situations and circumstances. Some of these behaviours may become deeply embedded and seem almost 'permanent' while others are more rapidly changing. We can see this clearly if we think about young graduates going through assessment centres and then into the workplace. It is important for them to make a particular impression during the assessments and interviews in order to persuade the organization that they will 'fit' in. Once accepted, they begin to assimilate into organizational life taking on a number of different role identities as they adapt to the culture and the environment. As they become more professional in their jobs their professional identity also evolves and becomes more prominent.

Identity can also be shaped by a perception of affinity, or similarity, as in those instances when employees believe there to be a close match between their own attitudes or beliefs and those of the company they work for. People may choose to work for companies they can identify with and they often thrive in those environments. This is what we understand as commonality: factors that we recognize in ourselves and elsewhere that create familiarity and proximity.

However, work identities can also be taken on that allow the individual to 'fit in' with the immediate environment. We can see this attempt to fit in acted out in the popular UK and US reality television show *The Apprentice*, where all the candidates are desperate to show how much they are 'like' Lord Sugar or Donald Trump, even if this involves doing things and behaving in ways that are unusual or even unprincipled. HR managers sometimes regard this characteristic as 'being adaptable' and often consider it to be a much sought-after skill for organizational effectiveness.

How does this relate to diversity? Some of the ideas that we absorb about how we should behave, or even what we should be like, are a consequence of often outdated stereotypes about what a good worker should be. As we assume roles as professionals, parents and partners, these social roles add to the base identity creating a more complex one that is often splintered to help us manage competing pressures. Mead and Freud (cited in Craib, 1998) refer to social identities as social 'selves' but not in the same way as having a cast of actors – more in the way of having different parts of our identity responsible (or best suited) for different roles in our lives. The face we assume then may not necessarily be recognized by people known to us, as illustrated in the case study below.

CASE STUDY   Window on practice: Malcolm's different social identities

Malcolm is a chartered engineer in a highly pressured telecoms organization. He has tight objectives and his bonuses are linked directly to his achieving these objectives. He has a reputation for getting things done but often through frequently raising his voice and behaving in an intimidating manner to his staff. He claims that in this industry this is the only language that is understood and you have to make your presence felt and your voice heard otherwise the staff will laze around and underperform. At his last performance review, anonymous upward feedback indicated that staff were afraid of Malcolm and found him threatening; some called him a bully and, although they liked working for the organization, if they could find another job they would quickly leave.

Malcolm's friends are surprised when he shares this information with them as they find Malcolm accommodating and extremely helpful though sometimes a bit steadfast and 'right-minded' in his views.

In this example we see what is termed as a social identity being formed: Malcolm absorbing the pressures of his job to produce an impression of himself that gets results. It is believed that we become performers in organizations – we are presented with a contract and a script upon which we must deliver an outcome or be 'dropped' from the 'film'. The Malcolm at home may be a different person or may well continue to rant and rave (personality extension) as a way of managing the stress from work. Individuals may become so caught up in this work identity that others in their personal lives no longer recognize who they are.

CASE STUDY   Window on practice: Mandy's different social identities

Mandy recently applied for a job heading up her department in a prominent university. No-one else had applied and Mandy was successfully interviewed and given the job. At the time Mandy was the only female academic in her department and there was resentment from her male colleagues that they would have to answer to her. One went as far as suggesting to HR that her track record of performance and research was not good and that they were making a mistake putting her in this role. Mandy realized that in order to manage this group of professional men who would constantly try to undermine her she would have to adopt a more masculine approach to this role.

According to Craib (1998) one of the ways in which we reduce anxiety in everyday living is to identify ourselves with something else – trying to make our social identity into our identity, often to reduce any biases against ourselves. For example, we see female CEOs acting more masculine (in dress, language, posturing, aggression even) in order to be better accepted into the boardroom. These coercive pressures to conform to images of the ideal worker may cause people to try to adapt to unrealistic expectations, or even to deny important aspects of themselves. For example, a devout Muslim woman who wishes to wear a hijab to work may struggle to reconcile this desire with her perception that the organization will not see her as ambitious and aspiring to senior management.

However, another response to these pressures may be anger and alienation. What is sometimes referred to as 'identity politics' is about seeking recognition for who we are and the struggles arising from what is perceived to be the discrimination, oppression or neglect. According to Schwabenland (2012) these struggles then become characterized by political platforms in organizations based on a shared sense of what people *are* (such as gender, race, caste, religion) rather than what they *do* (their professional role).

One of the organizational practices that has been subject to a lot of critique is that of monitoring employees by race, ethnicity, gender, etc (Mason, 2003). There are many arguments in favour of monitoring – for example it provides a benchmark against which progress can be measured. On the other hand, it can also be seen as an invasion of privacy. Also, the categories that are chosen for monitoring staff are always problematic. Mason analysed the categories used in the UK census and commented that they: '... represent a curious mishmash of principles of differentiation. Thus, they mix, in a variety of inconsistent ways, skin colour, geographical origin, and nationality or citizenship categories' (Mason 2003).

Another criticism that is made against monitoring practices is that in choosing to highlight certain characteristics over others the effect is to reinforce people's sense of difference. It is interesting to note that in France it is illegal for employers to monitor the ethnic diversity of its workforce because this is believed to reinforce a sense of separation and inequality rather than emphasizing the commonality of shared citizenship. However, in the UK public bodies are required to monitor the workforce in the belief that this will help to identify hidden discrimination and disadvantage.

Activities

Look at the job applications for five different companies that are advertising for staff.

Do they include an equal opportunities monitoring form?

If so, how similar or different are the categories that are provided?

Points to ponder

What are your experiences of monitoring?

Do you feel comfortable with the categories you are given to choose from?

Demographic, social and political trends are creating great changes in the composition of the labour market. For example, we are living longer, may well be working longer, come from increasingly different countries and places, have different expectations from work and have different allegiances.

Changes in terms of organizational mergers and political agendas will continue to strengthen these alterations, resulting in a complex range of possible identities and affiliations (Mullins, 2010). Managing people in organizations requires not only an understanding of the employees but also recognition of the environment in which they exist, especially of their cultures. Managers want to select the 'right' individuals to fit into the organization but they also have to be prepared to challenge their own assumptions about what makes someone 'right'. Managers also need to understand the impact the organization's culture and, indeed, their own personality will have on others.

Processes of identity formation – summary

Our sense of identity rests not only on what we bring to the organization but also on how we respond to the expectations that the organization has on us. These can be explicit (such as dress codes) or implicit (whether people behave differently towards men and women), intentional (how the organization thinks its workers should behave) or unintentional (involving assumptions taken for granted, such as that all couples are heterosexual) that may reinforce traditional stereotypes. We may react to these coercive pressures to conform by adapting our behaviour, even to the extent that our self-image is altered and transformed. Or we may choose to resist and challenge them. Managing diverse identities requires employees and managers alike to develop greater awareness of how these dynamics of identity formation are created, maintained, challenged and experienced at work.

Diversity in a global context

In this section we will suggest some critical questions that managers could ask themselves that would be useful in identifying the most relevant diversity issues for their different contexts. Such questions could include: who is privileged in this organization? Who is disadvantaged? How is that disadvantage maintained? What behaviour is or is not acceptable and how is that supported? What are the possibilities for changing operating systems that have a discriminatory impact? The aim of this section is to help managers and management students relate to the more theoretical debates about diversity (some of which have a very Western-centric orientation that may be of little direct relevance to people working in different contexts) to their own situations.

When you read about cross-cultural management you will find a lot written about the importance of managers respecting cultural differences (Hofstede, 2001a; Trompenaars and Hampden-Turner, 1997). The international manager should recognize that people from different cultures may have developed different understandings of such concepts as authority and respect. Branine writes that researching cross-cultural management: 'helps to establish the ways by which national cultural differences influence employment policies and practices of different countries and the ways by which national and international organizations have responded to them in a world that is determined by a globalizing power of business on the one hand and a localizing power of culture and politics on the other' (Branine, 2011).

This brings us back to Edwards' (1987) comment: when is it more equitable to treat people differently because of their differences and when does different treatment become unfair discrimination?

Managing diversity as a concept originated in the United States (Kirton and Greene, 2005). Indeed, the underlying idea that it is desirable to challenge inequality and that every human being is equal to all others and is entitled to certain basic rights, is part of a certain political philosophy that is very deep rooted in Western societies.

However, even in the United States these ideas have not always been shared – until the 1960s it was illegal for black people and white people to marry in some southern states. In South Africa that was also the case until the 1990s.

Applying diversity management approaches in different contexts may require great sensitivity to the local context. They may be controversial, even illegal. For example, in the United States and the UK it is illegal to discriminate against people on the basis of sexual orientation; in parts of the Caribbean and Africa it is illegal to enter into a same-sex relationship; in Iran people who are openly gay or lesbian are executed. In the UK it is illegal to discriminate against people with disabilities but for many years people with disabilities were sterilized in the United States so that they would not be able to have children. In the United States and in Europe it is illegal to discriminate against women, while in parts of India and China female children are regularly killed.

One important consideration is that the groups who are protected under legislation in the United States or the UK may not be the groups facing the most significant disadvantage, either there or in other countries. For example, diversity management is more concerned with horizontal inequalities than vertical inequalities. Horizontal inequalities are the differences across groups (such as gender, race, ethnicity and religion) while vertical inequalities are those of power, status, class and income. Very little diversity literature has much to say about income differentials and the gap between rich and poor.

Another important aspect is the relative disadvantage of minority and majority groups. Although much of what is written about diversity tends to assume that people who are experiencing discrimination are likely to come from minority groups, that isn't always the case. For example, in South Africa only 11 per cent of the population is white and yet the wealth of the country is still disproportionately concentrated in their hands. In the Philippines 1 per cent of Chinese control 60 per cent of private income (Chua, 2004). Chua describes 'market dominating minorities' as the 'Achilles heel of free market democracy' (Chua 2004).

Other people who may not be recognized in strategies to promote diversity are nomadic or tribal people, whose relationship to land is unconventional. In Europe Roma or Travelling communities continue to experience ongoing discrimination, as do people from First Nations in the United States, Australia and Canada. In many countries refugees or asylum seekers, who may have lost their connection to their homeland, may also be disadvantaged in many ways, including access to appropriate employment – many refugees are highly qualified and were doing demanding and skilled jobs in their own countries before being forced to leave.

Activity

Applying the business case for diversity to your own country, if your organizations were more 'diverse' would that bring you greater competitive advantage?

Points to ponder

Which groups of people in your country are disadvantaged in employment?

What do you think are the long-term consequences of inequality in access to jobs and promotion?

If you work in an MNC, especially if the parent company is a US or European company, the ideas and practices described in this chapter will be very important to its culture and you will need a basic understanding of them. But it is for you to decide how best to apply them in your own setting.

Key learning points and conclusions

- Managing diversity is part of the job role for everyone working in organizations not just for HR practitioners.

- Understanding diversity is key to enabling good practices to thrive and become part of the culture of organizations.

- Essential to unpicking diversity issues is to understand the nature of the individuals involved and their specific identities.

- As society is becoming more individualistic there is more emphasis on fairness and equitable treatment, a greater emphasis being placed on the ways in which workers are managed.

- Each of us will bring different aspects of our being to work and how we participate in organizational life will depend on how our individual identities are perceived and accommodated.

- Organizations and individuals each manipulate their understandings of their own and each other's identities to aid, or increase, performance.

- Managing across diverse cultures requires preparation as well as deep understanding of how other people wish to be treated.

Case study and discussion questions

CASE STUDY   How to manage across cultures

Bernard Smith is the newly appointed general manager of international marketing for a large UK company. His first challenge is to chair a meeting. The participants are John Miller, the American marketing manager; Hans Schmidt, the German operations manager; Nato Suzuki, the Japanese distribution manager; Mohammed Salleh, the Arab financial manager; and Li Chen, the Chinese manager of market research.

After a brief introduction by each manager on his group's activities, Smith formally and politely opens the floor to discussion. Schmidt questions the information that Suzuki has presented and its sources. Suzuki responds briefly, but senses an argument. Not wanting to destroy the harmony of the meeting, he suggests that the two of them meet later for lunch.

Miller then tries to defend Suzuki's position, at which point Miller and Schmidt get into a heated debate. Salleh tries to intervene, pointing out that everyone should listen to what each other has to say. In order to proceed with the meeting, Salleh invites Suzuki to present his rationale, experiences and final opinions again. Believing in teamwork, Suzuki takes the opportunity to ask the other managers to clarify some of the points discussed before giving his opinion.

In a bid to alleviate the tension, Smith makes a joke and then asks Chen to elaborate on the data he has presented, realizing that the Chinese representative has been waiting for an invitation. Like Suzuki, Chen responds without drawing any conclusions and leaves the decision to Smith. He then turns to Salleh and requests more money for research. Salleh categorically refuses, stating that he is in charge of finances and that the entire budget has already been allocated. Chen bows to his authority.

Smith now decides to wrap up the debate and come to an agreement. Miller immediately recommends a democratic vote, but Schmidt insists on delaying any vote until all the information is in. Suzuki smiles nervously and points out that the debate should continue until everyone is in agreement. He suggests that more time should be taken to help everyone settle down, perhaps during lunch and even a round of golf. For his part, Salleh supports Miller's suggestion for a vote, stating: 'God will help the majority.'

Smith finds himself in the middle of a multicultural clash and calls for a coffee break, wondering what he will do to break the deadlock. Luckily, his secretary reminds him of his flight to Asia in two hours. Smith excuses himself and heads out to Heathrow airport, hoping that the problem will take care of itself while he is gone.

Smith then visits Malaysia, Korea and Japan, where he attempts to tie up sales agreements. But in every city his hopes are dashed. In Malaysia, his 9.00 am appointment with a senior manager is changed to an 11.00 am lunch with a junior manager, Noor Ismail, who is more interested in learning about Smith's company's past activities in Malaysia than he is in product details.

Two days later, without confirmation from Ismail, he flies to Korea. Following tentative agreement with a Korean junior manager, Smith has brought a contract for final signature. To his surprise, the junior manager says the vice-president has not agreed the terms of the contract and has requested a 30 per cent discount. The meeting ends with no agreement.

In Japan, Smith fares little better, despite having laid the groundwork with his agent. He invites the potential clients to a sushi dinner and is bombarded with questions.

But no formal order is made. Sitting in the taxi on the way to the Imperial Hotel in Tokyo at 11.30 pm, Smith is not sure that the £300 sushi bill will ever pay off and wonders where he went wrong.

SOURCE Elashmawi, F (2000). First published in People Management magazine 30 March 2000 (http://www.people management.co.uk/pm/articles/2000/03/2668.htm)

Discussion questions

- What preparations could Smith have made to ensure a more successful outcome?

- What questions does the case study raise about managing across diverse cultures?

- What advice would you offer a new manager taking up a similar international role?

02

Perception, making decisions and people management

RAISA ARVINEN-MUONDO

LEARNING OBJECTIVES

- Understand what perception is as a sensory process and the implications of common errors.
- Gain a sense of what perception means on an individual level and as a socially constructed phenomenon.
- Understand what perception means for organizational members, both managers and the managed, in culturally diverse environments.
- Learn to identify and evaluate critically the potential impact that individual perceptions may have on decision making when developing and using people management processes and practices.

Introduction

Perception – that is, the way in which we as individuals see and interpret the environment around us and others' behaviour in it – has an impact on and guides the kind of decisions we make about our own subsequent actions. Think of organizations as living breathing organisms: although structured around processes, practices and policies, they are inherently sustained by individual people, all with unique ways of seeing and interpreting the world around them, working together in groups to achieve a purpose. Therefore, the ways in which people, both managers and those who are managed, perceive others' behaviour, as well as the practices used and structures in which they work, are likely to have a wide-reaching impact on organizational effectiveness. So when talking about people management, the impact of perception, a concept that has been explored in the organizational behaviour rubric but by and large overlooked as a concept in its own right in the area of HRM, warrants attention as we as thinking living human beings attempt to navigate through organizational contexts in which we place ourselves. Like a pebble thrown into a pond, the impact of perception ripples through to all facets of organizational life, including practices and processes such as recruitment and selection, reward management, performance management, training and development, and succession planning.

We are constantly making sense of our surroundings and choose to act or react based on what we perceive as happening around us. The assumption is that, based on our interpretations of observed phenomena, we as individuals then consciously or unconsciously make judgements and take decisions to react or behave in a given manner. As the focus of this chapter, and indeed the book is human behaviour, in organizational contexts I argue that the way in which people make sense of the world in which they interact with inanimate objects, structures, practices and processes as well as other social beings is contextual. Our environments, both social and organizational are occupied by other human beings, albeit in different capacities and to varying degrees, but nonetheless we do not behave in isolation. We are social actors in constant interplay with our environment and other social actors within it. From a managerial perspective, the question then arises, given the contextual nature of perception and consequent behaviour, what are some of the signals that managers need to recognize and act upon to manage individuals and teams to meet shared organizational goals that are conducive to optimal business performance?

The Introduction stated that in this book the intention is to adopt a normative approach as we explore various key OB concepts and their relevance to people management and the practice of HRM. So if perception is contextual, what can we learn about the concept as a process that you could potentially apply universally within practice to help you navigate the world of organizational life in a way that will make you an effective and motivated organizational member? This chapter cannot give you an entirely prescriptive list of instructions that would account for every possible scenario in the world of work. However, by adopting an OB lens and explaining what the perceptual process entails, its potential impact on individual judgement and decision making, and demonstrating these through vignettes and case studies, the intention is to equip you with the skills to ask the 'right' questions. These are the questions that will enable you to assess the potential impact individual perceptions have on the way people are managed in the contexts you will encounter beyond your studies and certainly beyond this book.

Social perception and cultural perspectives

Although the mechanics of the perceptual sensory process will be explained to lay the foundations, this chapter attempts to move away from positivist notions premised on an idea of single observable objective reality. The focus of this chapter will be on the role of social perception in individual judgement and decision-making processes and the implications for people management practices. Social perception refers to the perceptions people have of other people as opposed to their perception of inanimate objects. Adopting a social behaviouristic perspective (Ryckman, 1997), the underpinning logic presented in this chapter is that most of our behaviour is socially learned and geared towards achieving a specific goal, rather than innate. In other words, interaction between people is multidimensional and influenced by the external environment. Therefore, it can be logically argued that our behaviour and perceptions of others' behaviour also depends on our previous socialization experiences (Bandura and Walters, 1963). The increasing multicultural and multinational nature of labour forces and indeed business operations means that the norms and values of the environment into which we have been socialized and which we are conditioned by are constantly being redefined and challenged by behaviour that we may see as foreign. Think of yourself and some of the values and traits you see as important and how you may have come to think this way. Perhaps you value timeliness as it was instilled in you by your parents' expectation that you be home every evening by 5.00 pm for dinner, or your teacher dismissed you from class for being five minutes late. Our attitudes towards time are culturally contextual, as research by well-known writers on cross-cultural management such as Hofstede (1991) and Trompenaars and Hampden-Turner (1997) among others has shown. A manager who comes from a culture that values punctuality would perhaps struggle to understand why employees from cultures that hold very flexible attitudes towards time, for example many African and Latin American cultures, are what he or she perceives to be consistently late. The manager might mistakenly interpret such tardiness as laziness, which in return may have significant consequences on the performance management of the employees. The employees in turn would perhaps struggle to understand why their manager has appraised them in ways that they perceive to be harsh, since for them time is flexible and maintaining and building relationships are qualities that are valued over punctuality. Thus, we are constantly challenged to interpret our surroundings in a way that makes sense to us and, vice versa, communicate our actions or reactions in ways that makes sense to the person at the other end of the communication equation. In other words, successful intercultural communication (verbal and non-verbal) in business requires that parties are able to understand how their decisions and subsequent behaviour may be perceived and interpreted by others.

Points to ponder

What are the implications for our interpretations of behaviour when our understanding of 'acceptable' behaviour is based on distinct cultural values?

How do perceptions of fairness and equality in an employment relationship differ in different cultural contexts?

What are the potential implications of 'mismatched' perceptions?

If decision making is reliant on individual interpretation, then what are the potential consequences in the organizational environment and on HRM policy and practice?

Perception

Definitions of perception seem to vary depending on the dictionary one refers to, but one thing they all seem to have in common is the notion that perception is inherently about how we receive information through our senses (sensory organs) and how we then go about analysing it to make it meaningful. In order to understand what perception may mean in the context of organizational behaviour, it is helpful to elaborate on this a little and as such perception is defined here as a mental process, which involves selecting, receiving, attending to, organizing, structuring, interpreting and storing information in order to make sense of the world that surrounds us. The perceptual process is how we make sense of the environment external to us, events that occur within it and the behaviour of other social actors that occupy the space with us. First we select, receive and attend to stimuli (a thing or an event that evokes a specific reaction). Then we organize and interpret the stimuli in a way that is meaningful to us. Finally, we store our interpretations so that they can be retrieved later as the basis of new perceptions. Perceptions are inherently interpretations we make about what we see, hear, taste, smell and touch, a subjective reality, rather than an objective one that could be interpreted the same way by all social actors. The perceptual process is very much individualized and two people observing and experiencing the same thing are likely to infer different meanings. Therefore, the world we experience is never reality *per se*, but one individual's personalized version of reality (see Knights and McCabe, 2000).

The individualized way in which we perceive starts at the very beginning of the process, where we select (consciously or unconsciously) what information to process as we are confronted with more information than we can possibly handle at any one time. Our attention to and selection of information to process depends on both external and internal factors. What we are inclined to notice through our senses is determined on one hand by internal factors relating to us as individuals (our physical abilities, personalities and past experiences, for example, make us receptive to different things). On the other it is determined by external factors relating to the environment, which we may have very little control over. Take our sensory system; for example, we are inclined to notice sudden sounds like the doorbell or a sudden shriek from another person over constant humming of a computer, heating system or a fish-tank filter. An individual growing up in a Western developed country travelling around in underdeveloped countries, confronted with images and narratives of poverty in reality for the first time, is likely to react differently than someone who lives it on a daily basis. Our sensory system also changes and evolves, particularly if we are exposed to certain stimuli for longer periods, or vice versa. We also learn to adapt to our environments. Situations that may have felt alien to us previously, through continuous exposure become familiar and as we learn to interpret them 'accurately' we are better able to appreciate them, if not perhaps like or agree with them. Think about how we use technology to communicate with others as an example. In the UK, many people are what I would refer to as 'texters'. Rather than actually calling a person, they prefer to send a text message from their mobile phone. Indeed some people only call others if it is an absolute necessity and manage to maintain their friendships through a series of mobile phone SMS messages. However, many individuals coming from more interpersonal relationship-focused cultures may see this as odd and very impersonal or even offensive when directed at them. One might interpret continuous 'texting' as disrespectful as the sender does not appear to value the receiver enough as an individual to take the time to call in person. Text messages may be seen as practical for relaying a practical message, but insufficient for sustaining a relationship between friends, which would require face-to-face time or talk time at the bare minimum. However, if an individual from a relationship-focused culture (see Glossary) comes to appreciate that 'texting' in a more transactional culture (see Glossary) is seen as a normal way of communicating between friends and acquaintances, they are less likely to interpret it as lack of interest or take offence when directed at them, even if they do not fully agree with it.

An essential part of the perceptual process is the way in which we organize and structure the information that we receive according to schemas. Here it is helpful to refer to Clegg, Kornberger and Pitsis's (2008) summary of the variety of schemas (or schemata) that we as individuals use to structure meaning of the information that we constantly receive from the world around us. There are several types of schemas that structure the meaning we attribute to things, events or people, which I will introduce here. We hold:

- schemas about ourselves (self-schemas) that help us structure the way we see ourselves and construct self-conceptions;
- schemas about others (person schemas) that guide the way we see and behave with others;
- social schemas that structure our knowledge about the world and what is socially important;
- schemas that help us remember and understand information so that we can function in the world on a daily basis (script schemas).

Using the language of performance, we as individuals act out several scripts every day to carry out routine tasks, such as shopping for food and going to work. As social actors we act out these scripts through a variety of roles in constant interplay with other social actors performing their roles simultaneously. Not only do we structure the meaning we infer about the roles that we play ourselves, but also the roles others act out in a given interaction (role schemas). Schemas essentially contain information about our underlying values and beliefs and we base our interpretations of the world on the value systems that we hold.

Returning to the metaphor of performance is fitting here. The *Concise Oxford Dictionary of Music* (2007) defines interpretation (in music) as 'merely an act of performance, with the implication that in it the performer's judgement and personality have a share'. In the same way, individuals act out their roles in the environment they occupy structured by their underlying belief and value systems (schemas). Essentially the process of interpretation is about clarifying and explaining the stimuli that we receive through our senses and the resulting conclusions or assumptions are defined by the interpreting individual's personality and judgement. Here we refer to judgement as a process of assessment (of the situation and possible options) that leads to considered decisions about the course of action in any given situation. If we are unique individual thinking human beings, the assumption here is that no two individuals undergo the exact same process of judgement, even if they arrive at similar conclusions. The judgements we make are shaped by our previous experiences. We make assumptions about situations and other people in our environment all the time, often based on pre-set assumptions that we hold and may not even be aware of. Although not particularly politically correct to admit – and certainly organizations should devise measures that seek to manage people across the board equally – it is impossible to eliminate the impact of individual judgement in people management practices. A survey of 300 senior managers carried out by an executive communications and management development consultancy, for example, showed that 70 per cent of surveyed managers prefer thinner workers (Phillips, 2007). It was reported that appearances and weight had an impact on the chances for success in the workplace as thinner individuals were seen as being self-disciplined and having more self-control. It is not clear in which cultural context this survey (Phillips, 2007) was carried out, but it raises an interesting question about context. The findings of the study reported that the senior managers surveyed equated thinness with success, a common modern and Western ideology. However, in many cultural contexts where fatness may be perceived as a sign of wealth and prosperity, managers might be inclined to equate being overweight with success. A newly published Malawian novelist, Thumbiko Shumba, captures this sentiment well in his novel *Worklife* as he narrates a fictitious conversation between his main character and a friend: 'In Africa, a leader should look fat or pot-bellied. Generally, Africa associates fatness with good things. A sign a child will be a leader is if he or she is fat. You will notice that many cabinet ministers and corporate managers in Africa are fat' (Shumba, 2010).

Judgement, the process of evaluating our options, is the interconnecting link between perception and decision making, be that in terms of individual or collective decision making. In organizational contexts that transcend cultural, linguistic and geographical borders, employees and managers should develop both an awareness of bias in their own cultural value system as well as endeavour to understand the values that underpin other systems at play in their environment. Mutual understanding of different cultural value systems is needed in order for organizational members to make decisions at individual level as well as at corporate level about action in a way that allows them to be understood by other organizational members as they were intended. I will return to the topic of perception and decision making later in the chapter. Consequences of judgement will be discussed further in the next section, which explores some of the common errors of perception and examines practical implications for people management practice.

The final step to the perceptual process, as mentioned earlier, is storing and retrieving our interpretations of observed stimuli or experienced phenomena. By this I mean that the observations we process together with our experiences act as the basis of new perceptions we have; they are stored, retrieved and reinterpreted. Our previous assumptions are updated and new ones created, implying that the perceptual process is an iterative and a dynamic one and that perception does not happen in isolation. Our continuous construction and deconstruction of the world around us through the perceptual process defines our behaviour and interaction with other social actors.

The way that we perceive others' behaviour influences how we choose to behave in return. Within dynamic social interaction we attribute different traits and characteristics to people. We judge their behaviour relative to other actors in our environment and based on our previous experiences. Therefore, an essential component of the perceptual process that requires further elaboration is the process of attribution. Attribution theory, developed by Heider (1958), is about how we attribute cause to our own behaviour or to the behaviour of others. It is essentially about asking 'Why do I behave the way I do?' and 'Why do others behave the way that they do?' According to attribution theory, behaviour is essentially determined by internal and/or external forces. Internal attribution (internal locus of control) therefore refers to the process whereby we attribute certain behaviour of individuals to internal factors such as skills, ability, effort or perhaps dispositional traits (for example being happy, kind, angry, mean). External attribution (external locus of control) refers to the process whereby we attribute the cause of certain behaviour to external environmental factors such as the organizational structure, culture, the disposition of others or even the climate. Locus of control (see Glossary) has significant implications for organizations. Research conducted among managers in Skanska, a Swedish multinational organization (MNC), reported that individuals with a high external locus of control preferred participative decision making, for example (Selart, 2005). Research has also shown that individual personality traits such as locus of control correlate to job performance and success (Verbeke, 1994). Individuals with an internal locus of control, who equate their personal effort with success, are likely to be higher performers than those who believe that their success depends on external factors (Patten, 2005). However, attribution comes with its own set of errors, which we will discuss in the next section with other common perceptual errors.

Common errors of perception

Having established what perception is and what the perceptual process entails, it is time to have a look at some of the common errors that we frequently make in our interpretations and judgements, and to explore some of the possible implications in organizational contexts for how people can be managed. In this section I will explore common errors such as stereotyping, the halo effect, self-fulfilling prophecies, perceptual defence, attribution errors and cognitive dissonance.

Stereotyping

Stereotyping is a process of ascribing characteristics (positive or negative) to a person or thing based on widely held but oversimplified ideas. By stereotyping we categorize people or objects into groups according to our general perceptions, usually when we don't have sufficient cues to make an informed judgement. Stereotyping is generally seen as negative, an error, but are there situations when stereotypes can become helpful generalizations? In intercultural consultancy, expatriates embarking on an assignment in a new country are on the one hand encouraged to steer clear of stereotyping and making preconceived value judgements about their local employees and peers. Clients are guided on picking up social cues and taught to question why things are done perhaps differently in their host country than back home before jumping to possibly the wrong conclusions. Trainers encourage new expatriates to have an open mind and develop an understanding for the local context. However, when advising on specific cultural contexts, intercultural consultants and trainers inevitably rely on some form of generalization or helpful stereotyping to assist clients to make sense of the cultural customs and values of host country. After all, it would not be helpful to any relocating expatriate to be told: 'Well, in France it just all depends.' Instead, trainers need to be able to communicate helpful generalizations without judgement such as 'In France (or Italy, Portugal or Spain) it is customary to greet people with kisses on both cheeks' or referring to research: 'Many African cultures tend to be interpersonal rather than transactional and therefore relationships are important.' Stereotypes become unhelpful when they infer negative value judgements about others based on broad generalizations. Most widely used examples of this would be cultural and racial stereotyping where individuals are judged negatively based on their belonging to a particular racial or cultural group.

The halo effect

The halo effect, a concept first coined by Thorndike (1920), refers to the generalization of a whole based on a single perception, trait or characteristic. The belief that thin and attractive people are somehow more successful in work is an example of the halo effect. If we see someone being helpful to a homeless person on the street, we easily make an assumption that the person must be a generally altruistic person, kind and considerate in all situations. This may be the case, but we make this assumption based on a single situation we observe without any evidence to show that it will be the case in other situations also. We might perceive some organizations as more ethical than others and we might infer that because the organization's purpose is good (for example not-for-profit organizations), they must also be good employers and provide a good working environment. In other words, if we ascribe traits or characteristics to a person or organization in one situation, we assume that they are true or applicable in other situations too for that person or organization.

Self-fulfilling prophecies

Similar to the halo effect is the perceptual error that arises from self-fulfilling prophecies. The self-fulfilling prophecy refers to a belief or expectation, regardless of whether it is true or not, that influences one's own behaviour and that of others in a way such that the belief or expectation becomes true. In other words, a self-fulfilling prophecy is like a prediction of behaviour, regardless of the validity of the perception: if it is believed to be true, it will become so. The self-fulfilling prophecy is also referred to as the Pygmalion effect after George Bernard Shaw's stage play about a phonetics professor Henry Higgins who sets out to transform a very Cockney Miss Eliza Doolittle into a refined young lady. Self-fulfilling prophecy is also known as the Rosenthal effect, after a study of the effects of teachers' expectations of students' performance by Rosenthal and Jacobson (1992). Rosenthal and Jacobson's experiment showed that if teachers believe that students are high achievers, regardless of whether this is true or not, they are likely to act differently towards the students they see as gifted and therefore, in time, as the students perceived to be gifted are given more attention they become higher performers. Needless to say, the findings of the study have significant implications for the possible effects of supervisors' expectations on employees' performance. If individuals are identified as 'high flyers' at an early stage of their careers, according to the Pygmalion effect, their future success is predictable. However, who determines which individuals have high potential? What are the characteristics of a 'high flyer' and are they transferable across cultural contexts? Or as you enter the world of work as a graduate, is it just a case of meeting the right person at the right time, who sees your particular potential, which another person might miss? The idea that people's potential can be realized through the power of perception is actually quite incredible. It raises a whole world of questions and debate around how talent is managed, particularly as organizations tackle global human resourcing. (Talent management will be explored in Chapter 6.)

Perceptual defence

We also have a tendency to screen out information (stimuli) that we find perceptually threatening or difficult to process. This is called perceptual defence. We often use the term 'selective hearing' jokingly when we notice we have not heard information that we should have or when we feel that others have not listened to us. However, people may in fact be selective of what they want to hear or see and unconsciously prefer to process information that is supportive of their own viewpoint rather than information that challenges them to think about things differently.

Fundamental attribution error

Attribution theory was mentioned earlier. Attribution comes with its own set of errors, the fundamental attribution error being that when we interpret the behaviour of others, we have a tendency to attribute behaviour (particularly what we perceive as failures) to internal factors (for example disposition, personality or attitude). However, when we attribute cause of our own failures, we have a tendency to attribute them to external factors and when identifying causes of our successes, we attribute them to internal factors (a self-serving bias). In other words, if we fail it's someone or something else's fault, but it we succeed we tend to see it as a personal victory made possible because of our own skills, abilities and exceeding personalities. Therefore, the way in which we perceive others and the traits we attribute are not free of subjective value judgement.

Cognitive dissonance

Cognitive dissonance refers to the feeling of discomfort or anxiety that we feel when we hold contradicting schemas. When this happens we often reconcile by reinterpreting the conflicting information or we may even perhaps change our beliefs. Imagine parents who are particularly religious. They have always lived with the hope, perhaps even an assumption that their child will marry someone of the same faith as they feel that two people of different faiths cannot possibly have a successful marriage and raise a family. One day their daughter comes home and tells her parents that she is going to marry a man of another faith. At first the parents are very upset. They meet their future son-in-law and find that he is kind, intelligent and successful and clearly makes their daughter very happy as the young couple share the same vision for their future. The parents cannot help but like him. Despite holding a very strong belief of what they believed to be the right life choice, they change their priorities (a happy daughter is more important than an pre-set assumption they held based on a cultural or religious bias than practical evidence about the makeup of successful marriages) as they are confronted with information (a likeable and successful man and a very happy daughter) that conflicts with their previous beliefs. Cognitive dissonance carries implications for employee–supervisor communications. If employees, for example, feel that they have provided significant input to a task and performed well but, for whatever reason, the feedback they receive from their superiors is perceived as not showing the recognition that the employees feel they deserve for their efforts, this may have considerable consequences on their sense of motivation and commitment and therefore have an impact on their performance. By encouraging critical self-evaluation prior to task appraisal, managers would be in a better position to eliminate negative effects of cognitive dissonance. Following the underpinning logic, where employees have low self-confidence in their abilities cognitive dissonance via positive feedback has the potential to encourage employees' motivation, engagement, commitment and therefore future performance.

In summary, although the perceptual process can be framed in a series of logical stages, the resulting perceptions we have are distorted by a variety of errors. This takes us back to our original argument that perception is about individuals creating a unique sense of reality for themselves. However, without getting too philosophical, as the environment that we occupy where we interact with other people is not one objective reality, we cannot assume that in an organizational context, despite policies and structures designed on 'best practice', the outcome will be the same for all people. In the same organizational structure, navigating through the same process and practices, individuals are likely to draw different (and given the room for error, possibly incorrect) conclusions about the people they interact with and the purpose and outcome of practices applied to them. Subsequently, the decisions they make will differ.

Decision making

The decision-making process is often described as rational and logical, a series of steps taken to define, assess and develop solutions, and finally implement the solution that is thought to bring optimal results. However, the underlying assumption is that the choices we make depend on the ways in which we attend to, organize, interpret, store and retrieve information (stimuli) that we perceive in our surroundings. I argue here that our interpretations of others' behaviour influences how we choose to behave as a reaction, and vice versa. Communication is a complex and multidirectional process. Within dynamic interaction we are required to receive and decode both verbal and non-verbal messages and the way we approach this process of decoding and coding can be culturally specific (Adler, 2002). Research in cross-cultural communication has shown that cultures place different emphasis on context and non-verbal messages in social interaction (for example Hall, 1990). In a high context culture it may be assumed that individuals are more perceptive of non-verbal behavioural indicators. In such a culture the context in which messages are delivered and who they are delivered by is significant and therefore the recipient would make a decision to react based on their appraisal of all those factors rather than purely on the words used to deliver the message. Contrastingly in a low context culture (for example in the United States) emphasis is placed on the words used to relay the message and communication is considered more direct. In the course of my fieldwork exploring perceptions of personal career development of professional Angolans working in the oil industry, I observed that in Angolan culture (in the most generic sense) behaviour and decision making seem to be largely guided by unspoken but commonly assumed social rules. For example, in urban Angolan culture appearances seem to be important. Individuals are likely to portray the image they want the observer to see. Material wealth, expensive cars, lavish parties, designer clothes and friends in high places are seen as status symbols. However, most Angolans will know that just because people wear designer suits does not necessarily make them rich or successful or even mean that they have a house of their own to live in. Therefore, people do not seem to act or react purely based on observed physical behaviour or the words used to communicate, but rather based on what they anticipate the 'reality' of the situation to be given their knowledge of the contextual factors. For an outsider, particularly one who is accustomed to direct communication, interpreting the behaviour of those that come from a high context culture such as this, would likely find interaction confusing due to their inability to recognize, or their misinterpretation of, contextual factors. The perception–behaviour process therefore is continuous and multi-dimensional. The next section does not endeavour to cover group or organizational decision making *per se*. Rather, it will explore what the perception–decision-making dynamic means for individuals working in organizations and discuss the implications of such decisions in the context of HR processes needed for effective people management.

Implications for HR practice and people management

So, now that I have established what I mean by perception and how perceptions are both individual and socially constructed, what kind of impact do individual perceptions and resultant decision making have on the way people manage or are managed in organizations? I mentioned earlier that the way we perceive the world around us and other social actors in it implies significant consequences for HR processes. HR processes, starting from attracting and recruiting to managing performance and retaining people, are influenced by individual interpretations of the world. Aycan *et al* contend that 'managers implement HRM practices based on their assumptions about the nature of both the task and the employees' (2000), therefore developing an understanding of how and why we perceive is critical to effective people management. Let's start by exploring some of the ideas around how individuals choose to work in given organizations and then discuss what perception may mean for recruitment and selection processes, maintaining the employment relationship and HR development.

Organizational choice

Here I will briefly introduce the idea of organizational choice, as it is perhaps the point where perception comes into play as individuals make decisions about the kinds of organizations they visualize themselves working for and the kinds of individuals organizations seek to attract. That said, the discussion will be limited to the role of perception in terms of employer branding or corporate branding and perceived fairness of the employment relationship (for example the psychological contract). I argue here that individuals make decisions about positions to apply for and seek to become a part of organizations based not only on how fair they perceive the potential employment relationship to be, whether in terms of extrinsic or intrinsic rewards or development opportunities in exchange for effort expended (for example Vroom's (1964) expectancy theory), but also on their perceptions of opportunities available and corporate branding.

Granovetter's (1995) study conducted in the United States in the 1970s suggested that social structure plays a role in the job opportunities available; the more contacts one has, the more likely one is to be aware of new job opportunities. Although this idea has probably changed somewhat since Granovetter's study (conducted more than 40 years ago) given the explosion of technology, online advertising and recruitment, the basic assumption that we apply for positions that we perceive as attainable to us still applies. Whether that perception is based on a realistic self-appraisal of our skills is irrelevant in terms of the intent to apply. If we see ourselves as under-experienced or under-qualified, we might be inclined not to apply at all and thus the proposition that individuals apply for employment opportunities they see as available to them is reasonable. In developing countries where the technology may not be as widely available due to poor infrastructure – and in societies that are relationship focused – logically deduced, social structure would be a significant determinant of perceived opportunities available, perhaps even more so than in the West.

In attracting new talent, organizations need to consider what kind of image they want to market to potential employees. Employer branding (see Glossary) is key to attracting and retaining key talent (Brewster, Sparrow and Harris, 2005). HR's search for credibility as a discipline and realization of brand power during a time when unemployment was relatively low and competition for talent was high (Jenner and Taylor, 2007), has given rise to employer branding literature. In the simplest terms, this literature is concerned with exploring how tools traditionally adopted to market consumer brands could be used to market organizational qualities to prospective and existing employees. The Chartered Institute of Personnel Development (CIPD) defines employer branding as: '... a set of attributes and qualities – often intangible – that makes an organization distinctive, promises a particular kind of employment experience, and appeals to those people who will thrive and perform best in its culture' (CIPD, 2010a). Understanding the possible perceptions and consequent behaviours of applicants is therefore crucial in developing a brand image that not only attracts the right people with the right skills, but is also realistically sustainable once the employment relationship begins by not promising what it cannot deliver. Despite scepticism with the global financial crisis of 2008, since unemployment is on the up and there are more applicants then there are jobs, employer branding still appears to be relevant, particularly for those who have realized its power as a tool for sustainable engagement. (The next section discusses what employer branding means for employee engagement.)

In terms of organizational choice, a study conducted by Freeman (2003) concluded that gender differences exist in the traits men and women attribute to organizations they visualize as 'ideal' employers. In considering potential employment opportunities, according to Freeman's study, women are more likely to look for organizations that display 'feminine traits' that are focused on fair working conditions and are people-oriented, for example a friendly and a relatively stress-free working environment, concern for employees' well-being, diverse mix of people, where men are likely to place greater importance on salary. In other words men and women 'structured their perceptions of the organizations differently' (Freeman, 2003). However, the study also found that the majority of the female respondents did not perceive 'male domination of certain organizations as a factor in their decision-making regarding job application' (Freeman, 2003). Freeman suggests this paradoxical desire of women for 'feminine constructs' in organizations but lack of conscious preference for gendered organizational cultures may be explained by females of the current age being brought up in the belief that they are equal to men and will be treated as such. Although the national or cultural background of the respondents is not specified, the data for the study was collected from final year undergraduates at major UK universities.

Points to ponder

Do you think the findings or Freeman's proposition would differ if the study was conducted in a different cultural context and if so how?

Do you think differences exist in the kind of organizational or job characteristics applicants from the UK, for example, would seek in comparison to say a Nigerian, Chinese or Russian counterpart?

Recruitment

Earlier we considered the role of pre-set assumptions in recruitment decisions with the example of managers who equated thinness with success. Since recruitment is a process of social interaction between two or more people, the interviewee and the interviewer(s), there are likely to be a multitude of pre-set assumptions at play that will inevitably have an impact on the decision to recruit or not and on the interviewee's decision to accept the employment offer or not. The recruitment situation is therefore a process where both parties try to find a fit between their own expectations and their perceptions of the situation and of each other. Hurley-Hanson and Giannantonio (2006) found that the image norms that recruiters have of applicants influences their evaluations and decision making during interview processes. In this case 'image norms' refer to the pre-held conceptions of 'normal' or 'typical' appearance or image of an applicant that the recruiter holds, which may be defined by organizational image norms. Empirical evidence suggests that applicants whose appearance or image do not meet the pre-set expectations of recruiters are likely to be stigmatized during the recruitment process and 'experience a subtle, yet unacceptable form of employment discrimination' (Hurley-Hanson and Giannantonio, 2006). This is a somewhat simplistic scenario, but consider a man in his twenties, with a pierced lip, tongue and eyebrow and spiky dyed hair attending an interview for a carer position in a nursery. Although the man is dressed appropriately and has all the relevant qualifications and experience, do you think the nursery manager interviewing might be inclined to draw misconceived conclusions about the candidate's ability to perform based on his 'unconventional' appearance? Even if the manager can look beyond the exterior, what kind of conclusions do you think some parents who leave their children in the nursery's care might make? As uncomfortable as we sometimes may be in admitting our biases, it would be naïve to think that our decisions are uninfluenced by the stereotypes we hold. Even when there are no conflicting image norms, the candidate and the interviewer come from a similar cultural background and the organizational cultural context is familiar, there is still room for plenty of personal differences that will make the recruitment and selection process a challenging one.

Consider then when there are multiple cultural contexts in play, when the recruiter and the candidate each come with his or her own set of cultural values and expectations of what the other is looking for. Imagine the room for misinterpretation if no real understanding of each other's cultural value systems exists. A study on the hiring decision perceptions of Hispanics in the United States showed that Hispanic and non-Hispanic respondents held significantly differing perceptions about the hiring criteria used, which implied that the two groups held different values about what is important (Peppas, 2006). The Hispanic respondents perceived subjective traits such as loyalty, initiative, motivation, enthusiasm and self-confidence as significant factors in hiring criteria. Their non-Hispanic counterparts, although they also valued motivation, self-confidence and enthusiasm (to a lesser degree than the Hispanic candidates), perceived more objective criteria such as oral communication and work experience as significant hiring criteria. If we look at cross-cultural management literature, the differences in Hispanic and non-Hispanic perceptions can be explained by the US business environment being highly competitive and thus more transactional as opposed to Latino cultures where loyalty is key to any successful relationship, business or otherwise (Peppas, 2006). In practice then, a Hispanic candidate when interviewed for a position might be more inclined to emphasize his or her eagerness to work, ability to take initiative and his or her loyalty to the new employer. However, a US manager might dismiss such pledges as he or she is focused on whether the candidate has the required work experience and technical skills to perform on the job. If the candidate fails to explain his or her technical abilities to the prospective employer who values oral communications skills, there is a good chance the Hispanic candidate in this case could lose out on the job opportunity, despite having the technical skills, qualifications and motivation to succeed.

Once the challenges of the recruitment process have been overcome, with interviewee and interviewer perceptions reconciled, managers' and employees' perceptions of the ongoing employment relationship define the sustainability and success of that relationship.

Sustaining the employment relationship

The perception that employees have of their employers or prospective employers has consequences not only for recruitment, but also for employee engagement and retention. The way internationally operating organizations manage their key human resources is no longer just about 'plotting out a series of international assignments for young high flyers', but rather about attracting and retaining talented and skilled people by presenting a positive and attractive employer brand (Brewster, Sparrow and Harris, 2005). However, as Jenner and Taylor point out (2007), creating a sustainable employer brand that works in multinational organizational environments is challenging, but if created and communicated successfully, internal branding can increase organizational commitment. If members of an organization perceive that the system in which they work views them as individuals and consider themselves as being treated fairly in the employment relationship, they are more likely to strive for better performance. For example, the successful delivery of corporate social responsibility (CSR) programmes and initiatives in organizations has been shown to depend on the extent to which the employees buy in to the initiative (Collier and Esteban, 2007). Collier and Esteban's study indicated that employees' commitment to the implementation of CSR is complex and influenced by corporate social factors as well as employees' perceptions. In other words, if members of an organization do not perceive the ethical image being promoted by their organization, they are unlikely to be committed to 'implementing ethical corporate behaviour in the daily working life of the company' (Collier and Esteban, 2007).

We can turn to motivational theories (see Chapter 3) to develop our understanding of what drives people and why they may or may not be inclined to expend effort to perform in organizational settings. Such theories provide a useful general backdrop against which HR professionals can begin to design strategies to engage their workforces. However, as the majority of motivational theories were developed in the 1960s and 1970s, or are variations of these, it may be questioned whether they still stand their ground today. Moreover, such theories were developed in Western contexts and it may be questioned to what extent they are applicable in contexts that are underpinned by a diverse range of cultural values. Hence I argue that in order to build sustainable engagement, HR strategies need to be designed based on an understanding of how the promotion of given organizational cultures, values and attributes may be perceived and interpreted by employees and stakeholders alike in specific cultural and socio-economic contexts. By identifying relevant motivational factors, organizations can create processes that enable commitment and engagement, thus driving people to perform well.

Even the degree to which we consider ourselves successful in our careers depends on how we perceive ourselves. Although success can be appraised objectively to a degree by someone's title, salary or promotion, personal and subjective feelings towards the individual's own achievements play a significant role in defining overall career success (Gattiker and Larwood, 1989, 1990), particularly since the two experiences do not necessarily correlate (Lau and Shaffer, 1999; Poole, Langan-Fox and Omodei, 1990).

However, ultimately the success of the employment relationship depends on how fair and equitable an individual perceives the relationship to be and how that is reflected in the way he or she is appraised, rewarded and developed in the organization. The employee–organization relationship (see Glossary) is equally concerned with micro factors such as the psychological contract (see Glossary) and perceived organizational support as well as macro factors such as the employment relationship (see Glossary; Coyle-Shapiro and Shore, 2007). Coyle-Shapiro and Shore suggest that the relationship between employee and organization is founded on the concept of social exchange and essentially involves 'recurring exchanges of benefits in which both parties understand and abide by "the rules of engagement" – the bestowing of a benefit creates an obligation to reciprocate' (2007). The problem, I suggest here, is that in organizational contexts where members interpret and behave based on a variety of values and priorities (whether derived from previous cultural socialization experiences or socio-economic context), HR practices such as recruitment, performance management and reward strategies are often implemented without mutual understanding of the 'rules of engagement', thus potentially contradicting the perceived or implied psychological contract between the member and the organization. Moreover, in different cultural contexts varying emphasis may be placed on the transactional or interpersonal nature of the psychological contract. Research conducted in the context of ITES (Information Technology Enabled Services) companies in India suggests that a more relationship-based psychological contract is needed to develop employees' engagement and better talent management (Bhatnagar, 2007). Therefore, corporate decision makers need to give more consideration to both managerial and employee perceptions when creating and implementing HR processes. HR processes need to be created in a manner that develops the mutual understanding of the 'rules of engagement' between managers and the managed and does not take for granted that the understanding already exists.

Key learning points and conclusions

- Perception, that is the way in which we as individuals see and interpret the environment around us and others' behaviour in it, has an impact on and guides the kind of decisions we make about our own subsequent actions.

- Our perceptions are shaped by our environment and past socialization experience.

- The increasing multicultural and multinational nature of labour forces and business operations means that the norms and values of the environment, both social and organizational, into which we have been socialized and are conditioned by, are constantly being redefined and challenged by behaviour that we may see as foreign.

- Our perceptions are frequently subject to common errors that have potential consequences for how people can be managed and how individuals experience management practices applied to them.

- Developing an understanding of how and why we perceive is critical to getting the right people in the right places, developing the skills needed and sustaining the employment relationship by ensuring that expectations are communicated clearly between manager and employee.

Case study and discussion questions

CASE STUDY Cultural understanding

In most if not all African cultures interaction is premised on the importance of relationships rather than a transaction. This emphasis on the interpersonal nature of relationships is reflected in both social and business interactions. Somewhat simplistically put, in African cultures people often prefer to do business with people whom they are familiar with and whom they trust. This idea is very significant for the way in which people in such cultures may view the employment relationship between themselves as an employee and their manager or organization. In cultures where value is placed on relationships, a sense of responsibility and obligation towards one's family, friends and colleagues is prevalent. This is in stark contrast to the way in which in many Western cultures, particularly in the United States and to a great degree in the UK, the employment relationship is viewed as a transactional agreement between the employee and the employer.

Now, imagine a scenario where John, an operations coordinator of a Nigerian subsidiary of a US multinational freight company, has just been offered an international assignment in Houston for three years. John is thrilled and tells his wife about the exciting opportunity. His wife is very happy, but as a professional working also for a local freight company as an accounts manager, she cannot help but feel a little anxious at the prospect of leaving her own job to follow her husband. John fully appreciates the dilemma and the two discuss their options. As John's wife works for a national company, there is no possibility for a temporary transfer to Houston. After considerable research, they come to the conclusion that the only company in which John's wife could potentially continue doing similar work in a similar position is the very company that John already works for. So John decides to approach his US manager and ask her for a job for his wife. The manager refuses point blank and explains to him that they do not have any positions to be filled so it is simply not possible and does not engage in any further conversation. John is very perplexed by the reaction as he has always got on well with his manager. John explains to the manager that his wife is not happy about leaving her job behind and becoming a homemaker for the next three years, not to mention it would not make financial sense, particularly as the pair are paying for their three nieces' education as the main earners of their families. The manager replies that although she appreciates John's dilemma, it is not really her concern as at the end of the day this is about a job and reminds John that he is being compensated well for the assignment and that should be sufficient. John is so upset at the manager's reaction that he loses any sense of loyalty and commitment he had previously had to the organization. He feels betrayed as the company did not make even an attempt to help him and his wife. John loses motivation to work for the company and his performance suffers. John feels as though he is simply being used and treated as a number, rather than valued as a person. Most of all, he feels offended as he thought that he and his manager had developed a relationship based on trust. As a result he starts looking for alternative work and soon leaves the company.

Discussion questions

- How do you think John's request for a job for his wife was perceived by the US manager?

- Why do you think the manager reacted as she did?

- How do you think John interpreted the manager's reaction? Why is John feeling confused and betrayed?

- Even if there were no available positions, what could the manager have done differently?

- What are some of the consequences for the organization of the manager's lack of cultural understanding?

03
Motivation at work: engagement and facilitation

NAHID ROZALIN

LEARNING OBJECTIVES

- Develop an understanding of the roots of some classical theories of motivation and how modern theories of motivation have evolved from academic and practitioner research.
- Critically analyse controversial debates surrounding the extrinsic and intrinsic motivation dichotomy and how managers may use these in practice in motivating individuals to work to a purpose.
- Identify and examine the relationship between employee engagement and the role of the psychological contract and their influence on employee motivation.
- Develop an understanding of the significance of devising appropriate HRM strategies in creating environments that nurture sustainable high performance outcomes and workplaces.

Introduction

Employee motivation has always been a central managerial problem in organizations and as the future unfolds the changing nature of business for multinational corporations (MNCs) poses increasing challenges for HR managers and policy makers. Researchers working in the fields of

OB and HRM have demonstrated that employee motivation varies according to individual employee expectations, evaluations, performance feedback, rewards and the nature of the work itself (Amabile, 1993). In order to create a high performance workplace, managers need to understand what motivation means to different employees and how job content, process and context factors are shaping employee motivation. Furthermore, work motivation is not stable and static often due to frequent organizational changes, which warrants managerial consideration (Amabile, 1993). For example, during the recent global downturn many organizations have undergone significant restructuring and downsizing, resulting in cuts in reward and compensation systems, and a decline in promotions, regular salary increases and investment in training and development. An annual employee reward survey that has been carried out since 2008 suggests that two-thirds of people who are made redundant and return to work are paid less in their new job (CIPD, 2012). The surveys also find that the proportion of employees receiving a pay increase in the year prior to the survey dropped from two-thirds in 2008 to less than half (45 per cent) in 2011. All these changes could have significant implications for the way people feel about their work, their willingness to do their work, the level of effort they are likely to expend, and the quality of their performance. The consequences of redundancy, lower pay and pay freezes may also be felt by employees' families, friends and former colleagues and thus affect morale and engagement (CIPD, 2012).

This chapter attempts to explore some of these issues and explain some of the variation in how motivation may be perceived with the help of a series of classical and contemporary motivation theories and models. This chapter aims to provide insight into the roots of some taken-for-granted 'classics' informed by economics and psychology, placing these into their institutional context, as well as assessing the continuing controversy in debates surrounding the extrinsic/intrinsic motivation dichotomy. Therefore, in the first section I provide an overview of motivation and motivation theories, followed by a multidisciplinary analysis of motivation literature to update and balance longstanding motivation commentary and its relationship with employee engagement. Such multidisciplinary analysis is intended to reframe enquiry into employee motivation in organizational settings reflecting the role of social justice, perceptions of fairness and mutual obligation of social exchanges under the psychological contract label. Finally, I will discuss the role of managers and employers in developing HRM systems to enhance employee motivation and engagement, job commitment and organizational commitment. A key aspect is the influence of 'leader–member exchange' and 'organizational support' highlighting the vital role of line managers in leading and guiding employees individually and in teamwork, creating environments with the aim of motivating sustainable high performance outcomes.

Employee motivation

Motivation generally refers to the willingness to exert a high level of effort to reach any goals or to satisfy any individual need. Daft and Marcic explain that motivation refers to 'the forces either within or external to a person that arouse enthusiasm and persistence to pursue a certain course of action' (2004). Motivation at the workplace or employee motivation refers to the willingness to exert a high level of effort to reach organizational goals, conditioned by the effort's ability to satisfy some individual need (Robbins, 2005). Simply put, unmotivated employees are likely to expend little effort in their jobs, have poor attendance and time-keeping records, resist change, produce low quality work and exit the organization if given the opportunity. The counter logic is then that employees who feel motivated towards their work are more likely to be consistent, creative, enthusiastic and productive, turning out high quality work that they willingly undertake. Besides the work content and process-related factors, other contextual factors such as family, society and culture can influence the motivation level of employees. The importance of differences in employee motivation and individual needs warrants consideration. Furthermore, priorities in individual needs are likely to change over time. Consequently, in order to manage a workforce made up of employees with individual and changing needs, HR practitioners together with middle and senior managers would benefit from understanding existing motivational models and the theories behind them. Understanding of the fundamentals can enhance their ability to identify appropriate HR systems that can be matched with employee needs.

Historical perspectives of motivation

The concept and role of management were first developed by Taylor in the late 19th century. Taylor (1911), an engineer, argued that managers should conduct scientific study of tasks to develop the most efficient form of work with the intention of teaching these to employees. The division of labour between managers and workers was seen as a separation of planning function from its execution and provided a rationale for managers to give training to the relatively less skilled or unskilled labour in the most efficient ways to execute a particular task. The onus was then on managers to monitor and control employees' performance and provide economic rewards to employees using a piece rates method (for example remuneration according to the number of units produced or job completed) to increase or maintain the productivity. Taylor therefore conceptualized motivation in terms of 'money as motivational factor' (Buchanan and Huczynski, 2010). This notion was later the subject of much debate in the management literature.

Mayo's Hawthorne study proposed an alternative view that focused on the 'social man' as opposed to Taylor's 'economic man' (see Linstead, Fulop and Lilley, 2009). Mayo's research, conducted in the Hawthorne plant of Western Electric in 1927–33, provided a new view of management that was concerned with developing 'good human relations' between managers and workers, as well as among co-workers. Mayo suggested that people had a need for belonging to a community as well as order and conformity (Linstead, Fulop and Lilley, 2009). In other words, managers are better able to exercise control over employees by encouraging or developing informal work teams or small work groups and by emphasizing social cohesiveness and conformity at the workplace. Mayo's approach gave rise to the 'human relation movement' and was marked as the 'coming of age' of industrial and organizational pschology (Linstead, Fulop and Lilley, 2009).

Rooted in the worldwide economic depression of the early 20th century and the Second World War, Maslow's (1943) hierarchy of human need theory proposed that individuals are motivated to satisfy a set of needs that are hierarchically ranked. Maslow's theory has been criticized by a number of researchers due to its lack of empirical evidence and the highly ethnocentric view that it perpetuates being based on research conducted in the United States during the Great Depression in the 1920s. Nonetheless, Maslow's hierarchy of need theory has been influential and has given rise to several subsequent motivational theories, such as existence, relatedness, growth (ERG) theory; achievement need theory; and Herzberg's job enrichment theory, also called his two-factor theory or motivator-hygiene theory (Herzberg, Mausner and Snyderman, 1959). The general distinction between the need theories and the more advanced theories rests on the difference between content and process. Need-based perspectives reflect a content perspective in that they attempt to describe what factors motivate behaviour, whereas process-based perspectives focus on how motivation occurs or the ways in which motivated behaviour occurs. The next section gives a further exploration of need-based perspectives.

Content theories of motivation

Hierarchy of need

Maslow's theory (1943, 1970) claims that at any point in time people are motivated to satisfy one of five important needs: physiological, safety, belongingness, esteem and self-actualization. According to Maslow (1970) the relative importance of needs varies depending on the individual's current state of well-being. Thus, the emphasis on these needs varies from person to person. The major implication of Maslow's hierarchy of needs theory is that an individual's need satisfaction can be influenced by different factors, depending on the individual's level in the needs hierarchy. Moreover, it implies that each individual is unique; therefore, the level of motivation can vary depending on the characteristics of individuals. Maslow's hierarchy provides a basic stepping stone for further research related to job satisfaction, 'a pleasurable or positive emotional state resulting from the appraisal of one's job or job experiences' (Locke, 1976), which will be discussed in more detail later.

In an attempt to address cynicism of Maslow's theory, Alderfer (1972) developed ERG theory:

- **Existence** relates to pay, fringe, and benefits.
- **Relatedness** refers to social interaction.
- **Growth** refers to esteem and self-actualization.

He assumes that individuals will increase their level of desire for a lower level need if their higher order need is not fulfilled. For example, if an employee is continually frustrated in attempts to satisfy growth needs (for example, promotion) in the organization, either the employee's desire to fulfil existence needs (such as salary) or relatedness needs (such as social interaction) will emerge as a major motivating force.

In line with Maslow's need theory, McGregor (1957), developed 'theory Y', which implies that employees will be deprived and will make insistent demands for more money if there are no opportunities at work to satisfy higher level needs. McGregor was initially inspired by Taylor's approach and provided 'theory X', which entails that a psychological contract is essentially a purchase of services where the organization gives employees economic rewards in return for their service and controls their behaviour through rules and regulations enforced by the designated positions of authority.

However, he later argued that this behaviour is not a consequence of people's inherent nature; rather it is the outcome of management philosophy and practice. Therefore, rather than using an external control of behaviour, organizations should facilitate employees' internal control or self-control (autonomy) and self-direction.

Similar to Maslow and Alderfer's theories, McClelland (1961) provided a dynamic view of needs where he focused on just three needs: achievement, power and affiliation. McClelland suggested that people with a high achievement need strive for personal achievement rather than rewards. They seek situations where they can attain personal responsibility for finding solutions to problems and receive rapid feedback on their performance so that they can set moderately challenging goals. Individuals who have a high power need enjoy being in charge, strive for influence over others, prefer to be placed into competitive and status-oriented situations, and tend to be more concerned with prestige and gaining influence over others than with effective performance. The need for affiliation is the desire to be liked and accepted by others. Individuals with high affiliation motive strive for friendship, prefer cooperative situations rather than competitive ones, and desire relationships involving a high degree of mutual understanding.

Job enrichment theory

Herzberg, Mausner and Snyderman (1959), based on Maslow and McGregor's theory, developed job enrichment theory, also termed as two-factor theory or motivator-hygiene theory. Herzberg concluded that:

- The opposite of job satisfaction is not dissatisfaction, rather it is no job satisfaction.

- The opposite of dissatisfaction is not job satisfaction, rather it is no job dissatisfaction.

- Hence job satisfaction and dissatisfaction lie on two separate continua.

Therefore, Herzberg argued that the presence and absence of job content factors such as achievement, recognition, work itself, responsibility and advancement lead to job satisfaction or no satisfaction but do not cause dissatisfaction. On the other hand, job context or hygiene factors such as company policy and administration, supervision, salary, interpersonal relations and working conditions lead to dissatisfaction or no dissatisfaction but do not cause job satisfaction. In order to develop the job content of motivation seekers, Herzberg proposed job enrichment, which involves giving employees whole tasks that require more complex skills and greater expertise (Linstead, Fulop and Lilley, 2009). However, Herzberg later argued that all jobs were not capable of being enriched or need to be enriched as the 'hygiene seekers could be productive and satisfied in their jobs even if they were monotonous and disliked ones' (1987).

A subsequent version of Herzberg's job enrichment theory has been developed by Hackman and Oldham (1976) in their job characteristics enrichment model, widely known as the Hackman and Oldham model. According to their model, three critical psychological needs of the employees have to be met in order to create job enrichment and job satisfaction:

- meaningful interesting tasks;
- responsibilities for the outcome;
- feedback or knowledge about outcome.

These psychological states lead to the work outcomes of high intrinsic motivation, high job satisfaction and high performance outcomes. The job characteristics of skill variety, task identity and task significance positively influence the sense of meaningfulness; the job characteristic of autonomy positively influences the sense of responsibility, and feedback as a job characteristic positive influences knowledge of results, energizing the self-regulation process of self-setting goals and monitoring, evaluating and reinforcing behaviour (Bandura, 1986). Unlike Herzberg's, the most important side of this model is that it recognized the individual differences among employees in the need for intrinsic motivation and self-growth. Therefore, Hackman and Oldham (1976) proposed that the positive effects of job enrichment should be greater for individuals with a strong, rather than weak, need for personal growth. However, it may be argued that this model emerged in the United States where people value a high level of individualism and a relatively low level of power distance (Hofstede, 2001a). Such cultural values shape the individual and develop a sense of self-worth and well-being by being distinct from others. Likewise, Erez argued that Hackman's job enrichment design only 'satisfies the motives of self-worth and well-being of those individuals whose cultural values prize high individualism and low power distance' (2010).

Despite some obvious differences between job content theories discussed in this section, each of these theories actually complements the others and gives insight into the desired individual behaviour for a high performance work organization. All content theories describe the factors that motivate behaviour; however, they have failed to tell us about the actual processes of motivation (Moorhead and Griffin, 1995). To give you a better understanding of how motivation occurs, the next section will briefly examine some process theories of motivation.

Process theories of motivation

Equity theory

Adams (1963) developed the equity theory of job motivation and proposes that individuals are concerned not only with the absolute amount of rewards they receive for their efforts, but also with the comparison of this amount to what others receive. Employees perceive what they get from a job situation (outcomes) in relation to what they put into it (inputs), and then compare their outcome–input ratio with that of relevant others. When people perceive an imbalance in their outcome–input ratio relative to others, tension is created. Adams' theory leads us to think about the significance of equity and fairness in organizations. Adams (1963) proposed that employees can reduce such tension by making any of the following choices:

- **Cognitive disordering of one's inputs or outcomes.** For example, they might decide that they actually work harder than other colleagues or that a colleague's job is not as desirable as they originally perceived it to be.

- **Changing one's own inputs or outputs.** For example, they can decrease the amount of effort they are willing to exert. Individuals paid on a piece-rate basis can increase their pay by producing a higher quantity of units of lower quality.

- **Choosing a different referent.** For example, they might decide to compare themselves with a friend in a similar job rather than a more successful work colleague, leave or quit the situation.

However, others have argued that there are numerous methods of reducing tensions or inequalities that are likely to be largely influenced by individual differences or the psychological profile of the individual (Pritchard, 1969). For example, some individuals will have a tendency to view other people as being 'better off' than themselves, regardless of the lack of efficiency or the actual situation. Indeed, Vroom's (1964) expectancy theory has a more predictive and explanatory power regarding the performance in paid work settings than equity theory.

Expectancy theory

Vroom (1964), an industrial psychologist, developed a cognitive theory of motivation widely known as expectancy theory. The theory explores the motivation concept in terms of three elements:

- **Expectancy**: specific effort leads to a specific level of performance.
- **Instrumentality**: a particular type of performance is likely to lead to a specific outcome.
- **Valance**: this is the value an individual attaches to a specific reward or outcome.

Vroom (1964) argues that an employee is motivated to exert a high level of effort only when he or she believes effort will lead to a good performance appraisal; a good appraisal will lead to organizational rewards such as a bonus, an increment or promotion; and the rewards will satisfy the individual's personal goals. However, employees may see the performance–reward relationship as weak, because organizations tend to reward based on factors such as seniority, length of service or being cooperative and not solely on performance (Latham, 2007).

Porter and Lawler (1968) developed an extended version of motivation theory based on expectancy theory. Like Vroom's expectancy theory, their theory consists of effort, performance and reward, but reward can be distinguished as intrinsic or extrinsic. Together, intrinsic and extrinsic rewards are argued to lead to satisfaction. Porter and Lawler's model is complex, consisting of a series of stages that essentially suggests that effort, performance and reward is an iterative cyclical process. Indeed, their model has been criticized for including too many variables and hence has failed to provide clear guidance for managerial action (Linstead, Fulop and Lilley, 2009).

Goal setting theory

The basic ground of goal setting theory as envisioned by Locke (1968) is that people's intentions play an important part in predicting and explaining their behaviour. Locke (1968) made three propositions:

- Setting specific high goals leads to higher performance than no goals.
- Commitment to goal is important (that is, the higher the goal the higher the performance will be).
- Variables such as monetary incentives, participation in decision making, feedback or knowledge of result affect performance only to the extent they lead to setting specific goal and commitment to that goal (see also Latham, 2007).

It has been suggested that self-generated feedback, where the employee is able to monitor his or her own progress, is a more powerful motivator than feedback from external sources, such as supervisors. Likewise, where employees have the opportunity to participate in setting their own goals, the effort they expend in achieving those goals will be greater than where the goals have been assigned to them (Moorhead and Griffin, 1995).

Locke and Latham (1990) later integrated the goal concepts into a longitudinal high performance cycle (HPC). They stated that two factors affect the goals that a person chooses: 1) the importance of the goal to the individual; and 2) self-efficacy, namely, self-confidence that the goal for a specific task is indeed attainable. For example, people with low self-efficacy are unlikely to choose or commit to a high goal whereas the opposite is true for individuals with high self-efficacy. Indeed, people with high self-efficacy not only commit to high goals, they typically set even higher ones upon goal attainment. The HPC model suggests that job satisfaction does not lead directly to job performance, but rather job satisfaction affects an employee's commitment to the employing organization, which in turn leads to employee commitment to future challenges.

Intrinsic and extrinsic motivation and the individual

Herzberg, Mausner and Snyderman's (1959) pioneering work on the model of motivational versus hygiene factors inspired countless studies on the relationship between intrinsic as well as extrinsic job characteristics and job satisfaction (Locke, 1976). Intrinsic rewards (rewards that determine intrinsic motivation) are those intangible rewards that influence feelings of achievement, responsibility and self-worth. In Hackman and Oldham's (1976) job enrichment model, job characteristics such as the levels of autonomy, skill variety, task significance, task identity and feedback may all be considered to be the intrinsic rewards of the job. Deci (1975) proposes otherwise that when extrinsic rewards are offered for work effort that had previously been intrinsically rewarding, the overall level of motivation is likely to decrease due to a decline in the intrinsic interest in the job in the mind of the individual. Deci's (1975) cognitive evaluation theory suggests that there are two processes by which rewards affect intrinsic motivation. The first process is through a change in the perceived locus of causality. When behaviour is intrinsically motivated, the perceived locus of causality is said to be internal. When individuals receive extrinsic rewards, their perceived locus of causality becomes external. The idea is that individuals behave in a given way in an organizational environment if they believe that the extrinsic rewards will be forthcoming (Deci, 1975).

Human behaviour is often unpredictable, sometimes irrational based on emotions rather than logic (Mosley, Pietri and Megginson, 1996), thus attempting to understand individual differences in human behaviour is challenging to say the least, if not impossible. Although the organization can endeavour to address intrinsic rewards available within the constraints of job design, how these are valued or perceived by the worker will be subjective. One worker may view a job as being highly significant, offering a high level of autonomy; while another worker may perceive the same job as being insignificant and restricting. Kovach (1987) argues that no standard motivational factor is applicable to all organizations because of individual differences. So managers are tasked with developing an understanding of how individuals differ in their needs and priorities to enable them to design and implement policies and practices that address the multiplicity of needs present in any one organizational context. By doing so corporate leaders, line managers and HR practitioners can work towards motivating employees in sustainable ways that are consistent with organizational goals. The levels of intrinsic rewards are therefore often seen as being beyond the direct control of the organization. However, Robbins (2005) argued that setting flexible organizational rewards linked to each individual employee's goals and allowing each employee to choose the compensation package can best satisfy individuals' current needs – whether extrinsic or intrinsic.

Furthermore, as highlighted earlier, individual differences, employees' choice or preferred factors of motivation may change over time. For example, Wiley's (1997) longitudinal study found that although some motivational factors (for employees) seem to have remained relatively constant over time, a significant portion of motivators have changed over decades. Wiley (1997) claimed that the reasons for these changes might be economic conditions, change of working environment or industries, labour market conditions, industry competitions, change in workers' attitude, etc.

Similarly, the values workers attach to intrinsic and extrinsic job characteristics have also been shown to vary substantially depending on national characteristics (Adigun and Stephenson, 1992), see, for example, the case study on page 99. Socio-economic and cultural factors have also been used to explain cross-national differences in people's values, attitudes, and behaviour (Hofstede, 2001a). Inglehart (1997) found that workers in richer countries may attach more value to the intrinsic aspects of work and, therefore, may be motivated more by intrinsic rewards, because they have taken survival for granted. In contrast, workers in poorer countries may be more motivated by extrinsic rewards, because the lower needs (for example food and money) are still more prominent than the higher needs (such as self-esteem and self-actualization). For example, British workers are more motivated by intrinsic job factors such as achievement, the work itself and recognition, whereas Nigerian workers are motivated more by extrinsic job factors such as pay, fringe benefits and working conditions (Adigun and Stephenson, 1992) and similarly Indian workers seem to be indifferent towards challenging jobs according to Kanungo (1990).

Motivation and HRM: the psychological contract and employee engagement

There is evidence that HRM practices, such as working in teams, greater discretion and autonomy in the workplace, and various employee involvement and pay schemes, do motivate workers and hence generate higher labour productivity (Cully *et al*, 1999; Boselie and Van der Wiele, 2002). In order to develop and maintain sustainable organizational performance, employers and managers must understand what motivates their employees to work. Kovach (1987) suggests: 'if an organization knows why its employees come to work on time, stay with the organization for their full working lives, and are productive, then the organization may be able to ensure that all of their employees behave in that way and would have a decided marketplace advantage over competitors suffering from absenteeism, costly re-training programs, and production slowdowns'.

However, managers need to understand that not only individual differences but also job content and contextual factors, such as job characteristics, as well as cultural and socio-economic context influence employee choices and therefore, influence HRM practices. HRM practices are a means for employers to communicate their expectations of the respective obligations of both parties (employers and employees), thereby establishing psychological contract by increasing mutuality and enabling a smoothly functioning exchange relationship (Guest and Conway, 2002). Guest (1999) assumes that the HRM practices of an organization can positively influence the psychological contract of employees, therefore positively increase their motivation. This has led to promote the idea of worker-friendly HRM and to encourage researchers to explicitly consider employees' positive responses to HRM (Guest, 1999). Given the cross-cultural factors, to maintain the sustainable high performance organization in this rapid pace of globalization, the managers of multinational and multicultural workforces should be aware of such factors before designing the HRM policies and practices for their organizations. This section will first explore what we mean by the psychological contract and how that relates to employee engagement. Given the international dimension of this book, we will then focus on the HRM practices of MNCs and their effects on employee motivation, and vice versa, to highlight some of the emergent issues when managing teams comprised of diverse individuals.

The psychological contract

A key component of employee motivation is the psychological contract; the explicit and implicit mutual expectations that shape the employment relationship. Both employers and employees need to have clear perceptions of what their mutual obligations are towards each other (Guest and Conway, 2002). Unlike a formal contract of employment, a psychological contract is often an unwritten and unspoken deal between an employee and an employer that addresses the concepts of mutual trust and confidence, fairness and the reality of delivering on promises and may be more influential than the formal contract in affecting how employees behave from day to day (CIPD, 2011d). Argyris (1960) defined psychological contract as unwritten expectations between an employee and the employing organization. Hence, the employee's expectation from his or her employer includes the sense of dignity, worth and having opportunities to learn and grow on the job. From the organization's perspective, the employer can expect loyalty, commitment and good performance from their employees. Therefore, psychological contract may have greater influence on employee engagement (see Glossary) and retention than the legal employment contract does. The psychological contract reinforces the need for managers to become more effective in communication and consultation, which will help in adjusting expectations and if necessary renegotiating the deal. In the context of international HRM, an empirical study conducted in Taiwan found that perceived fulfilment of the psychological contracts of expatriates significantly influences both their adjustment to foreign situations and their organizational commitment (Chen and Chiu, 2009). So in this context international managers should implement appropriate human resource measures to meet expatriates' expectations for their psychological contracts. They should provide adequate counselling and training to assist expatriates in minimizing any psychological barriers they might have to adjust to in a foreign environment (Chen and Chiu, 2009). Similar argument for intercultural awareness could be made for most workforces today that are made up of culturally, nationally and linguistically diverse individuals.

According to Rousseau (2005), employees derive the terms of their psychological contracts in three main ways:

- Individuals can receive persuasive communications about mutual obligations from others. For example, during the recruitment process, prospective employees receive implicit or explicit promises from recruiters or interviewers. Once hired, employees are likely to learn the opinions of co-workers and supervisors about the obligations that exist between employees and the employer.

- Employees observe how their co-workers and supervisors behave and are treated by the organization, and these observations provide social cues that inform employees of their contractual obligations.

- The organization provides structural signals, such as formal compensation systems and benefits, performance reviews and organizational literature (including handbooks and mission statements), that all play a role in creating the terms of the employees' psychological contract.

Successful development and maintenance of a positive psychological contract relies on the organization's HR policies and the attitudes of managers. According to Watson (2006) an organization can either build a 'low commitment' or a 'high commitment' HR strategy. The former is based on a 'hire and fire' strategy, in which labour is acquired at a point of need, trained very little as their tasks typically do not need much training, and dispelled when no longer needed. This strategy echoes Tayloristic work practices. In contrast, the 'high commitment' HRM continues the path of the human relations movement and is characterized by an attempt to involve its employees psychologically and emotionally in the company and continue in different tasks for a longer period of time (Watson, 2006). Furthermore, companies using a low commitment HRM strategy draw on management based on direct control, while those using high commitment HRM strategy use it in a manner that draws on indirect managerial control (Watson, 2006). Therefore, use of psychological contracts is likely to prove useful to practitioners as an intervention for fostering feelings of justice or fairness in the workplace and minimizing feelings of injustice. When employers deliver on their commitments (ie by their actions they fulfil employees' expectations) they reinforce employees' sense of fairness and trust in the organization and generate a positive psychological contract between employer and employee (CIPD, 2011c).

Employee engagement

Employee engagement can be defined as 'the extent to which employees enjoy and believe in what they do and feel valued for doing it' (Knights and Willmott, 2007). The term 'engagement' refers to something more than motivation and it can be seen as a combination of commitment to the organization and its values and a willingness to help out colleagues (organizational citizenship behaviour). Employers want employees who will do their best work or go the extra mile; employees want jobs that are worthwhile and inspire them. However, achieving such a win–win situation has become problematic due to increased workload and long working hours on the one hand and achieving work–life balance on the other.

Unlike the psychological contract, employee engagement is something that only the employee has to offer and that is not required as part of the employment contract. However, employers can enhance their employee engagement. Lucy McGee (2006), director of global HR at the consultancy firm DDI, suggests that in order to enhance employee engagement, employers first need to measure the commitment and organizational citizenship of their employees by using an attitude survey (see Knights and Willmott, 2007). The results of such a survey can provide the basis for understanding employee engagement and the ways to enhance engagement. McGee (2006) suggests six characteristics to identify the probability of an applicant to be an engaged employee:

- adaptability (openness to new ideas);
- passion for work (maintaining a positive view despite stress and frustration);
- motivational maturity (putting results before ego);
- positive disposition (eagerness to help others, outstanding teamwork);
- self-efficacy (confidence in one's ability);
- achievement orientation (the need to succeed and to excel).

Therefore, testing candidates on the basis of the above characteristics, the argument is that employers can increase the chance of recruiting a high performing engaged employee for the organization. However, as with many attitude and aptitude tests, it is critical to look at how suitable they are to the context in which they are to be applied. We should consider: What context were they developed in? Are there any potential cultural biases? Are the results likely to bias any particular cultural or national group?

CASE STUDY   Google's employee engagement recipe

Laszlo Bock, the Vice President of People Operations at Google, stated that freedom and curiosity is what popular employer Google is all about. Being open to ideas from employees is really what is central to Google's success as a workplace, Bock maintained, although people may assume it has more to do with the fact that employees can bring their pets to work or the availability of onsite car washes. According to Bock, Google's rules of engagement with employees are as follows:

- Hire learners. They are inquisitive, and when they fail, they will ask how they can do better.

- Give people the tools and resources to succeed; then let them work on small projects in small teams.

- Keep structures flat. Especially as the company gets big, information needs to flow up.

- Discuss everything you can publicly.

- Give performance-driven rises. This is helpful in controlling turnover and enhancing retention.

- Reward success, don't penalize failure. 'If you don't fail, you're not doing your job well.' Quarterly goals are set and performance evaluations are based on these; the company aims for a 70 per cent success rate.

(*HR Focus*, September 2008)

In the section below we will explore what our discussion thus far then means for critical HR practices in a global multinational environment – practices such as recruitment and selection, compensation and reward, performance management, and training and development.

Recruitment and selection

At present, the relocation of skilled employees across national borders has become a critical business issue for MNCs that seek to bridge managerial or technical skill gaps abroad, build global relationships, develop a common corporate identity and meet the challenge of developing effective global leaders (Briscoe and Schuler, 2004). Particularly in relation to globally mobile employees, corporate leaders should seek to understand their employees' motivational drive to accept or reject an offer of international transfer or assignment (Haines, Saba and Choquette, 2008) before selecting the expatriate for the foreign assignments for achieving the best results. For example, some employees would willingly accept an international assignment for the lure of financial rewards or for career progression (extrinsic motivation); others may have a personal interest in an international assignment and be in search of new experiences and challenges (intrinsic motivation). Research shows that individuals driven by internal or intrinsic motivation engage in seeking and conquering optimal challenges and typically have high levels of interest, excitement and confidence (Ryan and Deci, 2000). These characteristics are deemed important to be recognized by the MNC's corporate decision makers in selecting employees to work in an international context where performance is not only task-specific, but also entails dealing effectively with the larger cultural environment (Briscoe and Schuler, 2004). Hence, international managers should implement appropriate HR measures with their psychological contracts to meet expatriates' expectations. Managers should ensure that expatriates receive adequate organizational support, such as counselling and training, to assist them in minimizing any psychological barriers they might have to adjust in a foreign environment.

Corporate managers in MNCs are increasingly providing a variety of organizational support, such as training in cross-cultural skills, information sharing, mentoring from home or host, orientation and performance appraisals to ease the expatriation experience. However, further evaluation of employees' reactions after implementation of such organizational practices is also warranted to understand how the employee is motivated and to foster the organizational performance. Organizations that follow best practice HRM offer resources and opportunities to increase employees' motivation, skills, attitudes and behaviours and, subsequently, work performance (Kuvaas and Dysvik, 2010).

Combs *et al* summarize that 'organizational performance can be increased by high performance work practice which could be achieved by increasing employees' knowledge, skills, and abilities (KSAs); empowering employees to act; and motivating them to do so' (2006). Nonetheless, research findings imply that in order for perceived best practice HRM to be effective, employees need to be motivated to respond to those practices in a manner that benefits the organization. Such motivation may have its origin in a healthy employee–organization relationship (see Glossary) that creates pro-social motivation (Kuvaas, 2008), that is, the employees' desire to expend effort to benefit their organization. It may, however, also originate from the job itself, where employees become intrinsically motivated because they experience pleasure, interest and enjoyment in their jobs (Deci, Connell and Ryan, 1989).

Compensation and reward

Chang (2011) examines the effects of compensation practices on individual attitudes and motivation to work of Korean employees. Employees' perceptions of HR practices, or how employees perceive the effectiveness of practices, have been regarded as significant determinants of their behaviours. Employees' perception of an HR practice is an important factor in influencing their behaviour as it is believed that when employees have positive perceptions of HR practices they will be positively influenced by those practices (Chang, 1999). However, employees' perceptions of practice can be changed easily by management practices such as open communication or information sharing. More specifically in the compensation area, the perception of the practice of an individual pay for performance (PFP) scheme indicates an employee's perception of the functional role of the pay system in realizing its intended goals of retaining capable employees and boosting performance as well (Chang, 2011). Having said that, compensation practices in MNCs is still a challenging issue. Cross-cultural management research argues that in managing employees with diverse cultural backgrounds, the compensation method should be determined by their cultural values (Chang, 2011). Studies of the relationship between cultural values and HR practices, therefore, warn of the danger of using individual PFP in collectivistic societies (Kim, Park and Suzuki, 1990; Hofstede, 2001b).

Individual PFP basically links an individual reward to an employee's performance, and several theories such as expectancy theory (Vroom, 1964) and goal-setting theory (Locke and Latham, 1990) support this logic. While individual PFP has been recognized as one of the representative motivators in individualistic countries such as the United States (Gupta and Shaw, 1998), in collectivistic societies, people are more concerned about group harmony instead. This has been identified as the equality rule, which indicates members' desires to assure interpersonal harmony in organizations and to focus less on differentiation in individual rewards. Nonetheless, recent empirical research discloses that collectivistic employees such as Koreans may also be effectively managed by extrinsic motivators such as incentive systems (Chang, 2006). Similar results found in Asian collectivistic societies, such as the traditional practices of lifetime employment as well as seniority-based evaluation, promotion and compensation, have been declining in Japan (Keys and Miller, 1994) and individual performance incentives are reportedly increasing in international joint ventures in China (Björkman and Lu, 1999).

However, employees are more satisfied and committed when their values match with those of their supervisors or the organization in which they work. Therefore, a compensation scheme designed in accordance with employees' work values will trigger impacts on their perception of fairness of resource allocation methods (Fischer and Smith, 2004) and hence create more positive effects on employees' attitudes (Chang, 2011). The changing nature in the collectivist society, therefore, can be explained by the fact that when employees perceive that the individual PFP system will contribute to achieving the goals of motivating employees and boosting performance, they tend to be more motivated by the pay practice. Likewise, echoing with Kovach's (1987) findings of employees' strong preferences for intrinsic values, Chang (2011) found a strong effect of intrinsic values on work effort and concluded that both intrinsic and extrinsic values enhance the work effort of employees.

Performance appraisal

Performance appraisal is a tool to manage the performance of the employees where individual employees and line managers engage in a dialogue about each individual's performance and development, as well as the support required from the manager (CIPD, 2012). Unlike compensation practice, performance appraisal has been reported as a less successful HR system for motivating employees (Fletcher, 2001). Goal setting and feedback are key performance appraisal activities in organization (Fletcher, 2001). Since an important purpose of goal setting and feedback is to increase individual performance it is expected that employee motivation with performance appraisal would be positively related to work performance (Roberts and Reed, 1996). Moreover, because performance appraisal often includes equipping employees with new knowledge and skills, it may also contribute to employees' perceived investment in employee development. As per the psychological contract, employees who believe their organization is committed to providing them with developmental activities may feel an obligation to 'repay' the organization through high work performance. Though it has been addressed both in Hackman and Oldham's (1976) and Ryan and Deci's (2000) research, employees' intrinsic motivation explains how they are affected by performance appraisal and the existence of individual differences explains why all employees may not react the same way to performance appraisal.

As addressed in Locke's goal-setting theory (1968), the performance appraisal system should have the clarity of goal and the capacity to increase employees' perceptions of being valued and being part of an organizational team (Kuvaas, 2006). Therefore, if an employee can set his or her own goal, monitor performance and get the self-generated feedback it may lead to enhanced job commitment. Moreover, performance appraisal, as a means to communicate and translate strategic visions and goals to employees, may enhance intrinsic motivation through experienced meaningfulness of work, because superordinate goals have the capacity to convey to employees something in which they can believe (Latham, 2003). Research on the job characteristics model (Hackman and Oldham, 1976) has supported the relationships between the psychological states of experienced meaningfulness, responsibility of outcomes, knowledge of the actual results of the work, and intrinsic motivation. Similarly, and according to self-determination theory (Ryan and Deci, 2000), intrinsic motivation will increase if communication of organizational goals provides the rationale for behaviour at work.

Most people respond positively to performance feedback that is interpreted as autonomy supporting and competence enhancing (Deci and Ryan, 1985). Systematic feedback on work performance through performance appraisal may have an impact on intrinsic motivation through increased experienced responsibility of outcomes and knowledge of the actual results of the work and may increase employees' perceived competence (Deci and Ryan, 1985). Hackman and Oldham's (1976) job characteristics model also shows the motivating potential of the work characteristics in that employees with interesting, enjoyable and exciting jobs are less likely to be attracted by extrinsic rewards. Thus, the intrinsically motivated employees seemed to react positively to performance appraisal as they will learn more from the feedback they receive than the extrinsically motivated employees. However, as intrinsically motivated employees are more self-driven and more autonomy-oriented than those less intrinsically motivated employees, they will be more sensitive to negative performance appraisal experiences (Ryan and Deci, 2000). Where Boswell and Boudreau (2002) suggest that the ultimate goal of performance appraisal is to improve the effectiveness of employees, Kuvaas (2006) proposes that performance appraisal is more effective in influencing attitudes and behavioural intentions than in increasing work performance. This can be explained by job-specific task performance as it is relatively strongly influenced by individual abilities and skills as well as constrained by technology and work design. Therefore, perception of contextual factors may not impact as much (Kuvaas, 2006).

Points to ponder

As a student, how do you perceive your assessment feedback from your university tutor? How do you react if you receive negative feedback?

Does systematic feedback through performance appraisal give you a sense of increased responsibility of outcomes and knowledge of the actual results of the work? Do you feel more competent as a result?

Do you agree with Kuvaas's findings that the performance appraisal system is more effective in influencing employees' attitudes and behavioural intentions than in increasing work performance? Why?

Training and development

Employee motivation has a significant impact on training outcomes as research shows that less-motivated employees are reluctant to learn from the training and, as a result, it affects their post-training satisfaction and transfer of knowledge acquired in the work situation (Ford *et al*, 1997). Guerrero and Sire (2001) observed that employees do not respond uniformly to training. As work performance is influenced by individual abilities and skills, organizations attempt to introduce different training mechanisms to improve their employees' abilities and skills. For instance, MNCs use international assignments as an attempt to develop employees' global skills, knowledge and competencies (Kobrin, 1988; Tung, 1998; Konopaske and Werner, 2005). Although some employees may not be motivated to accept multi-year overseas assignments, organizations try to determine factors that increase employees' motivation to accept such short- or long-term international training. Consistent with much of the relocation literature, Konopaske and Werner's (2005) study indicates that gender, age and marital status have pervasive, consistent effects on willingness to accept global assignments. They also found that benefits are an important component for encouraging employees to accept international assignments and long-term assignees appear to value home-leave allowances, job assistance for spouses and foreign-service premiums more than short-term assignees. Along with Vroom's expectancy theory (1964), less-motivated employees will exert less effort in training to learn the course contents whereas the motivated employees will exert more effort to do well in a training programme which would ultimately lead to better job performance and consequently to valued outcomes. Therefore, Konopaske and Werner (2005) suggest that internal communication of benefits through training programmes or workshops is a vital part of motivating employees to global assignments. Konopaske and Werner found that 92 per cent of firms provide global assignees with, for example, tax equalization, yet only 30 per cent of respondents perceived that they would receive this benefit. Therefore, employees' self-efficacy (believing in one's own capacities) and instrumentality (knowing that the effort exerted will be rewarded) provide a measure of motivation that 'influences the direct outcome of a training programme – learning and satisfaction' (Guerrero and Sire, 2001).

Conversely, Kupka *et al* (2009) argue that MNCs with a socially responsible HR system should select employees based on their motivational strength and train them to overcome their motivational deficiencies for greater global success. As MNCs aim to acquire global knowledge and skills to enhance their worldwide operations and also to transfer the corporate culture and best practices to control and coordinate their subsidiaries, selecting adequately motivated expatriates for such global missions is a must. A motivated expatriate will engage in mutually satisfying relationships with locals and can consequently transfer the knowledge acquired abroad across the organization (Hocking, Brown and Harzing, 2004). As part of a socially responsible HRM programme, a fair and thorough selection process and the provision of intercultural communication training enable expatriates to work effectively and efficiently during international assignments (Caligiuri and Tarique, 2006; De Cieri and Dowling, 2006). Sufficient motivation enables trainees to apply their knowledge and skills appropriately and effectively and training can address identified motivation deficiencies in an employee (Earley and Peterson, 2004). In the training process international assignees can acquire knowledge and skills to manage their attitudes and emotions toward other cultures. Training enables expatriates to become aware of their strengths and weaknesses and they can make a conscious effort to reduce their anxiety and increase their levels of trust and self-efficacy in a foreign culture. Strategic and international HRM researchers have also highlighted the importance of training, specifically intercultural communication training, to improve expatriates' intercultural communication competence (Black, Mendenhall and Oddou, 1991; Brewster and Pickard, 1994; Scullion and Brewster, 2001). The motivation to communicate across cultural borders is particularly important for expatriates who frequently engage in face-to-face interactions. Caligiuri (2000) agrees and argues that expatriates who are motivated to establish intercultural relationships with both host nationals and other international assignees tend to adapt more quickly to the host culture, to be more productive during their sojourn, and to complete their missions successfully. De Cieri and Dowling (2006) point out the particular importance of trust in these relationship webs and agree with Tung (2002) that global organizations need to select and retain employees who are motivated to develop, maintain and extend a network of mutually satisfying relationships among stakeholders through collaborative work.

Key learning points and conclusions

- Employee motivation is a critical managerial issue and one that requires understanding and awareness from organizational leaders, HR practitioners and line managers in developing and implementing practices and policies that are conducive to organizational success.

- Content theories of motivation describe the factors that motivate employees, whereas the process-based perspectives focus on the means by which motivated behaviour occurs.

- By developing an understanding of the implicit expectations in the employment relationship (ie the psychological contract) we can begin to explain underpinning factors influencing organizational commitment.

- Addressing individual needs, for example intrinsic and extrinsic, is central to understanding the complexity and contextuality of the impact of motivation at work as well as central to developing effective ways to managing diverse workforces.

- Employee motivation not only depends on the management philosophy or HRM strategies, but also on employees themselves, culture and context.

- Motivational factors change over time. Therefore, to maintain the sustainable high performance organization in this rapid pace of globalization, the managers of MNCs or international corporations should be aware of such factors before designing the HRM policies and practices for their organizations.

Case study and discussion questions

CASE STUDY Cultural influence on intrinsic and extrinsic motivation

A country's national characteristics can moderate the individual-level relationship between job characteristics and job satisfaction. Obtaining data from 107,292 employees in 49 countries, Huang and Van de Vliert (2003) found that the link between intrinsic job characteristics and job satisfaction is stronger in richer countries, which are equipped with better governmental social welfare programmes, more individualistic cultures and smaller power distance. By contrast, extrinsic job characteristics are strongly and positively related to job satisfaction in all countries. In addition, intrinsic job characteristics tend to produce motivating satisfaction in countries with good governmental social welfare programmes irrespective of the degree of power distance, while they do not tend to work the same in countries with poor governmental social welfare programmes as well as large power distance cultures. Socio-economic and cultural approaches to explaining cross-national variation in work motivation are discussed.

In countries with a well-developed social security system, workers may tend to place more emphasis on higher needs and are therefore more likely to be motivated by intrinsic rewards. In countries without a well-developed social security system, on the other hand, workers may be motivated more by extrinsic rewards that satisfy basic needs. Specifically, intrinsic job characteristics are associated with job satisfaction in countries with high social security and small power distances, because in these countries (for example Denmark, the Netherlands, and the United States) socio-economic status and cultural norms predispose people to value intrinsic aspects of their jobs more. Moreover, there is a significant link between intrinsic job characteristics and job satisfaction in countries with high social security and large power distance (for example Malaysia, Colombia and Venezuela). In addition, in low social security countries people are unlikely to take survival for granted, but they may still value intrinsic job characteristics if their country has a relatively small power distance culture (for example Argentina and South Africa). Finally, if a country's socio-economic status and cultural norms constitute an environment in which intrinsic rewards from one's job are undermined, such as those countries with low social security and large power distances (for example Egypt, Mexico and the Philippines), intrinsic job characteristics are not related to job satisfaction. In a nutshell, intrinsic motivation might work in countries with higher levels of social security irrespective of the degree of power distance, while it might not function in larger power distance countries with lower levels of social security.

(Huang and Van de Vliert, 2003).

Discussion questions

- Are there any differences in the motivation between the employees from developed and developing countries? How and why? Justify your answer in terms of motivation theories and the cross-national variation in work motivation.

- Do you think that employees in countries with low social security, such as Pakistan or Afghanistan, may still be motivated intrinsically?

- What HRM strategies should MNCs take to motivate employees for the subsidiaries in countries with low social security?

PART THREE
Employing human resources to work together for a purpose

04
Managing performance

CAROLINE BOLAM and SARAH JONES

LEARNING OBJECTIVES

- Understand the key principles of performance management (PM) and performance management systems (PMS).
- Be able to evaluate critically how different contexts, values and environments influence the management of performance.
- Understand the role of individual identity and social identity in how individuals perform.
- Be able to identify the difference between individual PM and team PM and their contribution to organizational goals.
- Understand the concepts of self control, social control and administrative control and their implications for the management of performance.

Introduction

The aim of this chapter is to examine the concept of performance and practice of PM in organizations. The intention is to help readers develop a deeper understanding of issues surrounding the managerial challenges inherent in managing individual and group performance, including those associated with power, control and identity not readily found in normative PM handbooks.

Managing the performance of individuals and groups in an organizational context presents some very real challenges. The employment relationship is entered into by both parties with a tacit understanding of the deal being struck: the forgoing of leisure time and the application of effort in pursuit of organizational objectives (performance) in return for rewards (financial or otherwise). This is not to say of course that employees have sold their souls as labour market commodities (Rubery and Grimshaw, 2003). Human beings remain autonomous entities with, it is assumed, ultimate control over their actions and behaviours. So the challenge for managers is how to move people to apply their effort, skills and knowledge voluntarily under direction to achieve goals that will benefit the organizational whole. For this to occur, employees need to come to the conclusion that performing in the way the organization wants them to will be beneficial for them as individuals: individual and organizational needs are aligned. Both extrinsic and intrinsic rewards come into play here: an employee may decide that the tangible reward and recognition on offer in the form of pay, benefits and acclaim (extrinsic reward) are valuable enough to warrant the expenditure of effort required to produce the requisite performance – a purely 'transactional' basis for exercising choice. On the other hand, an employee may also feel rewarded by more intangible 'relational' elements of work and employment: developmental opportunities, perceptions of leadership qualities and identification with organizational values as well as feelings of satisfaction and accomplishment (intrinsic reward). The managerial challenge of PM then, centres on the following key questions:

- How do you convince employees that it is in their best interests to conform to the standards of performance and behaviour asked of them?

- How do you develop and implement policies and practices that reward employees both extrinsically and intrinsically?

- How do you encourage individuals to identify with the interests of the group, create cohesiveness and get people to work together towards a common purpose?

This chapter will explore these issues and seeks to provide some answers to these questions. To do this we take the approach outlined in Chapter 1 of this text in which our first recourse is to literature outside the immediate sphere of Human Resource Management with the intention of bringing different perspectives to bear on HRM challenges. It is within this framework that our approach to understanding the management of performance is by seeing it as a mechanism of control in organizations.

'Control' is not a word used comfortably by many authors of PM handbooks. Indeed one of the underlying principles of HRM has been a movement from management by control to management through commitment (Walton, 1985a) and it is 'commitment' rather than 'control' that is central to the discourse on managing people effectively. However, it can be argued that seeking commitment is just another form of control; a way to gain compliance without coercion. It can also be argued that this is just one form of control in organizations that can be used formally or informally, consciously or unconsciously by the organizational hierarchy, social groups within it and individuals themselves in order to regulate actions, behaviour and performance of employees.

What is performance?

A central question for our understanding of the management of performance must be: what is 'performance' in an organizational context? As Shields (2007) notes, the simple answer is that it depends who you ask; for different stakeholders in the organization 'performance' may well have different connotations. Shareholders of public companies may look at organizational performance purely in terms of profitability, while customers may see the performance of an organization as denoting quality products, value for money or level of customer service. In the not-for-profit sector, performance may well be defined as fulfilling social imperatives that bring positive outcomes for communities. From a managerial perspective, the answer may be that performance is whatever management says it is. And for individual employees, performance may not just be about 'getting the job done' but being seen to do so; the notion of performance as a 'show' of some kind. So, we can understand performance as a social construct; it is defined according to who is thinking about it and their own values, beliefs and attitudes.

Performance and control

Johnson and Gill (1993), in their work on OB and management, cite three aspects of control, which are worth drawing on in this chapter. These are:

- administrative control – how organizations attempt to increase efficiency;
- social control – how groups and society regulate the efforts of organizations;

- self-control – how individuals view themselves in work and society and therefore wish to be part of the organization.

Each of these categories of control will be explored in turn, starting with social control.

Social control

'Nowadays, men often feel their private lives are a series of traps' (Wright Mills, 1959). In this, the first line from his book, Mills is expressing how, as individuals, our lives are made up of unwritten rules that are enforced by social pressures to conform to a reality that fits with what those around us see as right; those with whom we identify and see an affiliation to our own identity. Foucault (1975), describes how society 'normalises judgement' by defining what is correct and proper, and therefore setting out a 'subjective ideology' of how the people in that society should behave. Foucault gives the example of prisons and mental institutions in the 18th century which acted as a mechanism for demonstrating to those that did not comply as 'docile bodies' how they would be treated. He saw this as corrective behaviour designed to elicit the appropriate response in people and to create a social structure which is regarded as orderly within the norms of that society. However, Foucault, unlike Mills, did not see discipline as just a coercive measure; he argued that although there are negative connotations to its usage, discipline or control also 'produces reality'. By this he means that it produces knowledge in the individuals who interact in the society, who in turn act accordingly and thus shape the society that they interact in. Foucault draws heavily on how issues are discussed and the role of discourse in the 'problematization' of things. By examining how we talk about such things as sexuality and mental illness (Foucault 1975, 1976, 1984a, 1984b) he demonstrates how it shapes our views. By defining what is seen as an 'issue' we also condone what is seen as the subjective norm. As Burr (2003) says, discourse serves to create a framework to help individuals to understand their experiences and as such, serves as a social control. Drawing on Foucault, she explains how power is focused through discourse to mask its coercive nature, thus persuading individuals that their choices lead to their actions, not societal constraints. When we look at it this way, this means that power may not lie with the individual, but in how the individuals or groups use language to create a culture. Foucault argues that society has moved from 'sovereign power', the ability of one individual (king or queen) to enact power over others, to 'disciplinary power', the ability of all to create power through discourse, in how they frame issues and concepts, in the language used. Goffman (1959) argues that this not only affects how we speak, but also how we act. This is substantiated by Foucault's (1975) work on panopiticism (see Glossary), where he argues that social control is enforced by how much we as individuals feel we are exposed to the gaze of others. If we feel we are being observed, we are likely to show conforming behaviours in our bid to seek approval from the society we are part of.

Foucault argued that control is a complex relationship between the individual and the organization and the key to holding power of control is in how the relationship works. His work was in direct contrast and disagreement with that of Marx, who felt that power and therefore oppression lay in the hands of the bourgeois, or in the organizational case, in the decision making of managers, not individuals. Evidence of both viewpoints can be found in organizations. The traditional mindset of work has been one where power has been with the managers and the workers are expected to conform, but are not trusted to do so. This leads to a culture of control through observation and systems of checking up.

In knowledge-intensive firms the power is seen much more with the individual and the discourse is more about engagement and commitment than control. What is important here is that workers feel trust towards the organization and therefore want to give their own knowledge freely in a bid to help the organization achieve its goals. Traditional organizational structures have been working on a mindset of sovereign power, or obedience to a clear set of rules, with consequences for non-compliance. This paradigm sees power very much in the hands of the authority, but Foucault's argument is that there has been a shift to regulatory power, where individuals are preoccupied with their own identity and the technologies of self, how they portray themselves and warrant approval from society. Regulatory power sees the power in individuals to improve their self through a clear understanding of the socially accepted ideal.

Purcell *et al* (2003) stated that organizations that are seen to do well, do so through transmitting their 'big idea' to all the staff through their structures and mechanisms. These companies have strong cultures based on strategic vision that is integrated into their policies and practices, thus setting up the social structures to influence behaviour and, in turn, results. Those attracted to the organization will see themselves as identifying with the values of the organization. Purcell *et al* go on to emphasize that policies must reflect the vision and be meaningful to the organization. Critical to the instrumentality of these policies is how line managers engage with them and the people to whom they relate. These organizations use observation mechanisms to reinforce and further communicate their vision and reinforce their subjective ideology. However, as both Purcell's research and Foucault's work highlight, this is not without its problems. Purcell refers to the critical role of line managers, the social actors who implement organizational policies and practices as agents representing the organization's interest. But, and herein lies the problem, line managers also bring their own set of interests, values and interpretations to these policies and practices which has the potential to subvert the organization's intentions.

The philosophies we have dealt with so far refer to how the socially constructed ideal has an impact on the organization and also therefore the worker. However, social control can also be found at a more micro level in organizations. Again, drawing on principal agency theory (see Glossary), micro social constructs may not always be to the organization's interest. Organizations are made up of teams of individuals that are formed to carry out the vision of the organization, for the organization's benefit, and ideologically speaking, for the team's members' own benefit too. However, these teams are made up of groups of individuals who bring their own set of values, worries, mistrusts and interpretations to the group, and therefore also influence the behaviours in the group.

In a classic factory experiment Roy (1952) discovered that informal groups had formulated agreements as to acceptable rates of production. To exceed acceptable rates or fall below them would lead to individual sanctions in the group such as ridicule, criticism or even ostracism. This experiment demonstrated the power of group influence; even though pay is seen as the prime extrinsic motivator, in this case despite the opportunity to earn more (as greater productivity would lead to more pay under a piece rate system), individuals' desire to conform to group norms prevailed, clearly demonstrating the complexities of individual motivation. Group membership and social acceptance can be seen to play a large role in job satisfaction and how individuals see themselves in their work environment. This experiment demonstrated that group influences can be stronger than the individual motivations that organizations elicit.

Milgram (1973) demonstrated how easily individuals are influenced by the group. He asked volunteers to teach people a series of word pairs.

The volunteers were tasked with punishing those who did not learn by giving them an electric shock. Each time the individual made a mistake the shock level would be increased and the individual learner would get a greater shock for each mistake made. During the experiment Milgram found that individuals were prepared to, and indeed did, administer shock levels way over what was deemed safe because they were told to by authority figures. No shocks were actually given, and the learners were actors, but the volunteers believed that they were giving a shock to people. When a group member dissented from the protocol, as Milgram orchestrated, he found that of the 40 times, where he asked an actor to dissent, 30 times out of the 40 once someone dissented, others in the group did so. Thus, Milgram demonstrates the power of influence in the group.

Huczynski and Buchanan (2007) state that how we understand ourselves is not based on an ultimate 'truth' but on how we interact with others around us, and our environment to make sense of ourselves in this environment. Using this social constructivist argument (see Glossary), it would also follow that group influences can either improve or reduce a member's productivity and performance.

Aronson, Wilson and Akert (1994) explain how social perceptions can lead to social facilitation or social loafing. When in the presence of others, if a person feels that he or she is going to be evaluated, this can lead to apprehension, which tends to lead to better performance on simple tasks but impaired performance on complex tasks; this is social facilitation. If a person perceives that his or her performance cannot be evaluated, there will not be any apprehension about evaluation that is likely to lead to impaired performance on simple tasks but better performance on more complex tasks; this is social loafing. It was also found that the larger the team, the greater the chance of variation of performance in the group, therefore the harder for the organization to ensure consistency of output or service.

Applying these theories of social control to international companies also has its challenges. Using Foucault's theories, Said (1978) argues that country cultures operate a relationship between economics, military and political interests. These are all interrelated and affect the culture of a country, which in turn affects its politics and its organizational cultures, so companies that cross borders will find that their management practices may need to diverge in order to be effective. These social constructions are temporary and changeable as economics and politics change.

Self-control

So far we have concentrated on ideas relating to social control processes. However, these ideas pre-suppose that in order for social control to have any effect, self-control must also be present.

It is generally argued that personality is relatively fixed with roughly 40–50 per cent of what makes up individual personality based on genetic factors (Loehlin, 1992). Even in this relatively fixed model, however, this leaves over 50 per cent that is thought to be directly affected by environmental factors. Social acceptance is just such an environmental factor.

Social acceptance has to be warranted and individuals seeking social acceptance must therefore control their own impulses in order to achieve group acceptance. The enormous success of self-help books such as *How to Win Friends and Influence People* (Carnegie, 1936 – and still in print in 2012) demonstrates the desire of individuals to be socially successful. Goffman (1959) argues that every reaction, movement and utterance is done consciously with a view to demonstrating to others our social positioning. How we frame our discourse and how we represent ourselves is a deliberate bid to gain social acceptance with others. We form groups and mix with others in an attempt to build our own social identity. Kelman (1961) proposes that there are three ways in which individuals present themselves to show they are conforming; these are compliance, identification and internalization:

- **Compliance** is the adaptation of one's behaviour in order to obtain gratification or avoid sanction. However, this is an instant response and will therefore only last as long as there is a threat of sanction or a promise of reward. This effect is seen, for example, as a drop in absence rates in organizations at a time of economic uncertainty, or an increase in productivity in response to the promise of a bonus.

- **Identification** is when individuals' behaviour is in line with a group that they identify with and wish to be part of, but again, this behaviour may be no more than a temporary state. For example, some students may appear more studious than they normally would in a bid to join a group presentation that they feel will be good for their development. This state may not change their values once the presentation is done, but serves the purpose to join the group.

- **Internalization** is when a value takes on a more permanent state, and becomes a significant part of an individual's belief and value system. Once a principle is internalized it becomes a more stable part of an individual's value system and is therefore much more likely to be repeated as a set of behaviours.

Individuals mix with groups and join organizations to validate their own beliefs, and develop their own concept of self. The self-concept sets the image of how we wish to portray ourselves and thus reinforces our self-image. However, Rogers (1947) argues that there is a two-sided self, and that the self-concept can also be influenced by how others see us, depending on how realistic our perceptions of self are. Individuals' self-concept takes on two forms; how the individuals see themselves and then how others see them. If both the individual's view and the other people's view are reasonably consistent, then the individual will be receptive to the other people's view and be influenced by them.

So, self-concept can be seen as temporary or more permanent, depending on how much the aspect of self is central to one's life interests (Dubin, 1956). For example, a workaholic will have such a strong concept of self around work that they will want to work hard all the time – this is a part of their identity that is unlikely to change. Professional workers tend to have a stronger identity to work than non-professionals. This would infer that non-professional workers have central life interests outside work that are stronger than their work interests. Self-concept is also affected by personality stability. Those who find that their view of self is very different to others' view of them are likely to find the views offered by others threatening and will seek to ignore them and seek out people who will help to validate their view of self. These theories of how individuals make sense of themselves are very much based on Western cultural assumptions that individuals can deconstruct their historical self to understand their current self – a psychological perspective. The psychological perspective presupposes a knowledge approach to understanding, based on a scientific approach, but this is not the case in all cultures; some are more based on faith or spiritual influences than psychology. Issues such as how workers see themselves as well as the social context will have an impact on the PM processes used by the organization. This will be further explored in administrative control.

Administrative control

We have seen how individuals in the organization are subject to self-control, the personal motives influencing their behaviour as well as social control from the group, the norms and pressures of group dynamics – the process of socialization. These controls often happen in an unconscious, unplanned and informal way. By contrast, in this section we look at how organizations exert control intentionally to regulate self-control and social control. Organizations do this through mechanisms, policies and processes that constrain, influence or motivate the individuals and teams who work for them – what Johnson and Gill (1993) term 'administrative control'.

The rationale behind administrative control was initiated by Weber (1978), who advocated bureaucracy as 'the most rational known means of exercising authority of human beings'. Weber believed that by creating bureaucratic hierarchy, an organization cascaded through departments and levels the organizational objectives and control. Using bureaucratic measurements, an organization outlined what was predictable and calculable. Weber argued that if decision making was made by strict rules which have to be adhered to then control would be predictable and orderly, as these rules are designed and construed by people, this turns social action into 'rationally formed action'. Administrative control is rooted in the approach of '*homo economicus*', using rational economic reasoning to make decisions to increase the efficiency of people (for example Taylor, 1947). Johnson and Gill (1993) outline three common types of administrative control: rules and procedures, output control and information control. If rules are defined and behaviours are outlined then it is clear what is expected and what is the punishment should these rules not be adhered to. This creates a rationality to de-humanize the decision making, as it is transparent and set in the rules. Rules and procedures are useful where behaviours predictably lead to desired outcomes, but sometimes this is not easy to analyse. In such situations measurements of output become more important – the results are what matter, not how they are achieved – but the organization must clearly define the expected outcome and how to measure it. Information control is elicited through the disclosure of organizational or individual data. By demonstrating knowledge through the publishing of data, on financial figures or even such figures as absence, the organization is demonstrating its power and showing its position in the hierarchy to make these rationally formed decisions based on collected data. Such organizational and individual data is gathered and used in a perform-ance management system (PMS).

Performance management systems

From the HRM perspective, the performance of individuals and teams in organizations needs to be assessed, rewarded and ultimately improved in the belief that this will lead to organizational success. In practice, we can understand administrative control as PM and the interdependent PM processes and practices as a PMS. These systems will inevitably vary from organization to organization and depend on the type of work, size and age of the organization and the culture of the business.

For many organizations, an output-oriented definition of PM is domin-ant; a quantitative measure of production or a qualitative assessment of achievement: income generated, units produced, levels of customer satis-faction, targets met or objectives achieved. Here, performance means results that can be relatively straightforward to measure. More difficult to assess systematically are inputs; the abilities, attitudes and competen-cies an employee brings to the role, and behaviours; the enactment of competencies in a way that translates inputs into outcomes. And yet these less tangible elements of performance are also key to PM.

Taking an open systems approach, we see that each of these three dimensions of performance is interlinked. Viewed in this way, perform-ance is a process; it is not just about the destination (the results) but also the journey (the inputs and behaviours) that gets you there. At an individual level, employees hold particular personal competencies that they bring to their job, a combination of knowledge and abilities that are required to perform the tasks allocated to them. In enacting those abilities, each employee behaves in a certain way, puts in work effort, demonstrates 'citizenship' behaviour and this results in satisfactory achievement of the task; a tangible performance outcome. Importantly for some of the issues in this chapter, this process does not just take place at the individual level; it is not just individuals who perform but teams and organizations too. For teams, inputs such as collective knowledge, experience and cooperative teamworking behaviour can result in high productivity and quality output. At organizational level, inputs such as cultural values and workforce capabilities lead to collec-tive behaviour, such as customer focus, that results in customer satisfac-tion and profitability.

Various definitions of PM from the considerable volume of HRM academic and practitioner-oriented literature can help us to gain a greater understanding of how organizations approach the management and control of individual and team performance. Appraising the five definitions of PM in the box below, we can immediately see some areas of congruence and slight differentiation. Perhaps most striking is Mohrman and Mohrman's argument that PM is 'managing the business', ie it is day-to-day management; what managers are doing as a matter of routine (1995). This is echoed in the IPM definition, which stresses that PM relates to 'every activity of the organization'; for Armstrong and Baron (1998) it is 'integrated'. What do we take from this? Perhaps simply that PM is an integral part of management; an embedded activity that happens during the course of organizational events rather than a discrete practice that managers put into operation. Certainly, from an administrative control perspective this would make sense; for employees to perform effectively, there has to be more than infrequent sporadic attempts to influence their behaviour and outputs.

Definitions of PM

'[PM is] a strategy which relates to every activity of the organization set in the context of its human resources policies, culture, style and communications systems' (IPM, 1992).

'Performance management is managing the business' (Mohrman and Mohrman, 1995).

'Performance management is a strategic and integrated approach to delivering sustained success to organizations by improving the performance of the people who work in them and by developing the capabilities of teams and individual contributors' (Armstrong and Baron, 1998).

'Performance management can be defined as a systematic process for improving organizational performance by developing the performance of individuals and teams. It is a means of getting better results from the organization, teams and individuals by understanding and managing performance within an agreed framework of planned goals, standards and competence requirements' (Armstrong, 2006: 1).

'Performance management is the system through which organizations set work goals, determine performance standards, assign and evaluate work, provide performance feedback, determine training and development needs and distribute rewards' (Briscoe and Claus, 2008: 15).

One way of understanding these issues is to look, not at what PM is, but what organizations are aiming to achieve in implementing PM practices. Armstrong, an influential author of many texts on PM, summarizes the key aim of PM: 'To establish a high-performance culture in which individuals and teams take responsibility for the continuous improvement of business processes and for their own skills and contributions within a framework provided by effective leadership' (Armstrong, 2006).

This emphasis on high performance working and continuous improvement of processes is heavily influenced by Japanese work practices that have been heralded in the West as a move away from management 'command and control' practices towards autonomous or 'self-managed' teams. The thinking behind such approaches centres on the organizational benefits of greater employee satisfaction, better decision making and more creative solutions (Pfeffer, 1998). Hence, 'teamworking' has become an almost universally adopted concept seen as a vital component of organizational success (Marchington, 1999). The implementation of teamworking, however, has not always lived up to the rhetoric, with the incidence of fully autonomous teams rare (Marchington and Wilkinson, 2009). Moreover, Barker (1993) suggests that teamworking is, what he terms, 'concertive' control; control exerted by workers (self and social control) rather than management control under the rational rules of Weberian bureaucracy (the 'iron cage'). Furthermore, control through teamworking practices are not only more powerful, they are 'less apparent and more difficult to resist', creating 'a new iron cage whose bars are almost invisible to the workers it incarcerates.' (Barker, 1993).

A modern, commitment-oriented PMS then, is not only a way organizations exert traditional administrative control on individuals and teams, it can also be a powerful tool for tapping into the mechanisms of self-control and social control explored above, with the potential for even greater influence on behaviour and performance of employees.

Managing performance in practice

Given this potentially very powerful means of managing performance, there is surprisingly little evidence of wholehearted agreement that a PMS successfully meets organizational needs. A 2009 CIPD survey of 507 of its members, for example, found very little agreement about what

PM is capable of achieving in practice. Only 30 per cent of respondents agreed with the statement that PM enables individuals to understand what they ought to be doing and this rather modest result was the highest rate of agreement in the study. When asked about claims that PM has a positive impact on individual and organizational performance there were slightly more respondents who disagreed than agreed (CIPD, 2009a). It is clear that HR professionals themselves are not wholly convinced that operational PM achieves its aims.

It seems to us that one reason for the lack of confidence in and success of PM in practice is the associated lack of understanding of the issues we have discussed in this chapter surrounding control – particularly the impact of self-control and social control on individual and group behaviour in organizations. While we are certainly not advocating a return to 'management by control' principles, we are suggesting that a greater understanding of the psychological processes underlying issues of control and commitment can benefit managers approaching the challenges of managing the performance of their teams.

Building on the PM process described above, we can classify PM practices in three categories:

- **Character inputs** – the organizational practices that are intended to create desired behaviours and outputs. These are the things organizations do to 'shape' the employee, for example gaining 'buy in' to corporate values during induction and the interventions that might be made (such as counselling or coaching) if performance levels are lower than expectation.

- **Task behaviours** – they way things are done. Organizations can set out behaviour standards in the form of competency frameworks, create rules about conduct and appearance, and lay down procedures and protocols to describe explicitly how tasks are performed. Deviation from the rules or procedures usually incurs punishment or sanction either in the form of formal disciplinary measures or withholding of social or work-related benefits.

- **Results** – the outputs commonly associated with 'performance'. By setting clear objectives to be achieved, formally reviewing performance in appraisals and incentivizing output with reward practices such as sales commission, organizations attempt heavily to influence the achievement of results.

TABLE 4.1 PM implications arising from the self-control, social and administrative control perspective of HRM practices

	HRM practice	Self-control, social or administrative control perspective	Implications for PM
Character inputs			
Recruitment and selection	Finding people with the right skills, qualifications and expertise to perform in the job.	The organization specifies pre-emptively attitudinal and behavioural characteristics of organizational members (Townley, 1989)	PM can start before the employment relationship begins with sophisticated and systematic recruitment and selection practices.
Induction and socialization	A process of employees' adjustment to a new job, establishing working relationships and finding roles for themselves within teams.	Individuals joining an organization are likely to be seeking social acceptance but may be demonstrating compliance or identification behaviours rather than internalization (Kelman, 1961).	Induction can form a vital part of PM processes as an early opportunity to establish desired attitudes and behaviours in new employees as internalized values.
Training and development	Employees acquiring new skills or knowledge by formal and informal interventions such as training, mentoring, coaching or on-job experience.	According to situated learning theory (Lave and Wenger, 1991) learning is the co-construction of knowledge as a social process embedded in a specific social environment.	Using discourse to influence behaviours through learning. This could be done through meetings, workshops, coaching, mentoring or action learning.
Managing the employment relationship	A range of practices associated with managing collective and individual employment relationships – emphasis on involvement, commitment, engagement and development of a positive psychological contract.	Commitment-oriented employee relations practices can be viewed as an extension of the 'iron cage' shifting responsibility for employee control to the individual and group rather than the organization.	While commitment-oriented practices may well be more pleasant to work under for employees, managing performance in this way still constitutes organizational exertion of control.

TABLE 4.1 *continued*

	HRM practice	Self-control, social or administrative control perspective	Implications for PM
Task behaviours			
Rules and procedures, codes of conduct, job descriptions	The organization makes it clear and explicit to its employees what is seen as correct and appropriate behaviour, how tasks should be carried out and also the consequences of non-compliance, eg the disciplinary procedure.	The organization is relying predominantly on self-control to regulate behaviour by explicitly defining its expectations but will exert corrective punishment (including expulsion) to force compliance of its members (Foucault, 1975). However, compliance behaviours are only temporary behavioural strategies to avoid sanction (Kelman, 1961).	Over-reliance on rules and procedures implies lack of trust and necessitates extensive observation and checking. The long-term consequence for PM is that employee behaviour may be arrested at the compliance stage and does not progress to internalization and commitment to organizational values.
Competency frameworks	Structures that set out the behavioural or technical attributes employees must have or develop in order to perform effectively in their jobs. They can form the 'language of performance' in organizations (CIPD, 2011a) and form the basis for assessment of employee performance.	These are mechanisms for reinforcing subjective ideologies in organizations. Additionally, line managers bring their own set of interests, values and interpretations to employee assessment of competencies.	Competency frameworks have the potential to be unfair and even discriminatory in their formulation or implementation by line managers.

TABLE 4.1 *continued*

	HRM practice	Self-control, social or administrative control perspective	Implications for PM
Results			
Output control and objective setting	Managers set desired output levels or objectives and monitor achievement against the plan.	Groups exert informal influences on individual members that regulate outputs and achievement of objectives and can disrupt extrinsic motivational techniques such as piecework schemes (Roy, 1952; Milgram, 1973).	The power of informal group influence cannot be underestimated in PM as an extrinsic motivational factor and should be borne in mind in the design and implementation of output-oriented PM practices.
Performance-linked reward practices	There are variable pay schemes, linking achievement of pre-set objectives aligned to business strategy with incentive or bonus payments.		
Performance appraisal	There is an opportunity for individuals and their line managers to review and discuss performance and development support requirements.	If there is little consistency between an individual's own view of self and that of others he or she is likely to find the views offered by others threatening and will seek to ignore such views (Dubin, 1956). 'Distortion' effects of individual assessment (Grint, 1993).	Appraisal is a key PM practice but can become confrontational and demotivating. Use of 360-degree reviews and developing employee and manager self-awareness through the use of personality questionnaires etc may alleviate these effects.

The PM process becomes a cycle when the results determine the organization's response in the form of new inputs to character, a training and development intervention for example, to influence the performance being achieved (see Figure 4.1).

To illustrate the PM process in practice we now focus on three managerial PM practices looking at how managers use this process and problems they may encounter.

FIGURE 4.1   Cycle of PMS practices

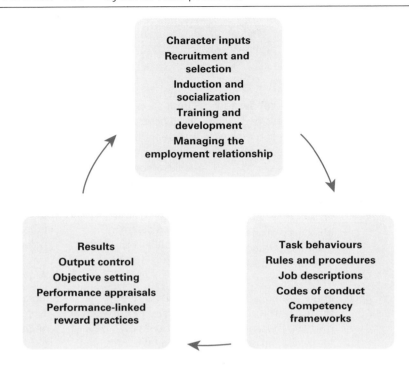

Character inputs – induction and socialization

Taylor (2010) states that 'there is nothing easier than giving new starters a poor induction'. He emphasizes how easy it is to neglect the early stages of the employment relationship and thus lead to disorientation and demotivation. Yet Armstrong (2009) makes it clear how important this stage is to new staff, by stating the aims of induction as being to establish a favourable attitude to the organization and obtain effective output of new staff as quickly as possible. This can be seen as a form of social control. By socializing the individual in the organization and influencing group formation, organizations can work to foster good relationships with new employees. Through arranging meetings with influential people in the company, managers are ensuring that the right relationships are built and thus influencing a strong organization commitment and work ethic. This depends on key players also working to organizational goals rather than their own agendas and on the social actors (managers) conveying the right messages. If one also factors in such issues as leader–member exchange (Dansereau, Graen and Haga, 1975), which is the early influence of managerial relationships, it is vital that managers use the induction phase sensitively to build up strong commitment with new members of staff. Achieving successful inductions can be difficult; they are time consuming and need to be tailored to individual need. Managers may complain about the amount of time and personal effort that induction requires, but this is important for leader–member exchange and building a reciprocal relationship. Often, companies run inductions for all new staff, which are a way of introducing important policies and rules, but these can be impersonal and do little to build relationships. It is, therefore, crucial to also draw up individual schedules to help people settle in. Drawing on knowledge creation theory, we can use Nonaka's (1994) model to demonstrate how induction acts as a form of PM. The first stage of this model is socialization; here the individual is given the chance to network with people and demonstrate his or her existing knowledge of the job. This is followed by externalization, where the individual is exposed to new explicit knowledge, both structured and unstructured. This new information is then combined with what the individual already knows in the combination phase, followed by the internalization phase where the individual can create new knowledge to help him or her to better carry out the role.

Task behaviours – competency frameworks

Another way in which an organization seeks to influence the behaviour of its members is by making explicit what are seen as desirable behavioural traits through the use of competencies. This is a form of input control, or rules and procedures. It makes clear and explicit what the organization sees as desired skills and behaviours. Boyzatis (1982) refers to competencies as behaviours that are associated with superior performance. He differentiates this from competence, which is a standardized level of performance, often used in NVQs. According to Armstrong (2009) the four most common uses of competencies are for learning and development, PM, selection and recruitment. Competencies break down behaviours into different categories, the most commonly used are team orientation, communication, people management, customer focus, results orientation, problem solving, planning and organizing, technical skills and leadership (Armstrong, 2009). They are time-consuming to develop and become out of date easily as they usually comprise what were seen as desirable behavioural traits in the past. As businesses change constantly this can be problematic, so in order for competencies to remain effective, organizations need to regularly review and update the categories. As with all PM techniques, they are only as good as the user. Managers can interpret their meaning and this can mean that some behaviours are seen as more important than others, depending who is administrating the process in the area. Therefore it is important to train managers in how to use them effectively.

Results – performance appraisal

The performance appraisal is the formal review and assessment of individual performance that happens annually or more frequently and usually culminates in a face-to-face interview between an employee and his or her line manager. There are various reasons why appraisals can be problematic for managers and their employees. First, there is long-standing research (notably Grint, 1993) to show that a variety of 'distortions' can occur in assessment of individuals by their line managers (for example, the 'halo or horns' effect when the appraiser only notes positive or negative attributes; or the 'doppelganger' effect when appraisers reward attributes that are similar to their own). The work of Dubin (1956) discussed above is also relevant here – challenges to an individual's self-concept may well be met by lack of cooperation or outright hostility, making the appraisal confrontational and an unpleasant experience for all involved. Clearly, this has profound implications for the organization's ability to operate fair and effective PM. Training for line managers and use of alternative PM techniques such as 360-degree appraisal may alleviate these effects but the capability of line managers is not the only problem. One of the more fundamental problems with performance appraisal is the potential conflict of purpose in what it is trying to achieve. Is the appraisal to assess performance over the previous year with a view to rewarding successful outcomes? Or is it to review performance to identify development needs in the forthcoming year? Many systems in fact try to do both and hence there is a conflict between reward and developmental purposes. The problem here is the likely impact on open and honest discussion between an employee and his or her manager about development needs and then how these needs are to be met. An individual whose annual bonus or merit pay rise depends on a successful performance review is unlikely to flag up areas where his or her performance needs developing. The performance appraisal becomes an exercise in convincing line managers that appropriate performance has been achieved and nothing more, which subverts the organization's intention to improve performance by identifying opportunities for development. Separating the process of appraising performance and identifying development needs is therefore vital for the PM process shown in Figure 4.1 to work effectively.

Key learning points and conclusions

- We have suggested that developing an understanding of power, control and identity in organizations is important for managers seeking to handle the performance of their employees effectively.

- Administrative control advocates the use of labour to maximize efficiency and increase organizational performance. The creation of rules and procedures, output control mechanisms and control of information disclosure are key administrative control techniques that are visible in many PMSs.

- Understanding the role of such techniques is important for managers but so is acknowledgement of their limitations and the drawbacks of heavy reliance on this type of PM. Both the failure to acknowledge motivational aspects of work and the dehumanizing impact on the worker have profound implications for the rights of the individual, as well as for basic levels of trust between worker and organization, which undermine organizational performance.

- Ideas relating to social control are rooted in the human relations movement where there is, by contrast, explicit acknowledgement of the importance of increasing morale and gaining trust of the individual.

- Socialization in the organization is seen as important in its contribution to building a sense of commitment to, and internalization of, organizational values in employees as well as group cohesion. But the forces of informal social-group influence stemming from individual need to form group bonds, social facilitation and social loafing are extremely powerful. These forces can all regulate behaviour and performance of individuals and teams in ways that may undermine both managerial control and organizational goals.

- Furthermore, we have seen how, if managers do not have the same interpretations of what constitutes good performance as the senior individuals in the organization, there is a risk that organizational intentions will be subverted. So a significant question for organizations centres on how they control the values and interpretations of the managers that are relied on to achieve organizational strategy through PM processes.

- It is important for managers to appreciate the role of self-control in PM. Individuals will act in order to gain social acceptance and this may be interpreted as adoption of organizational values by managers but may be mere compliance behaviour.

- We have also concluded that the development of self-concept and self-identity has important implications for how individuals perform at work. Undermining the needs of individuals to realize their true identity in a work environment, thus inhibiting growth and development in a traditional bureaucratic work structure, will be detrimental to individual, group and ultimately organizational performance.

Discussion questions

- How effective are PM practices in improving individual, team and organizational performance in your organization (or one with which you are familiar)?

- Think about how your organization (or one with which you are familiar) manages the performance of employees. Would you describe these practices as commitment- or control-oriented?

- Do you agree that managing performance is 'managing the business'?

- Do you think that 360-degree appraisals are a 'fairer' way of reviewing individual performance than through manager feedback alone?

Case study and discussion questions

Relationship between a team leader and
line manager

James was a team leader of a small group dealing with motor vehicle insurance in a company providing commercial insurance and financial advice. He had been with the company for six years, and three years ago was promoted to team leader, showing a lot of early promise. But James was unhappy with his line manager, Paul. 'When he took over as line manager two years ago,' says James, 'we were having problems with a couple of members of the team, who were not performing well, and who were a disruptive influence. My line manager was not happy with the fact that it took a long time to resolve the problems, and that team performance suffered. Paul didn't realize how careful you have to be if you want to discipline and dismiss someone. After that he always saw me as a poor team leader; he was constantly on my back, watching me and checking up on me. He just didn't let me run the team in the way I would have liked to.'

James went on to say that his line manager told him that he was weak, and not good at motivating his team. Paul often sat in on team meetings, talking directly to the team, undermining James' authority. He wanted to see target and performance figures regularly, and spent a lot of time telling James how to run his team, and how to get the best out of the team members. James started to doubt his own abilities and became an inconsistent team leader, sometimes coaching and supporting team members, sometimes criticizing and threatening them, particularly after he had had a difficult session with Paul.

The team members were unhappy, not sure whether to trust James, or see him as a failure, as his line manager did. They resented his inconsistent behaviour. One member of the team left, several attempted to move to other departments, and performance was poor.

Paul had been appointed from outside the organization and had built up a good record of getting teams to work hard and productively. By this point he was fed up with James, and had decided to get rid of him. 'He was too concerned with being liked by his team. He couldn't push them, or deal with poor performers. I couldn't rely on him to get work done, and I had to spend a lot of time monitoring him and the team. I had to set targets, and check performance. If I left the team to itself it wouldn't perform. I hadn't got the time to keep telling this team what to do but I just didn't trust James to performance manage this team effectively on his own.'

Discussion questions

Reflecting on some of the issues considered in this chapter relating to social and self-control perspectives:

- Why do you think the relationship between James and his line manager Paul had become so difficult?

- Without intervention what do you think would have happened?

- If you had been asked to advise on what actions to take that would have avoided James leaving the organization and to ensure the team worked more effectively, what would you have proposed?

05

Leadership, communication and organizational effectiveness

LINDA HOLBECHE

LEARNING OBJECTIVES

- Appreciate mainstream and critical approaches to leadership theory; how and where these vary and complement one another and why.
- Understand the key roles leaders play in ensuring organizational effectiveness.
- Explain why new approaches to leadership are called for.

Introduction

Interest in leadership as a concept and a practice is not new, yet in recent years leadership has become one of the most topical themes in the OB pantheon. Recently, a quick internet search on the subject of leadership yielded about 358,000 entries in 19 seconds!

This chapter considers why discussion about leadership has become so prominent in recent decades. Any discourse about people management must take into account the changing nature of organizational context, and while it is beyond the scope of this chapter to consider all aspects of the context in which organizations are operating, specific aspects will be highlighted that appear to influence how leadership is defined and understood in contemporary organizations. In particular, we will explore some of the dominant influences contributing to the development of a 'new' work culture and related calls for new approaches to leadership. These include 'background' factors such as the changing global economy, advancements in technology and the changing demographic which will continue to have an impact on the shape and nature of organizations, work and the employment relationship.

Recent developments and trends with regard to leadership theory and practice will be examined through a review of leadership literature post-2002. Mainstream and critical approaches to understanding leadership, management and HRM will be contrasted. This chapter will argue that traditional definitions of leadership, in which leadership is primarily associated with the characteristics, capabilities, behaviours and values of individual leaders, need to be expanded to meet the needs of 21st century organizations and networks.

Why is leadership so topical?

From the earliest times and in possibly every culture, tales about leaders and leadership have abounded. Arguably, humanity has always been pre-occupied with personal security, maintenance, protection, and survival (Van Vugt, Hogan, and Kaiser, 2008) which leaders helped secure. Quality of leadership by individual leaders is therefore conventionally assumed to be central to the survival and success of groups and organizations. Many of the historical images associated with leadership have their roots in conflict and are about great (mostly) military leaders such as Alexander the Great, Julius Caesar, Napoleon and Winston Churchill – generals who outwit their opponents, politicians who convince and channel groups into action, and people who take control of a crisis.

The current explosion of interest in the theme of leadership has arisen perhaps because leadership is assumed to be the 'solution' to a number of challenging issues facing contemporary organizations. For instance, perhaps because of the generally low levels of employee morale reported in various surveys, the links between leadership styles and employee engagement, and the notion of a 'great place to work' have become areas of growing HRM preoccupation. Similarly, in fast changing and highly competitive contexts, organizations may need greater agility and the ability to achieve 'more for less'. Other context factors are also driving the growth in interest in leadership. Over the last two decades, the increasingly knowledge-based economy has brought about a sea change in the nature of work and the skills required by workers. Organizations are becoming complex and networked, with speed of innovation seen as the means of staying ahead of the competition. In comparison to older economies, where growth was based on physical assets, such as facilities and equipment, growth in the new economy is said to occur through innovation rather than mass production; value is measured on less tangible assets such as intellectual capital, talent and patents.

Similarly, the more diverse and multi-generational nature of work-forces and the widespread use of social media by employees as a means of connecting with other people are factors driving the need for diffe-rent forms of communication and for different styles of leadership than in times gone by. Old style 'command and control' leadership styles seem out of place in such contexts where getting work done depends on collaboration and adult–adult, employer–employee relationships. How leadership theory is developing in response to these changing external environmental factors will be discussed in more detail later in this chapter.

More generally, the growing interest in leadership in the corporate world might also be explained by the seemingly high levels of change and restructuring taking place, often in response to the challenging business context. In their study of the top business leaders of the last century, Mayo and Nohria found that an innate ability to read the forces that shape the times in which they live – and to seize on the resulting opportunities – is a characteristic of successful top leaders. These writers argue that it is a lack of contextual sensitivity to the zeitgeist that can cause any leader to fail since, as they point out: 'Companies don't succeed or fail in a vacuum. When it comes to long-term success the ability to understand and adapt to changing business conditions is at least as important as any particular personality trait or competency' (2009).

The complexities of today's business environment, particularly the financial crisis and subsequent broader economic and social malaise, are contextualized as providing high levels of stress and ambiguity for almost all businesses and employees. It could be argued that the primitive human need to identify with a community that provides security, protection, maintenance and a feeling of belonging is as strong as ever, and that this need is now met by the informal organization and its emergent, or unofficial, leaders. And while it is inappropriate to anthropomorphize the organization (ie treat it as having a concrete existence of its own; Guest, Isaksson and De Witte, 2010), nevertheless, in one sense, for many employees, leaders and organization have become synonymous.

However, leadership has also recently become topical for the wrong reasons. The ethics of corporate, institutional and political leadership has been called into question in the wake of various corporate or institutional scandals, such as the Enron and WorldCom debacles, debates about rewards for executive failure, the MPs' expenses scandal in the UK, revelations about the power of media moguls over politicians, to name but a few. As a result, public trust in corporate and establishment leaders is reported to be at an all-time low.

What is leadership?

Leadership is a compelling, yet elusive, topic. Definitions of leadership abound, for instance: 'Leadership is about capturing attention and motivating people to follow your way – your vision and your dreams' (Augier and Teece, 2005). Leadership is about 'influencing others to accomplish organizational goals' (Tubbs, in Tubbs and Schulz, 2006). Yet, according to several commentators, in spite of the plethora of studies, we still seem to know little about the defining characteristics of effective leadership (Dulewicz, Young and Dulewicz, 2005). Indeed 'as a scientific concept, leadership is a mess' (Augier and Teece, 2005).

As a theme, leadership can be contentious, giving rise to many debates:

- Are leaders born, not 'made'?
- Is leadership synonymous with rank?
- How does leadership differ from management?
- Can you be both a manager and a leader?

While there is a large literature on the theme of team leadership, the bulk of leadership literature focuses on the roles of individual leaders, especially senior managers as leaders. Here there can be a lot of confusion. Some argue that not all managers, for example, are leaders; and not all leaders are managers. Moreover, many US texts treat leadership and management as synonymous (Mintzberg, 2009; Hamel and Breen, 2007).

Leadership 'at the top'

From an OB perspective, there is a degree of consensus among theorists that leadership by top management is one of the most significant factors affecting organizational health. Schein (2008), for instance, views leadership and culture as two sides of the same coin since, consciously or otherwise, leaders first create cultures when they create groups and organizations (see Chapter 8). Once cultures exist they determine the criteria for leadership and therefore who will or will not be a leader. But if elements of an organization's culture become problematic in a changing environment, Schein argues that it is the unique function of a leader to be able to perceive the functional and dysfunctional elements of the existing culture and to manage cultural evolution and change in such a way that the group can survive. Given the link between organizational culture and business practice, as evidenced by various corporate scandals, this raises the question of just who exactly governs leaders.

Many contemporary studies focus on links between leadership by top managers and employee engagement. High performance theory places employee engagement or 'the intellectual and emotional attachment that an employee has for his or her work' (Heger, 2007) at the heart of performance, especially among knowledge workers. Employee engagement has been linked in various studies with higher earnings per share, reduced sickness absence, higher productivity and innovation; the business benefits go on and on.

Sibson's (2006) research on employee engagement found two common features in organizations with high performance: knowing what to do and wanting to do the work. Topics such as clarity of business strategy, top level leadership and speed of decision making can have a big impact. For instance, Heintzman and Marson's (2006) Canadian research on a public sector value chain lists effective leadership and management among the most important engagement and performance drivers. Similarly, a government report into employee engagement in the UK (MacLeod and Clarke, 2009) concludes that 'engaging leadership' is one of the main drivers of employee engagement.

Leadership culturally defined

Definitions of leadership tend to vary over time, and the meanings attributed to leadership are culturally specific. Even whether someone is considered a 'good' or a 'bad' leader is culturally and politically determined and will vary according to the lens used to consider the question. For example, while Genghis Khan, Attila the Hun and Hitler may have been considered great leaders by their followers, those who feared them took a different view.

Yet a review of leadership literature, both pre- and post-2002, highlights how much of this reflects Western, particularly US theory. Arguably this is because the dominant form of global capitalism over the past 30 years is Anglo-American and is underpinned by neo-liberal ideology (see Glossary), which Hutton refers to as 'free market fundamentalism' (Hutton, 2010). This involves the deregulation of markets, reducing the size of the state, the pursuit of competitive advantage and corporate and individual 'survival of the fittest'.

Related to this ideology and the pursuit of shareholder value is the development of managerialism, which we will return to later in this chapter. Leadership theory and mainstream management writing, much of it by consultants, has burgeoned since the 1980s, a common characteristic of which is an acceptance of the prevailing conditions that require leaders to behave in certain ways.

Points to ponder

How might non-Western and non neo-liberal approaches to leadership change how we think about the 'legitimate leader'?

What other types of leaders or leadership in other cultural settings (for example ethnic, geographic, gender, organizational, political) can you think of?

Categories of leadership theory

The messiness in theorizing about leadership arises partly because leadership theories tend to fall into two broad categories: essentialist or contextualist, each of which may bracket off other ways of understanding leadership.

Essentialism

The ontology (see Glossary) of essentialism is that there are two realities of phenomena: one that is the essence (which is real and knowable) and the second that is perceived. While the essence is perfect and ideal, the perceived is that which is in a constant state of flux. The essentialist is committed to the view that the human mind can come to know the essence of things, if only partially, since society is fragmented and a natural science view of how it should be studied determines how it comes to be understood. To essentialists, because leadership is a natural effect, social scientists must search for leadership's ideal character, a general theory of leadership that permeates all human experience. Essentialists document idealized and universal personality traits and situations and match the individual leader's orientation with certain organizational situations. The leader's role is therefore often linked to some other role such as manager or expert. Four things stand out in this regard. First, to lead involves influencing others. Second, where there are leaders there are followers. Third, leaders often become visible when an innovative response is needed to a crisis or special problem. Fourth, leaders are people who have a clear idea of what they want to achieve and why. Thus, leaders are people who are able to think and act creatively in non-routine situations – and who set out to influence the actions, beliefs and feelings of others.

Over the last century four main categories of essentialist leadership theory have been influential, though it is important to note that none of these categories is mutually exclusive or lacking advocates today:

Trait theories

The 'essence' of leadership approach underpins trait theory. Trait or 'great man' theory is an individual orientation approach. In the past, the personal qualities, characteristics or traits of heroic figures or 'great men' were studied and used as templates against which leadership potential could be understood and assessed. In leadership development programmes, special individuals stand out in the popular imagination or memory as 'great leaders', for example Joan of Arc, Ghandi or Martin Luther King, people whose actions appear pivotal in moments of crisis. They have a vision of what can, and should be done, and can communicate this to others. From this, it would be easy to assume that the nature of leadership is common across all cultures. In leadership, the essentialist focus is on who leaders are, what they pay attention to, as much as what they do. Even today, we use idealized competency templates to assess potential for leadership.

Behavioural theories

In the 1940s theorists started to focus more on how leaders behaved with respect to other people, rather than on their traits alone. The assumption was that leadership can be learned. Influential proponents of the behavioural approach were mainly US-based, such as the Ohio State Leadership Studies, which focused on how leaders could satisfy common group needs. The research followed a psychological scientific method using quantitative analysis of questionnaires to leaders and subordinates (Ohio State University Leader Behavior Description Questionnaire, 1957–62). The findings indicated that the two most important dimensions of leadership were: 'initiating structure' (ie task-oriented: the extent to which a leader defines leader and group member roles, initiates actions, organizes group activities and defines how tasks are to be accomplished by the group) and 'consideration' (ie people-oriented: the extent to which a leader exhibits concern for the welfare of the members of the group). These characteristics could be rated as either high or low and were treated as independent of one another. (See **www.odportal.com/leadership/ fastlearner/ohiostate.htm**)

According to the Michigan Leadership Studies which began in the 1950s leaders could be classified as either 'employee centred', or 'job centred'. (Boje, 2000) These studies identified three critical characteristics of effective leaders: task-oriented behaviour, relationship-oriented behaviour and participative leadership. In their study of leadership behaviour, Blake and Mouton (1964) developed a managerial grid which described two extremes of leadership concern – for production, and for people. The stereotypical leadership styles thus identified were 'impoverished', 'country club', 'middle of the road', 'authoritarian' and 'team'.

As time moved on, theories that focused on leadership style, without taking into account the needs of 'followers,' came to be considered incomplete since the leader's task was to deliver results through people. Instead it was proposed that leaders' behaviour should flex to respond to the requirements of the followers in any given situation. Hersey and Blanchard's (1988) 'situational leadership' framework is still widely used in organizations today. This takes into account what followers need from leaders at any given time, and also leaders' ability to respond appropriately to these needs.

Contingency theory

Contingency theory is a class of behavioural theory that claims that there is no one best way to organize a corporation, lead a company or make decisions. Instead, the optimal course of action is contingent (dependent) on the internal and external situation. Fiedler's (1994) contingency model proposes that the leader's effectiveness is based on 'situational contingency' that is a result of interaction of two factors: leadership style and situational favourableness (later called situational control). For example, a task-oriented leadership would be advisable in a natural disaster, such as a flood or fire, whereas the considerate (relationship-oriented) style of leadership can be appropriate in an environment where the situation is moderately favourable or certain. In order to allow for complexity, good leaders need to be able to 'read' the situation specifically and sensitively and adjust their behaviour accordingly. Effective leaders are deemed to be those who are responsive or proactive in dealing with situational complexity.

Transformational theories

Weber (1947) was the first to distinguish between transactional leaders, such as bureaucratic leaders, and transformational leaders, such as charismatic leaders. Since the 1980s, the charismatic, visionary or transformational approaches – all individual orientations (ie consistent with the essentialist and atomist view) – have come to dominate Western leadership theory (Burns, 1978; Bass, 1985). Such approaches emphasize the leader's ability to influence others to act. Weber (1947) defined 'charisma' as 'a certain quality of an individual personality, by virtue of which he is set apart from ordinary men and treated as endowed with supernatural, superhuman, or at least specifically exceptional powers or qualities'. The charismatic leader gathers followers through dint of personality and charm, rather than any form of external power or authority.

The charismatic leader and the transformational leader have many similarities, in that the transformational leader may well be charismatic. The main difference is in their basic focus. Whereas the transformational leader's focus is on transforming the organization and, quite possibly, their followers, the charismatic leader may not want to change anything. Exemplar transformational leaders are generally viewed as having a clear vision, strong values and courage, together with the ability to inspire a devoted following and to develop their followers. This approach, being value- or principle-led is not always flexible.

Collins' influential book *Good to Great* (2001) describes the nature and characteristics of 'level 5' leaders who, in his view, are the leaders best able to help organizations break through to 'greatness'. In contrast to many conventional characteristics of heroic leaders, who are stereotypically assumed to charismatically, assertively and visibly take charge in given situations, level 5 leaders are described as humble and of low visibility in the organization. They work for others and themselves; they recognize the intrinsic worth of employees and other stakeholders, and support the development of associates. While transformational leaders bring hope to followers, they may also create emotional pain in others by the changes they bring about (Frost, 2004; McKenna and Yost, 2004).

Thus many of today's most influential leadership theories, and the assessment and development tools which derive from them, such as competencies, work within an essentialist frame of understanding.

Contextualism

In contrast, contextualist theorists (see 'contextualism', Glossary) believe that a complex system of cultural, social, psychological and historical differences constitute human experience (Owen Jones, 1996). They do not deny that phenomena such as leadership exist; however, they argue that such phenomena are more complex, multi-faceted, and varying than previously envisaged.

One concept underlying much of contextualist theory is that reality is socially constructed. Social constructivism is the belief that reality is developed through people's interpretation of the world, rather than representing a universal essence (Calas and Smircich, 1996). Contextualist scholars have challenged previously held universal truths and essences because, in this view, there is no objective vantage point (or reality) and our perceptions are the only thing we can come to know. Contextualists also question whether universal essences or truths even exist beyond our perceptions. Instead, knowledge is seen as contingent on local conditions and contexts, the phenomena under consideration being always in a state of becoming. Accordingly, reality is a social and cultural construction, not an idealized form beyond our immediate perception. By examining multiple interpretations, a shared sense of reality can be detected; nevertheless, our understanding of reality is always partial and imperfect. Each of us generates our own 'rules' and 'mental models' which we use to make sense of our experiences.

Similarly, there are no universal, essential, and transcendent aspects of leadership. For contextualists, leadership is shaped by individual, (local) conditions, circumstances, time, and variations of human experience. The emergent nature of leadership is emphasized, rather than the specific behaviours demonstrated by the leader. A leader is not a person who leads others but rather a person who is spontaneously followed by others before he or she is aware of it. A resonance and a swell of support, rather than a pseudo-organizational relationship, should be developed between leaders and followers (Noda, 2004).

In the contextualist leadership area, the foremost theoretical schools include cognitive, cultural and processual. Researchers in the field of psychology have investigated different psychological orientations, for example, different types of cognitive orientations among leaders (Antonakis, Avolio and Sivasubramaniam, 2003). Sociologists have examined social differences to understand whether race and gender affect leadership (Calas and Smircich, 2006). They have also examined cultural differences in an effort to understand whether different countries value different traits or influence strategies. Ethnographic and folkloristic studies illustrate that organizations and societies have particular histories and cultures that affect organizational phenomena, including leadership (Owen Jones, 1996; Kets de Vries, 1999). Historians have examined whether different (historical) periods require different approaches to leadership. Similarly, organizational theorists have studied whether different organizational contexts – including processual change that occurs in response to distinctive organizational histories and cultures (Bolman and Deal, 2008) – require different forms of leadership.

Points to ponder

Reflecting back on your earlier discussion, how do your own observations about leadership link with these various schools of thought?

For contextualists, leadership in each context is unique and is dynamic, emergent, and evolving over time. Because leadership is a process, it is volatile and sensitive to changes. Mayo and Nohria (2009) argue that great leadership is not a singular concept but is a function of the particular circumstances in which businesses and their executives operate. The latent opportunities of the context come into play at different times and may require different kinds of leadership. They identify three archetypes of executive leadership:

- entrepreneurs who are ahead of their time and not necessarily bounded by the context in which they live;

- managers who through a deep understanding of the landscape in which they are operating shape and grow businesses;

- leaders who confront change and identify latent potential in businesses or any organization.

With echoes of the conventional sociological debate about agency or structure, Mayo and Nohria argue that leadership and context are co-constructed.

The conclusion of these cultural studies, to contextualists, is that universal essences have little value in this emergent context and understanding of leadership. Despite this, many theorists take essentialist rather than contextualist perspectives, as we will discuss later with respect to 'new' perspectives on leadership. The general 'ideal' is for leaders to be able to respond to their changing environment by developing versatility, resilience, and emotional intelligence, thus enabling them to tailor their styles to specific people and situations. In other words, trait and situational leadership theories are alive and well. Later in this chapter you will have chance to consider a case study of leadership in a public sector context. When you read it, bear in mind these categories of theory as you evaluate the nature of the leadership challenge and the types of leadership you detect.

This polarity of categorization of leadership theory feeds through into policy frameworks that legitimize some forms of leadership and de-legitimize others. It also has an impact on how HRM and leadership might interface – with implications for the relative roles of those engaged in the employment relationship in organizations. Taken into MNC contexts, there are issues about how HQ staff judge leaders' fitness to lead subsidiary operations; about how leaders 'ought' to be developed as well as how leaders ought to think about themselves.

Points to ponder

Reflecting on your experiences and views about leadership, how would you categorize your own responses?

Are you more inclined to essentialist or contextualist views? Why?

What might you be taking for granted?

In the next section we will consider aspects of context that gave rise to the forms of managerialism and of HRM that are familiar today. In contrast to mainstream views about leadership, management and HRM, we will now consider these themes through the lens of critical management scholarship.

Critical management scholarship

Critical management scholarship (CMS) is a disparate field encompassing critical versions of postmodernism (Alvesson and Deetz, 2005) and radical humanist approaches (Burrell and Morgan, 1979), among others. For CMS scholars, the capitalist context is significant since some have explicitly Marxist leanings and seek to reveal the political and economic consequences of capitalism. These scholars aim to bring to light and challenge underlying philosophies and interests that produce the conditions in which leaders operate and to which followers are required to comply. According to Watson (2010), CMS's motivating concern is the social injustice and environmental destructiveness of the broader social and economic systems that managers and organizations serve and reproduce, rather than focusing simply on the practices of managers themselves. So by implication, critical scholars take a contextualist position, yet, for some of them at least, the agenda of conflicted employee relations might be viewed as essentialist.

The capitalist context: neo-liberalism and pursuit of shareholder value

The dominant form of global capitalism today was developed and promoted by the US and UK following the economic crisis of the late 1970s. The welfare capitalist model (see 'welfare capitalism', Glossary) of mass industrial production and capital accumulation was beginning to fail. There was a collapse in the rate of profit and a systemic crisis attributed by some to the successful pursuit by organized labour in the advanced industrial economies of high wage policies. Out of this crisis grew a new and invigorated global capitalism based on neo-liberalism (see Glossary) the dominant intellectual ideology of which is the efficient market hypothesis. This claims that individual competitive freedoms should be enhanced through the deregulation of markets, allowing capitalism to flourish free from state or other third party interference, such as the corporatist (see Glossary) settlements which the social partners in Europe, including the UK, arrived at after the Second World War. Successful competition, and the pursuit of competitive advantage, it was argued, would require new markets, greater efficiency and labour flexibility (see Glossary).

The development of this form of capitalism was assisted by the development of new information and communication technologies which began to transform traditional manufacturing and distribution systems. The utilization of knowledge and culture as economic resources led to the creation of new types of post-Fordist firms (see 'Fordism', Glossary), products and markets. Much traditional manufacturing capability migrated from the developed to parts of the developing world. The UK economy became predominantly service-based by the late 1990s, with three-quarters of employees employed in services and services accounting for two-thirds of GDP (Julius and Butler, 1998). Sennett (2006) argues that the capital-driven nature of Anglo-US forms of globalization resulted in short-termism and businesses themselves coming to be seen as short-term trading vehicles. By changing their investment patterns, international corporations could put local economies at risk. The pursuit of shareholder value became the rationale for corporate governance including how leadership in organizations was to be legitimized.

Managerialism

For many critical scholars, the prominence of leadership in mainstream theory from the 1980s onwards reflects the promotion of managerialism, an explicitly political project to better control and exploit labour in the interests of the capitalist class and its agents (such as corporate leaders). Effective management, and reducing the power of organized labour, came to be seen by governments from Margaret Thatcher's UK premiership and Ronald Reagan's US presidency onwards as the panacea for all economic ills. High levels of unemployment during the 1990s allowed managers to control recruitment and introduce more flexible structures, removing many aspects of the bureaucratic employment relationship, such as job security, and embed managerialism. The point was, of course, to unpack the corporatist settlement, which involved a critique of managers as a class, and to align what they are, who they align with, and what they do, with neo-liberal capitalist interests.

Top management's task was to increase shareholder value by providing customer value, stimulating innovation, finding new markets and driving down the cost of production, including employment costs. As deliverers of the mandate set by shareholders, 'leadership teams' focused on short-term value enhancements, through merger and acquisition, restructurings, outsourcing and divestments, driving down the costs of labour and finding cheaper ways of getting work done, such as through suppliers or via technology. The stage was set for the interests of 'leaders' and 'followers' to diverge.

Managerialism was further advanced in the UK as a political project and as a form of social domination by the New Right (see Glossary) including the 'New Labour' governments (1997–2009). This is reflected in the political attempts under New Labour to achieve a closer functional relationship between the state and a 'modernizing' of the public sector, as demonstrated in the centrally imposed public sector targets (Gamble, 2009). Conventional public sector leadership (akin to Weber's bureaucratic leadership and sometimes referred to as the 'trust us the professionals' model) was to be replaced by managers and their related tools, such as performance management, the rationale for which was efficiency as defined in relation to liberal market values. As a result, many professionals who had traditionally operated in a largely self-directed way, which managerialists considered negative, were obliged to comply.

Managerialism is now evident in diverse social spheres and in all sectors of the UK economy, its apparent legitimacy in the UK's neo-liberal economic context seemingly unquestioned. Deetz (1992) argues that the increased influence of management may be interpreted in terms of a 'corporate colonisation of the lifeworld' in that cultural and institutional forms become progressively subsumed in the logic of capitalism. This wholesale shift in power towards 'managers' (Parker, 2002), reflects the dominance of organizational interests in the employment relationship, arguably at the expense of employees' interests.

Thus, against this backdrop, the nature and task of leadership is riddled with paradox, complexity and ambiguity. It could be argued that 'old' management and leadership styles, based on a convention of low-trust and high control, sit uneasily against a paradigm of 'volunteer' knowledge workers, who are expected to be accountable and empowered, willing and able to create shared learning and intellectual capital. Moreover, high commitment leadership styles, especially if the 'walk' does not match the 'talk', are likely to be met by cynicism from employees. Not surprisingly, one of the key leadership challenges in today's organizations is that of employee engagement.

> **Points to ponder**
>
> In such a context, to what extent can leadership be both genuine and mutual (ie balancing the needs of external and internal stakeholders) when measures of success are short term and oriented to creating value for shareholders?
>
> Will the corporate governance context converging across business systems effectively determine how 'authentic' leadership is defined and assessed?

The HRM contribution

The discussion on leadership naturally progresses into a consideration of HRM as a particular form of leadership of people in organizational settings. To what extent is HRM playing a pivotal part in delivering sustainable performance through people (the Chartered Institute of Personnel Development's vision for HR)? Or could HRM itself be described as 'modern' management, and viewed as neo-Taylorism (see 'Taylorism', Glossary) dressed up as neo-human relations? The interests and objectives of many workers and their senior managers may have diverged. Yet mainstream management and HRM theory tends to ignore the essentially 'contested terrain of work' (Marchington and Wilkinson, 2009). This term refers to the complex interplay between the interests and objectives of workers and management, acting on behalf of owners or shareholders, typically portrayed as managers seeking to maintain control and generate workers' consent, creativity and commitment (Delbridge, 2007). While there is a growing interest in the management press in the practices of more mutual organizations, with the John Lewis Partnership being a well-known UK example of an organization with an ownership structure reflecting the principle of mutuality, on the whole such organizational examples are rare.

New approaches to leadership

Calls are growing for new forms of leadership, for a variety of reasons explored below.

Leadership for knowledge and service-based work

In mainstream organizations there is a growing recognition that new or evolved forms of management and leadership are needed that are better suited to the demands of a complex, fast-changing service- and knowledge-based economy. In such an economy, people are the source of production and, with the aid of knowledge technologies, knowledge is a tool to produce economic benefits as well as job creation. As workforces become increasingly diverse and multi-generational, the challenge for leaders is to engage employees in ways which produce discretionary effort.

As Pearce (2004) points out, 'With the shift to team-based knowledge work comes the need to question traditional models of leadership'. Hamel and Breen (2007) agree, asserting: 'Management is out of date' and that 'what ultimately constrains the performance of your organization is not its operating model, nor its business model, but its management model'. For them, 'management, as currently practised, is a drag on success'.

Leadership and ethical practice

Not surprisingly in this post-Enron age, business ethics and the reputations of some business leaders have been put under the spotlight. In the management press there are growing calls for more sustainable and ethical business and management practice, for greater transparency and accountability at the top, and for more equitable reward practices.

Critical scholars, in particular, approach mainstream management theory with deep scepticism regarding the moral defensibility and the social and ecological sustainability of the prevailing forms of management and organization (Watson, 2010). This is with a view to radically transforming management practice.

More progressive forms of management

Some critical scholars are also arguing for more progressive forms of management to enable the enhancement of mutual purpose and mutual gains between employer and employee (Spicer, Alvesson and Karreman, 2010; Francis, Holbeche and Reddington, 2012). These more mutual approaches, it is argued, are likely to produce more sustainably effective organizations since they focus on both the outcomes, and the means to achieve these, by reframing the employment relationship along more equitable principles. This means paying much more attention to the ambiguity about the goals and objectives associated with work and organization than classical models of leadership, OD and HRM tend to allow.

Quite what is required to lead successfully in today's organizations is the focus of extensive discussion in the literature post-2002. In the next section we look at the primary theme – the role of individual leaders as authentic moral leaders – and consider how the nature of leadership functions is being redefined and expanded.

Authentic leadership theories

In the 2000s, a wealth of theory focuses on the authenticity (ie honesty and integrity) of leaders. In some ways, such approaches reflect developments in the conventional 'heroic' leadership models. Forms and styles of leadership are variously described as 'authentic', 'moral', 'grown-up', 'differentiated', and 'prosocial' (Lorenzi, 2004). Goffee and Jones (2005), among others, argue that leadership demands the expression of an authentic self. People want to be led by someone real. People associate authenticity with sincerity, honesty and integrity. For Norman, Luthans and Luthans (2005), the authentic leader has confidence, hope, optimism and resilience, and also a moral or ethical transparency orientation. According to Gardner and Schermerhorn (2004), the theory of authentic moral leadership derives from Luthans' (2002) work on positive organizational behaviour (POB) and Luthans and Avolio's work on 'authentic leadership' (2005). POB is 'the study of, and application of positively oriented human resource strengths and psychological capabilities that can be measured, developed, and effectively managed for performance improvement in today's workplace' (Luthans, 2002). These writings point in the same direction as earlier work by McGregor (1957) on 'Theory Y' (participative) leaders. For Gardner and Schermerhorn (2004), authentic high performance leadership is something achievable by all managers, regardless of level or setting. They lead on strengths rather than viewing individual performance from the perspective of 'problems' that must be corrected.

The expanding functions of leaders

The traditional functions of leadership – such as inspiring people, providing direction, building culture, developing organizational capability and stimulating effective practice such as team working, learning and knowledge sharing – are continuously being expanded to reflect changing circumstances. Nowadays, leaders are expected to get people to commit to the organization at an emotional level, to produce high performance even in the absence of certainty, to act as 'steward' or moral compass for the organization.

Stewardship

Though Burns, Bass and others were writing about the moral purpose of leaders from the 1960s onwards, arguably the moral dimensions of leadership have had a relatively low profile in leadership literature until recently. In this post-Enron age, there is a growing literature with an emphasis on organizational ethics, with leaders expected to act as 'stewards' of their organization (Kets de Vries and Korotov, 2005). Moral leadership is seen as key to high standards in public life. Business leaders are expected to have strong values and to act as role models for ethical practice (Tubbs and Schulz, 2006). However, some theorists argue that leaving the ethical stewardship of organizations to individual leaders may be unwise or unrealistic. Augier and Teece (2005) propose that leadership skills should be channelled and checked in the political context by the instruments of political governance. Moreover, it could be argued that when leaders act in ways that imply mutuality of interest between employers and employees, when they are in fact acting in the interests of 'owners', this might be viewed as little more than a sophisticated and cynical attempt to persuade employees to do things that might not be in their interest.

Capability building

There is also a growing literature theme about leaders as builders of organizational capability and agility. The extensive scale and impact of the economic downturn has demonstrated that a step change in leadership thinking may be required away from the short-termism inherent in the pursuit of shareholder value. Prahalad (2009) and others argue that leaders should shift mindsets and increase their risk appetites, moving out of reactive or defensive or responsive mode with respect to the business context into a shaping mode. This will require building robust yet flexible business models and strategies that can be executed fast and well, helping organizations get ahead and stay ahead of the competition. This involves specific skills such as continuous scanning of the environment, collective intelligence gathering; processes for involving employees in thinking through the implementation implications of choices that have surfaced. Dive (2008) argues that leaders must simultaneously hold people (and themselves) to account for their actions and performance, and should use structures as a tool to define accountabilities.

Handling paradox

The literature suggests that leaders must be versatile, learn to embrace paradox, be strategic and operational, forceful and enabling (Kaplan and Kaiser, 2006). In line with popularized notions of emotional intelligence (Goleman, 1996), such versatile leaders have high self-awareness and self-control; they are able to bring out the best in others by their insight into what makes others tick. Developing this versatility requires leaders to find sources of advice they can trust and to handle uncertainty by reflective conversations. For Joni (2004), the first step of any leadership development journey requires leaders to look at themselves intensely and critically – leaders need self-insight and must grapple with their shadow sides. They need moral codes that are as complex, varied and subtle as the situations in which they find themselves.

Involving people

Rather than being about a set of traits, leadership is increasingly regarded as relational and contextual, reflecting the complexity of organizations. According to Spears: 'We are seeing traditional and hierarchical modes of leadership yielding to a different way of working – one based on teamwork and community, one that seeks to involve others in decision-making, one strongly based in ethical and caring behaviours' (2004).

There is a growing recognition that top managers may not have 'sufficient and relevant information to make highly effective decisions in a fast-changing and complex world' (Pearce and Conger, 2003). The principle of involving employees in issues that affect them was promoted by HRM discourse from the outset, but it might be argued that, since many employees no longer have their voice formally recognized through institutionalized means – such as the collective bargaining and consultative employee relations model used from the 1950s to the 1970s – the need for more direct employee voice mechanisms has become increasingly salient.

Communication must be of a high order, not just top-down but also two-way. Numerous case studies detail how executives are using social media to cut across hierarchy and engage employees in honest conversation about strategy and change. Such moves imply a potential rebalancing of power, not simply a new vehicle for top-down 'leadership communication' from bridge to deck.

Building trust and collaboration

An emerging approach to leadership and service emphasizes collaboration, trust, empathy and the ethical use of power. This began with Greenleaf's concept of 'servant leadership' (Greenleaf, 2002; Spears, 2004). Such forms of leadership are described as the most appropriate for knowledge-based organizations operating in these complex post-Enron days when a firm's reputation can be its greatest asset or its Achilles heel.

Kouzes and Posner (2003) emphasize credibility – how leaders earn the trust and confidence of their constituents. For them, credibility is conferred on leaders by their followers, reflecting a more mutual, less hierarchically distant approach: 'It is about what people demand of their leaders and the actions leaders must take in order to intensify their constituents' commitment to a common cause. But people still want and need leadership. They just want leaders who hold to an ethic of service and are genuinely respectful of the intelligence and contributions of their constituents' (2003: xviii).

So prevalent are such 'new' approaches that they might now be considered mainstream. The appeal of such models is their congruence between context drivers that many managers and employees will be familiar with, as well as their aspirations for a better working life. Unlike CMS, which is often criticized for having little interest in improving practice, such approaches are often promoted by consultants, along with methodologies accessible to practitioners. However, in these new mainstream studies notions of leadership power tend to be played down. Instead the new leadership focus is on dynamic, interactive processes of influence and learning that will transform organizational structures, norms and work practices (Pearce and Conger, 2003). That said, in contemporary organizations facing significant business challenges, these newer, more 'caring' and 'democratic' leadership approaches may be far less in evidence than are micro management and old-style command and control approaches (ORC International, 2011).

As we shall discuss in the next section, alongside the focus on individual leaders in the post-2002 literature review, a strong secondary theme is about more collective forms of leadership.

Collective forms of leadership

More collective forms of leadership are variously described in the literature as 'democratic' (Woods, 2004), 'shared', 'distributed' (Spillane, 2006;

Gronn, 2002), 'grown-up', 'we' (Block, 1996) leadership. Many studies of shared leadership appear to be centred on public sector organizations in particular. The essential characteristics of these various models are summarized by Turnbull James (2011):

- Leadership involves multiple actors who take up leadership roles both formally and informally, and importantly, share leadership by working collaboratively, often across professional or organizational boundaries.
- Leadership can be distributed away from top management and this distribution takes the form of new practices and innovations.
- Leadership needs to be understood in terms of leadership practices and organizational interventions, and not just in terms of leader attributes and leader-follower relationships.

Raelin (2005), for instance, promotes the concept of profoundly democratic 'leaderful practice', arguing that developing a community of leaders will be the key to sustainable performance. This is different from Block's (1996) 'stewardship' in which leaders step aside to let others take over when necessary. Traditionally leadership has been thought of as serial, individual, controlling and dispassionate. In 'leaderful' organizations leadership is concurrent, collective, collaborative and compassionate. Leaderful practice inspires genuineness among its community members so that they can bring their 'whole person' to work. Raelin argues that top leaders have four critical processes:

1 Set the mission (purpose).

2 Actualize goals.

3 Sustain commitment.

4 Respond to challenges.

Such shared approaches to leadership implicitly challenge power balances in prevailing command and control cultures.

Leadership in networked contexts

In new constructions of leadership, particularly with respect to public institutions, people who are normally thought of as leaders by dint of role, for example heads of departments, are now more clearly understood to be supported by a network of people – within and beyond the institution – engaging in leadership practices, even though these may not be officially called 'leader'. Pearce (2004), for instance, argues that high performing teams display more dispersed leadership patterns (ie shared leadership). Graetz argues that 'organizations most successful in managing the dynamics of loose-tight working relationships meld strong "personalised" leadership at the top with "distributed" leadership, a group of experienced and trusted individuals operating at different levels of the organization... [ensuring] ... integrated thinking and acting at all levels' (2000). This involves different people taking the lead depending on organizational circumstances, supported by conscious efforts among senior managers to examine what new structures and systems need to be introduced to extend employee involvement and participation in the workplace. Bryant's (2003) analysis is 'decentralized leadership' (ie that leadership is not located in a person but in a community, and that 'the leader' is a transient position). Everyone plays a leadership role at different times, and can make a significant contribution. Tate (2009) goes further, arguing that leadership systems ensure that organizations are not reliant on individual leaders since leadership is a collective practice.

Similarly, Ireland and Hitt (1999) note that as the global competitive environment becomes ever more complex, the nature of strategic leadership is starting to shift. Instead of being concentrated around a 'great leader', a more appropriate concept for strategic leadership in the 21st century is the 'great groups' view. This sees the organization as a community where strategic leadership and the foresight function are distributed among diverse individuals 'who share the responsibility to create a viable future for their firm' (Ireland and Hitt, 1999). Further, tasks that are highly interdependent, highly complex and require creativity call for shared leadership. If people's skills are brought together it is possible to forge a concerted dynamic that represents more than the sum of the individual contributors. Initiatives may be inaugurated by those with relevant skills in a particular context, which others will then adopt, adapt and improve in a mutually trusting and supportive culture.

The view of distributed leadership as concerted action through relationships allows for top leaders to act as strong partners with employees despite the power disparities between them. The vertical leader's role in developing shared leadership is designing and managing the boundaries of the team. Training, reward systems and cultural systems can facilitate shared leadership. The vertical leader needs to be able to step in and fill voids in the team and emphasize the importance of the shared leadership approach. The creation of a shared vision is an especially important manifestation of shared leadership in knowledge-worker teams.

Points to ponder

How widely applicable do you consider notions of 'shared leadership' to be?

What do you consider to be the benefits and risks of shared leadership?

To what extent do you agree that more democratic forms of 'shared' leadership require a different context? What conditions would need to be present for such leadership to emerge?

Is there any sense that a more collectivist, if not pluralist, environment for leadership is credible – or not?

Discussion questions

- On balance, how would you now define 'effective' leadership?
- How much do the leadership theories discussed above reflect predominantly Western views?
- What is the HR function's responsibility with respect to leadership?
- In many organizations, trust is often a casualty of change. What can individual leaders do to avoid losing trust during challenging times, or to regain it?

Key learning points and conclusions

- Given the complex context in which organizations are operating, definitions of organizational effectiveness will continue to evolve, as will definitions of what constitutes effective leadership. While many theorists continue to explore the 'essence' of leadership, there is increasing recognition that leadership is socially constructed. Moreover, as the workforce becomes increasingly diverse and multi-generational, as long as employers require particular sorts of skills and 'talent', labour power may force improvements in the employment relationship and require different kinds of leadership.

- Although the main emphasis in the literature remains on individual leaders, there is an important and growing sub-theme around more collective forms of leadership. Increasingly, the task of individual leaders is perceived to be about building communities of leaders at every level; at the very least 'top' leaders are expected to involve people actively in issues that affect them. These more democratic forms of leadership appear congruent with evolving definitions of organizational effectiveness that emphasize mutuality.

- For such forms of shared leadership to emerge, emphasis is placed on employee development and on managers creating the environment to allow staff to release potential and discretionary effort. As a result, organizations will be populated by employees working in high performing, highly motivated and committed teams, who can proactively shape some of the context around them, and successfully implement strategy.

Case study and discussion questions

CASE STUDY Leading change in the UK's national health service (NHS)

The UK's NHS has been subject to considerable government-driven change in recent years. Many of these changes have involved policy initiatives to 'modernize' the NHS and subject it to market disciplines. Foundation Trusts, which came into being under the Labour Governments (1997–2010), give NHS institutions a relatively high level of management autonomy, as well as a degree of independence from centralized financial control which makes this form of status highly desirable. Since Foundation Trust status is only granted to 'successful' NHS organizations, the pressure is on to improve standards and performance against national targets and outcomes, while increasing organizational scale and scope by taking over other institutions.

FT1 is a large, diverse NHS Foundation Trust which, at the time of writing, was on the acquisition trail. Directors and HR business partners at FT1 are experienced at managing integration and FT1 has developed a reputation for being able to convert what are by some considered 'failing' institutions into more successful bodies once they have been incorporated. Organization A, for example, one of FT1's acquisitions, had been previously judged to be failing to meet NHS measures such as the four-hour target on admissions and reducing infection rates of MRSA. The organization was considered to have 'cultural problems'. FT1 acquired organization A and embarked on a structured programme of integration.

Management capacity, national performance targets and cultural issues proved to be difficult challenges to address and FT1's overall performance suffered as a result. FT1 had taken a total integration approach to organization A and the structure of the organization did not recognize the needs of local sites. In times of trouble, FT1 adopted a more command and control style of leadership to address performance. FT1 recognized that organization A required better local leadership to engage local communities and staff. This needed to be balanced against the requirement for corporate efficiencies in entering an era of austerity. How did this happen?

A significant factor was developing a new approach to leadership. FT1's new CEO wanted both a coherent corporate strategy and also to do what was right for each hospital and its stakeholders. This can of course lead to tensions between local and corporate, but the CEO supported management teams in working through these. He set great store by building constructive relationships with stakeholders, especially the site management teams. The CEO encouraged site teams to create a local partnership, to get the hospital more connected to the people it serves. Indeed, the CEO sees his role as being a buffer to absorb some of the bureaucratic and other pressures on site managers to give them greater freedom to lead.

The CEO recognized the need to strengthen the site leadership team at organization A, and to develop a new approach to responding to the needs of the local community it served. For the first three months in his new job, the CEO made himself visible in organization A and FT1 by going 'back to the floor' and encouraging anyone in the workforce, at any level who wished to, to come to see him. He also met with external partners. To the workforce the CEO came across as genuine and he demonstrated the need for an engaging approach to leadership and culture.

For the directors, as part of management in a Foundation Trust, the overall pace of activity increased and became more concentrated. They were therefore pleased to receive support from members of FT1's organization development team, who provided 360-degree feedback, coaching and structured programmes such as 'back to the floor.' The focus was on building collegiate working among directors, then on building directors' capability to lead and become champions of change. Directors and senior managers were also able to access other forms of leadership development which helped them see the benefits of being part of a bigger whole and better understand their role in delivering a national agenda and in building capability.

For staff in FT1 as a whole, the fast and demanding pace of change can be wearing. Employee engagement surveys suggest that, while most employees remained willing to 'go the extra mile', their overall engagement scores during the acquisition period were down on previous years. The CEO acknowledged the pressures people were under in his frequent blogs. At the same time, he let people know that they would have to work differently so that FT1 could continue to deliver its purpose to its stakeholders. Staff engagement is now improving and plans continue to develop an inclusive, engaging leadership culture.

FT1 has recently acquired a community services organization and has put into practice the lessons learned from the acquisition of organization A. Local leadership and staff engagement have been fundamental and have had a positive impact on the success of the latest acquisition.

Discussion questions

- How would you assess the role played by the CEO's role in leading this integration?
- What kinds of leadership does this case study demonstrate?
- What do you see as the key leadership challenges of this case study? How would you address them?
- What do you consider to be the strengths and limitations of the approaches taken to strengthen leadership at FT1 and organization A?

06
Talent management

RAISA ARVINEN-MUONDO and QI WEI

LEARNING OBJECTIVES

- Develop an understanding of various definitions of talent and what these potentially mean for employee perceptions of self and others, engagement and motivation.
- Identify the main approaches to talent management and conceptualize potential implications for HR practice and organizational strategy.
- Learn to identify challenges faced by organizations in identifying, putting into operation and retaining talent.
- Develop a critical understanding of talent management as a strategic tool in developing human resources.
- Identify and critically assess challenges arising from applying talent management approaches to the development of employees in intercultural contexts.

Introduction

Talent management has received increasing attention from academics and practitioners alike in HRM, global HRM and OB commentary. Talent management has been associated with core HRM processes such as recruitment and selection, performance management, retention, career development and succession management. The assumption here is that managing talent effectively would generate value to an organization's performance and development. Although the notion of talent management has been around for over a decade, there seems to be an air of ambiguity about it. It has been criticized for being merely a fad with nothing truly novel to offer to people management practice. However, we suggest here, as Scullion and Collings (2011) imply, that part of the difficulty in situating talent management in the broader management discourse, and the reason why it is left open to critique, is that talent management not only lacks consensus in definition and theoretical development, but is also often equated with HRM. One can argue, as we will later in this chapter, that the two are inherently distinct despite their numerous similarities. However, in building the case to demonstrate that talent management warrants attention from academics, practitioners and corporate leaders alike, this chapter will argue that talent management must be seen as part of the wider HRM agenda, rather than somehow separate or in competition with it. The purpose of human resources is to add value to organizations, but for some reason HR as a function seems to be continually trying to prove that it is worth the investment and position as a business partner rather than merely an administrative function (Lawler, 2005). It is the HR function's job to create policies and practices that enable the recruitment, development, deployment and retention of the kind of human capital that will improve organizational effectiveness and create value for the company (Lawler, 2005). In this chapter we argue that one of the ways in which HR can contribute to organizational effectiveness is by enabling the recruitment, development and retention of key talent through talent management processes. Furthermore, it is HR's responsibility, together with middle and senior management, to identify key roles for which talented individuals are needed. Most importantly, we propose that although the development of processes and practices from a traditional HRM perspective can contribute to the management of talent, successful talent management requires a more holistic approach that recognizes the influence of and consequences for individual perceptions, behaviour and motivation to work. Talent management as strategy, practice and method can be applicable to all areas that are traditionally grouped under the OB cannon, but in this chapter the discussion focuses on just a few: perception, motivation and employee engagement. Successful management of talent requires multiple perspectives in that it is relevant as much at organizational level (structural and functional) as it is at individual and group level.

Simply put, organizations have the opportunity to build sustainable competitive advantage by selecting, developing and retaining the right people. There is an entire body of literature dedicated to demonstrating the link between HRM, human resources development (HRD) and competitive advantage (for example Ulrich, 2001). If we follow the logic of 'an organization is only as good as the people in it', then we can assume that organizations would endeavour to select the most capable and talented individuals. However, this raises several questions. How *can* and *do* organizational leaders and HR professionals determine who is talented and who is not? Three practical management problems can be identified:

- The first is definitional and relates to identification of talent. Even if the parameters of talent are somehow narrowed and agreed upon, how can organizational leaders then develop strategies that put these 'talented' human resources into operation in a way that is conducive to organizational success?
- The second problem is therefore concerned with developing strategic approaches to talent management.
- The third problem is then concerned with implementation of practices and policies defined by strategy that will be effective in creating and sustaining talent pools as well as recruiting, developing and retaining the individuals organizations have invested in.

In starting to address the practical management issues highlighted here, we feel that exploring some basic concepts from OB, such as perception and motivation, is helpful in understanding what are some of the consequences of how talent is managed and, as a result, they will also enable us better to understand why talent management approaches are useful for organizations and people management practitioners. Furthermore, it will help us understand why talent management warrants a place in the people management rubric.

In the course of exploring the three management problems that we have identified, we will discuss what perspective the OB lens can offer to the talent management debate, particularly in relation to experiences of being talent managed, what we mean by 'talent ideology', definitions of talent, the concept of talent management and what it means for organizational strategy as well as for people management practice. Let's begin by setting the scene for you and briefly introducing the ongoing debate on talent management versus HRM, which will enable you to understand where our discussion sits in the wider management rubric. We will identify and explore some of the emerging issues from the

OB perspective in terms of the consequent experiences of being talent managed for individuals, such as employee self-perceptions, motivation and potentially on performance. We will then critically explore how talent may be defined and how its definition consequently influences the kind of talent management strategies available to organizations. Finally we will conclude by discussing how talent can be managed.

Talent management versus HRM

The talent management rubric is often accused of merely trying to rebrand what is essentially HRM. Although talent management and HRM are both concerned with how people are recruited, managed, developed and retained in order to achieve organizational as well as individual objectives (Cascio, 1998; Chuai, Preece and Iles, 2008) it could be argued that talent management is a more detailed and focused approach to managing individuals (human resources) that have been identified as having the potential to contribute to an organization's core competencies (Chuai, Preece and Iles, 2008). HRM may be argued to adopt a more egalitarian approach to the management and development of people in organizations (Chuai, Preece and Iles, 2008). The focus of talent management on the other hand is to differentiate the skills and capabilities of individuals and develop their talents strategically in line with the company's corporate strategic objectives. However, talent management is also about identifying key positions that have the potential to contribute to organizational effectiveness and ensuring that such positions are fulfilled with the right people. Talent management is often also equated with strategic HRM; however, talent management offers a more 'segmented approach to managing people in strategic roles' and therefore the emphasis is on integrated approaches to 'attracting, developing and retaining key employees and potential organizational leaders' (Kock and Burke, 2008). That being said, we argue here that talent management, although distinct, is a component of the broader HRM agenda in one way or another.

Iles, Chuai and Preece (2010) identify a set of policies and practices to attract, retain and engage key talent, as opposed to a focus on HR in general that can help us make sense of differences between the two:

- Talent management involves getting the right people in the right job at the right time and managing the development of people, which does not necessarily make it different from HRD or HRM.

- However, talent management may use the same tools as HRD but focus on a relatively small group of employees – the talent pool.

- Finally, talent management involves organizationally focused competence development through managing and developing talent. The focus here is on talent continuity that is linked to succession planning and HRM planning, which we discuss later in the chapter.

For some organizations systematic approaches to talent management are limited to individuals in leadership roles (Barlow, 2006), in which case it is hard to tell the difference (if any) between talent management and leadership or management development. To distinguish talent management from HRM or management development, we should consider talent management to be based on some form of exclusivity, but one that is not merely defined by leadership or managerial positions. Furthermore, an organization may have more than one 'pool' of talent that are each defined differently. For example, according to a Chartered Institute of Personnel and Development (CIPD) report on talent management, Cargill, an international provider of food, agricultural and risk management services, has divided its talent into three different 'pools': 'Next generation leaders', 'Emerging leaders' and 'High impact performers' and therefore make varying decisions about how each of these 'pools' are resourced, developed, deployed and retained (Tansley *et al*, 2006). Identifying and accordingly recruiting, developing and retaining individuals who have been somehow deemed to be higher potential or specifically capable from the rest of the work population seems to be key in differentiating talent management approaches from other HR activities, even if the terms by which talent is defined is somewhat ambiguous and contextual.

The OB perspective

We would encourage you to look back at Chapter 2 on perception and decision making and Chapter 3 on motivation. Although these chapters do not discuss talent management explicitly, it is easy to see how the notion of perception and motivation are inherently linked to the way talent is identified, managed and developed as well as the resultant consequences as you work your way through this chapter. The underlying assumption here is that the way in which we perceive the world around us influences the decisions we take and the options we see as available to us. It should not, therefore, be difficult to see that the way in which we define ourselves and the way we think others in the organizational context, particularly managers, perceive us and our efforts would influence our motivation to work and our efforts in the workplace. If we feel valued and our efforts are noticed and recognized through intrinsic or extrinsic rewards (see Chapter 3), we are inclined perhaps to work harder and perform better. Therefore, if individuals have been identified as 'talented' by management and are aware of such classification, one might argue that their self-confidence may be enhanced, they may feel that their capabilities and efforts are being recognized and, as a result, they may feel more motivated to produce results. What are the consequences then if one is aware of *not* being identified as 'talented' in organizations that clearly have a formal or at least a semi-formal approach to managing and developing 'talented' individuals? In the realization that one's efforts and skills are not recognized or that managerial expectations of an employee do not match the employee's self-perception, considerable room exists for dissatisfaction and potentially loss of motivation and effectiveness. If we take an intercultural approach, for example, in some cultural contexts that are considered hierarchical, status and position can be very important in determining where one sits in not only the organizational hierarchy, but in wider society (see Hofstede, 1980; Trompenaars and Hampden-Turner, 1997). Being perceived and categorized as somehow talented potentially means better development and promotion opportunities, or at least one may perceive these to be better. Therefore one could assume that the lack of the 'talent status' implies limited opportunities to develop and progress professionally.

The talent management discourse seems to further perpetuate a managerial perspective rather than an employee perspective. What we mean by this is that very little research seems to be focused on how individuals feel about being identified and, consequently, managed as talented. It has been argued that in order for talent management to succeed, organizational objectives must coincide with the employee's personal objectives (Kock and Burke, 2008). There is little point in planning out an employee's careers: no matter how great a plan, if it does not fit in with the future that those employees had envisioned for themselves; any investment by the company may be a wasted one. So in addition to encouraging discussion on why organizations should pay due attention to strategically recruiting, developing and retaining talented individuals, we also want to explore what it means to the individual to be talent managed.

The notion of being identified as talented is interesting and relevant not only for its implications for corporate success, but also because of what it potentially means for individuals and their perceptions of themselves and others. Are individuals aware that they have been identified as high potential and placed in some kind of a 'talent pool'? Is the talent identification process somehow explicit and evident, for example by individuals being placed in particular development programmes? This may be the case in organizations that have adopted a more formal and strategic approach to the way their key human resources are managed. However, our suspicion is that in many companies that lack a formal approach to talent management, some individuals are implicitly assumed to be high flyers based on the kinds of attitudes and personality traits they display coupled with the 'right' professional experiences and educational background. In such organizations, development opportunities are likely to be presented on a more ad hoc and haphazard basis and the relationship between employees and managers becomes an increasingly important factor in talent management decisions.

Chapter 2 looked at perception and explored the notion of self-fulfilling prophecies. Following this logic, it could be argued that if individuals feel that they have been identified as high achievers, they are more inclined to behave and take action in ways that are conducive to professional success. On the flipside, the reverse may also be true. If the skills and abilities of talented individuals remain explicitly unacknowledged, this may have a negative effect on their level of motivation and even self-confidence. As McLean (2009) points out, the basic idea of a 'talent pool' is that ideally the 'pool' should be greater than the demand and therefore inevitably there would be high flyers who are passed over for promotion. Attention therefore also needs to be paid to the reaction of key human resources that are not utilized in what they themselves may see as key positions and significant to their professional career development. Employees in such positions may have low morale, feel less committed to their jobs and underperform (McLean, 2009). Although the impact on employees' morale of being passed over for a position is a concern, there is some evidence to suggest that it is not as 'detrimental' as often assumed (CIPD, 2010b; McCartney, 2010). A recently published CIPD report on talent management experiences suggests that participation in talent management programmes is associated with high engagement levels and that 'structured selection processes serve to increase talent programmes' perceived value and the motivation of participants to perform' (McCartney, 2010). However, over and above formal talent management activities, the CIPD research findings suggest that among the senior level participants, mentoring, coaching and networking were particularly valued methods in talent management programmes (McCartney, 2010).

Ensuring that employees feel engaged is an essential part of long-term talent management as employee engagement has been linked with commitment, job satisfaction, performance and retention. There seems to be little question that people who feel engaged with their work and organization are more productive than those that feel disengaged (Bhatnagar, 2007). It is also recognized that, in addition to financial reward, development opportunities are a increasingly significant factor in engaging and retaining talent (Bhatnagar, 2007; Orr and McVerry, 2007).

However, as the discussion to follow will show, there is no one set definition of talent and even when we think we have arrived at one, particularly in international contexts we should question to what extent our definitions are applicable or perhaps shaped by Western ideology. Moreover, each organization and industry differs and requires different approaches to the way in which it selects, manages, develops and retains individuals or groups of individuals (ie talent pools) that corporate leaders think possess the kind of skills needed to enhance their company's business success. In the next section we will introduce the concept of talent ideology and how it shapes the way in which talent is defined and what are some of the implications for individuals and organizations.

Talent identification

The talent ideology

How has the talent ideology developed in the corporate world? Generally talent implies rarity. After Penrose (1959) ascribed importance to managerial and technical talent for firms' growth and sustainable returns, the talent ideology was formally set out in an article 'The war for talent' by McKinsey consultants. The term 'war for talent' was originally coined by McKinsey & Company in 1997 as a result of its research on talent management practices and beliefs (McKinsey & Company, 2001). The term has been widely used by practitioners and academics to describe a phenomenon that most organizations had been experiencing, but one that remained unnamed and in need of further clarity. Three major points emerged from the article:

- Talented employees have a highly disproportionate impact on a company's performance.

- Talented leaders are required by the increasingly complex global economy.

- The search for extremely effective employees has become even more challenging due to demographic changes.

Following the above, companies would contest an ever intensifying 'war for talent' with their competitors. The authors' very definition seemed to provide us an ultimate foundation that a more complex economy demands more sophisticated talent with global acumen, multicultural fluency, entrepreneurial skills and the excellent ability to manage organizations.

McKinsey & Company's talent ideology perhaps not only provided a sharp insight of the importance for having talented individuals, but also promoted people's interests of those who have highly paid knowledge jobs. Therefore, ever since McKinsey & Company coined the phrase 'war for talent', managing talent has received remarkable attention by both academics and practitioners in the United States, Europe and Asia (Aston and Morton, 2005; Bennett and Bell, 2004; Berry, 2007; Buckingham and Vosburgh, 2001; Pianmsoongnern and Anurit, 2010). In the UK, the CIPD recently claimed that 'most organizations believe talent management is more not less important in periods of economic uncertainty and it is even more important to have a well-developed talent strategy' (CIPD, 2010a). Indeed, it has been suggested that during times of economic uncertainty individuals may be reluctant to change employers: 'employers should consider "growing their own talent"' (CIPD, 2011b). Therefore, attracting new talent and developing and retaining existing talent has become increasingly important.

Following on from this, let's examine what we mean by talent and how organizational leaders might go about identifying talent.

Defining talent

What is talent? How do we define it and once we have defined it how can we be sure that what we mean by it is interpreted in the same way by others? What are the benchmarks? The rubric at times implies there are some universal truths, but anyone thinking logically can see that talent depends on a multitude of factors whether industry, company or discipline related, so why do we talk about it in general terms? Is the talent pool bound – when individuals once enter, are they in it for the duration of their careers, or can they dip in and out, and who decides that? Or is being defined as talented really just about having the qualifications and meeting the right person at the right time, who for whatever reason thinks you have what it takes?

The original concept of talent by McKinsey & Company is not clear, and how the word has been used has become more complex. In ancient Greek, a talent described the amount of silver required to pay the monthly wage bill of a crew of a large warship known as trireme. Thus, the original meaning of the word 'talent' can be interpreted as something that donates value. The concept of talent has been defined in various ways (Buckingham and Clifton, 2001; Rath and Conchie, 2008; Robertson and Abbey, 2003). The CIPD defines talent as consisting of 'individuals who can make a difference to organizational performance either through their immediate contribution or, in the longer-term by demonstrating the highest levels of potential' (CIPD, 2011b). Buckingham and Clifton (2001) identify that talent refers to a natural recurring pattern of thought, feeling or behaviour that can be productively applied. When talent is augmented with knowledge and skills, the results become individual strengths. In other words, individuals could never possess strengths without requisite talent. Morton (2004) and Goffee and Jones (2005) define talent as a handful of employees' skills, knowledge and cognitive ability and potential. Ingham (2006) considers that talent is a critical ability set that is difficult to obtain in the labour market. So talent is regarded as a scarcity of skills.

Some other researchers define talent as a core group of leaders, experts and other key employees who are the best performers in the organization. For example, Huselid, Beatty and Becker (2005) describe high performance employees who hold strategic positions as talent. They further note that organizations need to adopt a portfolio approach to management, placing such talent in support positions and dismissing non-performing employees and jobs that do not add value.

Based on a comprehensive literature review of the term 'talent', Pianmsoongnern and Anurit (2010) identify two categories. The first is individual potentials – talent is a quality possessed by people that drives outstanding performance. The second is potential people – talent is a generic term for people who hold key positions, such as organizational leaders, high performers who make unique contributions to an organization and those who possess excellent knowledge and skills. Thus, on the one hand, maximizing people's inherent talent may drive them to perform well. On the other hand, a group of employees having above average educational qualifications, skills and performance, and defined as talent should be well managed and developed in the organization.

In the context of management of internationally mobile talent, D'Costa (2008) defines talent in terms of technical competency and in accordance with a definition from the Organisation of Economic Co-operation and Development (OECD), as professionals with a minimum of four years' tertiary education beyond primary and secondary education in fields such as physical and life sciences, social sciences, engineering, health, education and business. Although to some this may seem a little limited, it reflects the notion that talent is often associated with educational attainment and implies that the skills, capabilities and knowledge that can differentiate one individual from another as talented are consequent of higher education. However, we are then faced with another dilemma. If talent is defined by the skills and capabilities that organizational leaders seek in their employees, then we must ask on what basis are the 'desirable' skills that they seek defined? The argument here is that in multinational and multicultural contexts the criteria used to define the 'ideal' candidate for recruitment or employee for development may be based on a set of cultural values and assumptions that may be inherent to the manager or recruiter but not the candidate or employee (see the case study example of African candidates and US recruiters in Chapter 2, page 72).

Points to ponder

What about countries where educational infrastructure is poor in comparison to developed Western countries, where individuals may have four years of higher education behind them, but do not necessarily have the same skills set as a UK or US graduate?

Will these individuals be perceived as somehow less talented or differently talented by leaders of MNCs where practices are largely underpinned by Western values?

In a recent article in the online magazine *HR Review*, a writer suggested that the skills that organizations should be developing in their high potential employees, in their talent pools, should not be bound purely by formal talent programmes (*HR Review*, 2011). The author contends: 'Instead we must look for those individuals with the universal skills that will enable them to take advantage of the uncertainties of the future'. In essence, in order to be defined as talent now as well as in the future, an individual has to be three things, according to the article's author:

- An information seeker. It is impossible in today's world, where we are bombarded with information, to remember everything. One must understand how and where to look for information and importantly distinguish what is reliable and what is not.

- A multidimensional learner. One has to be someone who is open to new experiences and is capable of reflecting on them.

- An enquiring mind. One must be capable of both problem solving as well as asking the difficult questions (*HR Review*, 2011).

We realize the assessment of such qualities is an impossible task, as is the measurement of talent. However, we argue that the qualities highlighted by the article's author offer a useful qualitative perspective to anyone attempting to decipher the notion of talent.

Having explored what talent is, how it may be defined and what are some of the implications for employees' perceptions and motivation, in the next section we will address the second management dilemma we highlighted at the beginning of this chapter that relates to how organizations use these high potential individuals to enhance organizational performance by adopting a strategic approach to their management and development. We will begin by highlighting some of the challenges organizations are faced with that necessitate some kind of systematic approach to the management and development of talent if organizations want to develop a competitive edge.

Strategic talent management

Defining talent management

Like the notion of talent, the term 'talent management' has been criticized as a management fad and as ambiguous because there appears to be no single concise definition of the concept (Aston and Morton, 2005; Lewis and Heckman, 2006; Reilly, 2008). Often the terms 'talent management strategy', 'succession planning' and 'human resource planning' are used interchangeably (Aston and Morton, 2005). In the substantial academic and practitioner literature, Lewis and Heckman (2006) and

Pianmsoongnern and Anurit (2010) identify three main talent management approaches that have also been highlighted by Scullion and Collings (2011) to which they have added a fourth approach as identified by Collings and Mellahi (2009). The four approaches are:

- Traditional HR practices are used.

- There is a new term for succession planning with an emphasis on developing talent pools and tracking the progress of employees through positions.

- People's natural capability or learned skills that benefit an organization are managed (HR development). A distinction is made between top and poor performers and people are managed accordingly.

- Key positions that have the potential to make a difference to business success are identified.

A further definition of talent management provided by the CIPD has been widely adopted by academics, HRD managers and consultancies: 'the systematic attraction, identification, development, engagement/retention and deployment of those individuals with high potential who are of particular value to an organization' (2009b). Therefore, many of the existing studies on talent management tend to be from an HR planning, selection and HRD perspective (for example Garrow, 2008). While focusing on definition and delivery of talent management, Reilly (2008) and Chuai, Preece and Iles (2008) suggest that talent management should not stand alone from other people management practices. The challenge for organizations is how to design the focus of their approach to talent management and how their approach fits in the organizational context. It is important for managers to recognize that the organization's definition of talent determines their talent management programme, and how talent management is emphasized may have an impact on the organizational management system and procedures. For instance, if the organization defines talent as employees who are in senior management positions or the potential employees to be in such positions, then the organization has to decide what criteria should be used and which level of managers should be included, as well as the criteria on which to identify high potential.

Seemingly the adoption and implementation of formal talent management strategies remains piecemeal for many organizations. That being said, according to a 2010 survey report by the CIPD, nearly 60 per cent of organizations do engage in some kind of talent management activities, but only approximately half of these consider such activities effective (CIPD, 2010b). This could suggest that organizations are not necessarily consistent in their approaches. Although much debate surrounds how talent or talent management is defined, there seems to be some consensus that organizational success in today's changing and financially challenging times requires some kind of systematic approach to the way key human resources are managed.

Challenges and changing contexts in talent management

In addition to the recent global recession, what are some of the other changes that suggest that talent management approaches are needed to maintain a competitive edge in today's market? Why do we need talent management? In summary, from an extensive review of literature on talent management the following challenges have been identified and we will explore them in more detail next:

- labour shortages;
- changing demographics;
- greater demand for work–life balance;
- skills gap;
- experience gap;
- increased professional mobility;
- lagging educational attainment.

Research has indicated that the competition for talent has been created as a consequence of labour shortages (Boudreau and Ramstad, 2005; Brewster, Sparrow and Harris, 2005). In addition, competition for talent arises from the changing demographics of the labour market as well as a greater demand for work–life balance (Tansley *et al*, 2006).

Galagan suggests that an increasing skills gap, that is a gap between 'organization's current capabilities and the skills it needs to achieve its goals', a consequence of the recent financial down turn, challenges organizations to think more strategically about how they manage their key human resources who hold the knowledge and skills needed to create and sustain competitive advantage for their organization (2010). Bridging the increasing skills gap is not only a challenge for organizations, but industries, communities and entire nations, as Galagan (2010) points out. Moreover, this skills gap seems to be a persistent problem world-wide. As the generation of people born since the Second World War (often referred to as the baby boomers), who possess knowledge and experience and hold a significant portion of senior leadership positions begin to retire, the existing skills gap is likely to be further exacerbated (Galagan, 2010; McKinsey & Company, 2001; Orr and McVerry, 2007). In developing countries lacking resources, inadequate educational infra-structures and a large gap between the rich and poor do little to enable the development of home grown talent to meet the needs of companies working to meet the demands of an increasingly consumerist society (see Glossary) worldwide.

Organizations are also facing an experience gap and struggle to find and retain qualified people with the adequate experience and capabilities (for example, in the oil and gas sector; Orr and McVerry, 2007). The retire-ment of 'baby boomers' is not only likely to leave a gap in technical knowledge and experience, but the retirement of such a significant segment of the working population in a relatively short number of years may also mean a loss of supplier and customer relationships as well as a loss of understanding of the complex informal networks that often keep organizations functioning (McQuade *et al*, 2007). Somewhat contrastingly and perhaps on a more optimistic note, the changing demographics of the workforce also means that the labour market in-creasingly consists of individuals of the 'net generation', a term coined by Don Tapscott to describe individuals born between 1977 and 1997 who have grown up with computers and digital media and now make up the largest group in the US workforce (Galagan, 2010). This generation of people is said to demonstrate higher IQ and different learning styles, work habits and a new notion of collaboration, thus changing the nature of the way a large portion of today's working population work. However, we would like to point out here that this notion of a 'net generation', a generation of people that somehow have internalized the use of computers and take for granted the availability of technology, currently remains one that should not be universally assumed to apply to all parts of the developing world where such infrastructure simply remains unattainable for the majority. It raises an interesting question in that if the notion of talent in Western MNCs is somehow explicitly or implicitly shaped by the expectation that all graduates entering the job market have internalized the notion of technology and access to it long before reaching university, then would that not mean that individuals who have not would inevitably be to some extent excluded from 'talent pools', whether implicitly or explicitly?

Points to ponder

Are individuals who have grown up without access to information technology unintentionally, but inevitably, left sitting by the side of the pool instead of paddling in it?

Returning to the earlier point of organizations losing tacit knowledge as people leave, is this new generation of people with new learning habits and technological knowledge enough to create and sustain intellectual capital needed for organizations to stay ahead of their game?

Furthermore, relative to 50 or even 20 years ago, professional mobility nationally and internationally is becoming increasingly the norm as individuals search for new opportunities to better their own development, despite suggestions that professional mobility is likely to slow down in times of economic distress (*HR Review*, 2011). There is no longer a stigma attached to changing organizations (McKinsey & Company, 2001) and as recent findings of the Inspiring Talent 2011 Survey indicate approximately one-third of the people interviewed intend to leave their current jobs in the next five years (Churchard, 2011). Hence, retaining individuals in whose training the organization has invested becomes an increasingly significant challenge. In a global context, a shift has also occurred in the direction of internationally mobile talent. The flow of talent is no longer limited to movement from the West to East, but rather multidirectional (D'Costa, 2008; Solimano, 2008). This shift in direction poses talent management strategists and HR practitioners with further challenges in attracting, developing and retaining individuals with key skills, know-how and experience in a way that is culturally appropriate. So, regardless of national, cultural or industry context, organizations need to adapt, in terms of their internal culture as well as strategically to the needs, values and habits of their changing workforce.

Coupled with this notion of a demographically changing workforce, another reason attributed to the lack of available talent is reported to be lagging educational attainment, in that during times of financial difficulty, it is anticipated that organizations are more likely to reduce the amount of low skilled, low paid jobs and these are likely to be replaced by more knowledge-intensive positions that require more highly qualified people (Galagan, 2010). Indeed, there appears to have been a shift in the nature of work where more emphasis is placed on knowledge workers and innovative thinking, which is creating a higher demand for qualified and experienced individuals with high degrees of expertise. A study conducted in the South African public service, for instance, indicates a severe skills gap across middle and top management with vacancy rates at deputy director-general level reaching 59 per cent (Kock and Burke, 2008). The demand for top managerial talent is a global phenomenon.

Key components of strategic talent management

As you can see from our discussion so far, organizations are increasingly in competition with each other to attract, develop, deploy and retain individuals with key skills needed to maintain a competitive edge. As such, organizational leaders need to develop strategies and practices that not only address their current business needs for specific talent, but also their future business needs. However, it appears that the degrees to which talent management initiatives and practices are actively used in organizations varies from informal and incidental approaches to approaches that incorporate strategic talent management with wider corporate strategy (Tansley *et al*, 2006).

Oakes and Galagan (2011) argue that talent management comprises several key areas of HR: recruiting, compensation and rewards, performance management, succession management, engagement and retention, and leadership development. The authors further propose that the talent management framework in its entirety is underpinned by a notion of learning and development. However, the degree to which organizations choose to emphasize each of the key components is determined by the organization's individual business needs (Oakes and Galagan, 2011). Therefore, talent management is also about succession planning for the future as it is about recruiting and deploying the 'right' people with the 'right' capabilities in the present. In other words, talent management can be used at different stages of career development, such as when graduates who enter an organization for the first time are earmarked for fast track development opportunities or middle managers are developed for future leadership positions as part of a longer-term organization-wide succession plan. Indeed, the boundaries between talent management and succession management, of which succession planning is a component, are somewhat blurred. Succession planning refers to the process of identifying successors for key positions in the organization and developing and deploying such individuals accordingly. Succession management as a process (see Glossary) seems to be most often relevant at executive level positions and not something that is necessarily applied throughout the organization except perhaps for positions that are considered hard to fill or otherwise vital (Tansley *et al*, 2006). Successful adoption of a much needed integrated approach to talent management requires addressing the various key components of talent management (Oakes and Galagan, 2011), which is precisely the view that we wish to promote here.

We would like to add to the list of challenges a further concern for MNCs operating in some developing country contexts: nationalization. By this we mean the pressure from governments to nationalize workforces, particularly at management level. The implication for MNCs is that in countries where they have previously been able to fill the experience or skills gap with expatriates, this is becoming increasingly difficult due to restrictions on expatriate quotas placed by the host country government. This phenomenon is particularly evident in the energy sector and oil and gas companies operating in the Middle East (for example 'Omanization', Al-Lamki, 1998) and African countries such as Angola are all too familiar with it (for example 'Angolanization', Bjerke *et al*, 2004). That being said, the problems brought about by nationalization differ from country to country, which we do not have space here to delve into any further.

Emerging issues in managing talent

Danger of narrowly defining talent

Based on McKinsey & Company's talent ideology, talent employees must have a high level of mental ability and a high level of proven performance. However, can we really say that today's high level of mental ability will be tomorrow's source of competitive advantage? Many companies tend to believe so, recruiting young graduates with high marks in top universities and business schools, and paying them a premium. Organizations may put themselves in danger when highly associating their talent pool with younger people and demotivate those who are older and more experienced. Moreover, sometimes a high level intellectual ability can have a negative impact on people's behaviour. For example, a high powered job may require employees to have a high tolerance of humdrum and the constant repetition of similar tasks. A highly active mind might be more likely to become dissatisfied with such a job.

A high level of proven performance as a criterion for talent could also be problematic, since companies first have to identify precisely types of high level individual performance. If we cannot identify high level individual performance we cannot reward it and the talent ideology becomes meaningless. Second, companies have to provide appropriate measurements for the defined performance. Once again, if we cannot measure it, we cannot reward it.

Nowadays, more organizations have adopted a competency-based method to recruit employees with certain skills and knowledge to be the future talent in the organization. The advantage of this is that the organization may provide more opportunities to develop employees' skills and competences. However, the danger of this is obvious too. Cappelli (2008) points out that the competence-based assessment process does not sufficiently acknowledge people's strengths and weaknesses. For instance, leadership is situational and such approaches may not value charismatic leadership.

Goals and resources in managing talent

One of the key questions for organizations managing talent is: where do we want to be and what are our resources to get there? As we have shown, there is a need to ensure that any talent management strategy is in line with broader and longer-term business needs. Therefore, as part of this process in the first stage it is essential to identify the organization's goals and the capabilities (ie human resources) needed to achieve them. The second stage involves evaluation of current available human resources internally in the organization as well as from external talent pools. The third stage involves bringing the two together to identify areas where skills gaps appear or indeed where there might be so-called surplus of talent. Depending on the outcome of this analysis organizational leaders would then need to decide how to structure and organize their human capital, whether it be on a local, national, regional or global basis.

There seems to be a consensus among researchers and commentators that a top-down approach is needed for successful management of talent. Although HR plays a critical role in driving the talent management agenda forward, it is essential that it is driven from the top down and supported by leadership. Talent management, after all, is a component of HRM, but should not be the sole responsibility of this people management function. Rather, it should be a shared priority to line managers and top leadership (Chuai, Preece and Iles, 2008; Kock and Burke, 2008).

The need for an integrated approach to talent management mentioned earlier in the chapter is also emphasized in Kock and Burke's (2008) approach to managing talent, based on research conducted in the South African public sector. Kock and Burke's (2008) 'talent wheel' model (see Figure 6.1) depicts a cyclical process consisting of:

- **talent planning** – identifying the gap between demand and supply of talent;
- **talent identification** – assessment of employees' performance, potential and readiness to advance;
- **talent categorization** – classifying individuals as 'high performers, solid performers or poor performers' based on the talent identification process;
- **career management** – a process that involves matching employees' visions and career plans with organizational needs reflecting their talent classification;
- **talent balance sheet** – a consolidation of data collected about the employee.

All these elements are underpinned by continuous employee engagement. Although we are not prescriptively promoting this model, it offers useful insight into the practical aspects of the talent management process.

Sustaining quality talent

Boudreau and Ramstad (2005) argue that two paradigm shifts have occurred that carry implications for how organizations define their people management strategies. The authors refer to the first paradigm shift as talentship, which entails identifying key talent pools in areas where strategic success is influenced by the availability or quality of human capital (Boudreau and Ramstad, 2005). As you will have noticed, we have discussed aspects of talentship, albeit using slightly different vocabulary. The second paradigm shift is referred to as sustainability.

FIGURE 6.1   'Talent wheel' (Kock and Burke, 2008)

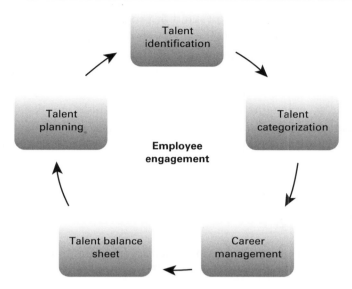

Figure 6.1 Talent wheel. Reproduced from Kock, R. and Burke, M. (2008) Managing Talent in the South African Public Service. *Public Personnel Management*, *37*(4), 457–470. (For further information on *Public Personnel Management* see www.ipma-hr.org)

It is no longer sufficient to define HR's contribution and organizational effectiveness in financial terms, but rather in broader terms that enable 'success today without compromising the needs of the future' (Boudreau and Ramstad, 2005). In other words, although financial success is required to achieve sustainability in an organization, it should be defined in broader terms that include notions of transparency, ethics, diversity, support for employee and human rights, corporate social responsibility and contribution to the community, according to the authors. We therefore suggest that succession planning, an integral part of talent management, is not possible without achieving sustainability in an organization and it is specifically these notions that go beyond financial definitions of success that contribute to employees' sense of organizational commitment and motivation to work, which in return are key factors in managing talent to meet future business needs. Moreover, as it is suggested in an online article, when organizations look at developing their talent or indeed recruiting new talent, the kind of individuals they need are not merely defined by their technical or practical knowledge, albeit they too are important, but by their potential ability to adapt to changing conditions successfully (*HR Review*, 2011).

This is as far as we intend to provide any kind of step-by-step guide to talent management as we strongly believe that the talent management process is not a 'one size fits all' kind of process. Indeed as Scullion and Collings (2011) contend in their edited volume on global talent management, we too argue that understanding the significance of contextual factors is key to successful talent management. What we do aim to provide you with is the ability to ask the right questions when looking at possible approaches to managing people with key skills and expertise that have the potential to enhance organizational performance. We also want to emphasize the holistic approach that is needed – it is not simply enough to address one component of HR when managing talent.

Key learning points and conclusions

- Despite criticism and scepticism, talent management does have a place on the strategic HRM agenda. There seems to be little doubt that developing the right human resources, intellectual capital, skills and competencies are more important now than ever for organizations to achieve competitive advantage.

- Any successful talent management strategy must be holistic and due consideration should be given to these key components: recruitment, selection, learning and development, performance management, retention, pay and reward as well as employee engagement.

- More insight is needed on employees' experiences of being talent managed. Although we have only touched on perception and motivation in this chapter, it is evident that talent management, like HRM, cuts across all areas that are traditionally grouped together under the OB canon. If organizations are to develop effective ways of developing and retaining their key human resources, more attention needs to be paid to how individuals experience being talent managed and what are the consequences of applying talent management practices and policies in terms of behaviour in the organizational context.

- Particularly as organizations increasingly operate across geographical and cultural borders, the approaches used to manage key employees in today's economically challenging environment must be adapted to be contextually fitting. Moreover, the expectations and consequent experiences of those being talent managed are likely to differ in different national and cultural contexts.

Case study and discussion questions

CASE STUDY   Talent management in MNCs in Angola

Angola is one of Africa's largest producers of crude oil, along with Nigeria and thus attracts foreign MNCs to its shores. Angolan government's policies and practices have historically had a significant impact on the way in which MNCs operate and thus strategically manage their own human assets in the country. MNCs are under increased pressure to localize their workforces as work permit regulations are seemingly tightened, thus restricting the number of expatriates companies are able to deploy to Angola. Such barriers carry implications for the success of knowledge transfer processes in MNCs and potentially places increasing pressure on MNCs to send local employees abroad for training rather than relying primarily on expatriates to transfer skills and know-how to their local counterparts. The dynamic is further complicated and made topical by the acute shortage of local skilled professionals (Kreeft, 2009) as a result of Angola's 27-year civil war that only ended in 2002 and the rapidly growing oil business. Talented and experienced Angolans appear to be in short supply and high demand.

A number of interlinked factors have been identified in contributing to current talent management and development practice in the Angolan oil economy. First, the nature of Angola's struggle for independence from its Portuguese colonial rulers and subsequent declaration of independence in 1975 resulted in a mass departure of Portuguese professional and semi-professional settlers, leaving a severe lack of skills and abilities across industries (De Oliveira, 2007; Hodges, 2004). Second, the subsequent civil war between Angolan nationalist movements has resulted in the destruction of much of the country's original subsistence industries (mainly agricultural), and had severe economic and developmental consequences for the country's other sectors such as education, healthcare, tourism, retail and communications. Thus, the development of Angola's infrastructure is highly reliant on oil exports, foreign direct investment in exchange for concessions and oil-backed loans creating a path dependency (eg Buckley and Casson, 2001). A shortage of educated and skilled Angolans is a consequence of the lack of access and the quality of education to name two problems and this is proving a major resourcing challenge not only for MNCs operating in Angola, but also for national companies. The lack of skills supply and restrictions on expatriate quotas could potentially slow down economic growth by making the economy difficult for foreign investors to invest in.

Furthermore, accessibility to educational and career opportunities in Angola has to an extent traditionally been determined by ethno-linguistic divisions (Oyebade, 2007). From a cultural perspective, family obligation, often perceived as nepotism in the West, is practised in Angola and thus the socio-economic position of one's family, in many cases rooted in ethnic heritage, can be a significant determinant in accessing educational and career opportunities.

The Angolan government is driving forward a nationalization agenda, referred to as 'Angolanization' and thus foreign MNCs are having to put into practice strategies that will develop local talent to meet their operational needs. 'Angolanization' has been associated with the development of future leadership potential, not only for its practical implications of developing technical expertise, but also in increasing corporate capacity for local know-how to establish 'constructive relationships' with local stakeholders and the Angolan government (Ernst & Young, 2004). However, Angolanization has been criticized in the media and online forums for its limited and short-term scope (Kreeft, 2009; Paulo, 2006) and bias towards foreign-educated Angolans, implying that the agenda in itself is selective (Paulo, 2006) and perhaps perpetuates the social and economic divisions that are prevalent in Angolan society.

Nationalization in this sense is generally examined from a corporate perspective. In other words, what does nationalization mean for organizations, business performance and the nature of the labour market? The employee perspective is overlooked. Research carried out by one of the authors of this chapter in to the career development experiences of Angolan professionals working in the oil industry suggests that the Angolanization agenda carries many more personal implications for individuals who are being talent managed in this context. Participant narratives suggest that although the development of local talent is seen as a positive concept in principle, it is also accepted in practice with a degree of scepticism. MNCs' perceived inability to treat people as individuals is contradictory to the Angolan cultural value of human relationships. Western transactional approaches to employment relationships in the Angolan context seem counterproductive. Narratives suggest that a perception exists among some Angolan professionals that their Angolan nationality has been a factor when being recruited by foreign MNC. This realization has led to feelings of cynicism and of being used, which in turn has implications for organizational loyalty and motivation. It is therefore easy to see that if individuals feel that they are merely a resource to their organization, there is a greater likelihood that they will move between companies in search of the most financially rewarding deal for themselves. The positive side of the Angolanization agenda that has been acknowledged is the increased training and development opportunities for local talent and rapid career progression. Although status and position are highly valued in Angola, rapid career progression is also met with a degree of scepticism and it is questioned whether promotions are based on skills and merit or governmental pressure on MNCs to localize at management level.

Discussion questions

- Can you think of other countries where differences between local and typically Western cultural values inherent in MNCs may influence the way talent management or development practices are received by the individuals that have been identified as somehow talented? Discuss using examples.

- How would you define 'talent'? Using cross-cultural management knowledge, can you recognize any characteristics in your definition that would reflect your specific cultural values?

- What kind of qualities and skills do you think MNCs are looking for in their high potential employers? What kind of similarities do you see in your definition of talent and in the qualities and skills you think corporate leaders of MNCs are looking for?

PART FOUR
Shifting contexts for organizational behaviour

07
Conflict, power and politics

PHILIP DAVIES and ROD SMITH

LEARNING OBJECTIVES

- Understand the key terms and nature of the contemporary debate about conflict, power and politics.
- Be able to analyse critically the key debates in existing literature.
- Identify the implications of politics, power and conflict for managers.

Introduction

The study of conflict, power and politics has engaged the interest of scholars and practitioners for centuries. The intention of this chapter is to show how a linked approach that uses the twin lenses of OB HRM can offer richer insights than a single track approach. Politics is, however, often difficult to discuss in organizations. It is often said by practitioners to be 'the elephant in the room' – a term in general use meaning that you are ignoring the obvious problem. In some respects the term 'politics' has acquired the status of a taboo that refers to someone or something that cannot be named. For example, Crozier's classic study of organizational politics (1964) had to use anonymous organizations.

Our unease about discussing politics has been heightened by recent financial problems in the Eurozone and United States as well as global issues such as environmental change, that challenge our view in the West of the world as beneficent. Can politicians be trusted to put the problems right or are they beyond repair? So when the term 'politics' is used in the context of organizations it arouses complex and contradictory responses. To help answer such questions about the role of politics in organizations we first need to be clear about the terms as well as what is currently known.

So what do we mean when we use the terms – either separately or together – 'power, politics and conflict'? What are the roots in OB and HRM discourses of our current theories? Have we reached a consensus or are there still unanswered or indeed unanswerable questions? And finally, what are the implications for executives, and for future research by HRM and OB scholars?

Since the topic is very broad, we will use a case study of Easyjet, a budget airline, which should be familiar to readers, to illustrate what the various terms we highlight here mean in practice. But first we need to be clear about definitions.

Definitions – power, politics and conflict

In practice the terms 'power', 'politics' and 'conflict' are often used interchangeably. They tend to be used to describe a situation in an organization where there is conflict and the appearance of power and politics is no longer hidden but is visible. Often, for example, newspapers will use phrases such as 'boardroom coup' to describe a sudden dramatic change of directors. Therefore politics, power and conflict are commonly seen in a negative light and as something by implication that managers should avoid or at least seek to limit. This chapter argues, and this follows the current consensus among scholars, that the phenomena is neither positive nor negative, but rather a normal part of organizational behaviour. But obtaining evidence that is publishable concerning the topic is difficult (Crozier, 1964; Mintzberg, 1985). Often researchers use anecdotal or unattributed evidence instead. Often it is only with the benefit of a historical perspective that a true picture emerges of politics in action and the records for business leaders are not as rich as those for political leaders. This can be seen in an excellent biography of former US president Abraham Lincoln (Kearns, 2005) that makes extensive use of new evidence. The topic of politics in organizations is also frequently used in films and television dramas as a recurring theme that tends to emphasize its negative side to the popular mind.

Power

Power is a social process by which outcomes can be achieved. It is related to Weber's concept of authority which is the 'legitimate exercise of power' (1947). The exercise of power can occur in a variety of ways: directly or via reward, obedience to authority, or compliance to norms. Lukes argues that 'consensual authority with no conflict of interest is not a form of power' but this is disputed (1974). Power exists in three dimensions: direct power, indirect power and meaning power (Lukes, 1974). Modernist scholars tend to focus on the first two dimensions while critical and postmodern scholars tend to consider the third dimension or the power of meaning (Hatch, 1997).

Politics

How national politics should be organized is disputed. Some states argue that only where everyone has a vote is there real political freedom. Others disagree and argue that what works in one culture may not work elsewhere so that a benevolent party or one who rules alone might be better. Ways of describing politics can be traced back to Aristotle in fifth-century BCE Athens. However, most observers would agree that all politics is basically about how disagreements involving the allocation of resources can be resolved. The political struggle usually concerns who succeeds in getting power, the process through which they get power, and how the ends of the organization at whatever level from small firm up to a nation state are then determined. Organizations are political when there needs to be agreement over the use of scarce resources (Pfeffer and Salancik, 1974) or their future direction (March, 1962). For organizations the most convincing theory is that power in the form of strategic choice is exercised by the dominant coalition – defined as 'the small number who exercise authority within the organization' (Child, 1972).

Conflict

Conflict can arise from disagreements between the actors in an organization whether at individual, group, team or departmental level (Weiss, 1996). Conflict can be short term or long term, open or hidden. The ultimate conflict is of course war, which is a continuation of politics by other means (Clausewitz, 1968). Businesses do compete but they do not wage war, although war-like language and metaphors are sometimes used for rhetorical effect. Conflict can arise at any level up to and including between organizations or groups of organizations when formed into alliances, as currently occurs with airlines (Weiss, 1996).

Main arguments in the literature

OB, as Hatch (1997) argues, has essentially three research approaches: modernist, postmodernist and critical. All have an interest in the linked topics of conflict, power and politics but each have a fundamentally different set of underlying assumptions about how to analyse the phenomena. Each research approach also has preferences as to how to acquire knowledge, ranging from statistical analysis to the qualitative analysis of discourse. We will cite examples where relevant in the text. These different approaches have been well summarized by Alvesson and Deetz (1996) who consider how the three approaches see power. Modernists tend to see power as about how organizations exercise legitimate authority and resistance as something to be managed. Postmodernists see resistance to power as inevitable as well as a source of creativity. Critical scholars distrust power and take a variety of approaches from Marxist to feminist and generally try to reflect the views of the silenced or powerless. There has been a long history of scholarship on politics and power from the perspectives of actual states. This includes: the best way to organize states (Aristotle and Plato in the fifth century BCE), power in renaissance states ruled by a Prince (Machiavelli in the 16th century), and social conflict in states resulting from changes to the ruling classes from feudalism through the bourgeoisie to the industrial proletariat or working classes (Marx in the 19th century). Each class loses power in a crisis. Marxists assert that the current era of capitalism will end in a crisis. Machiavelli in his advice to princes summarized the disconnect between how princes should behave in theory and what happens in practice very well when he argued that 'the gulf between how one should live and how one does live is so wide that a man who neglects what is actually done for what should be done moves towards self-destruction rather than self-preservation' (Machiavelli, 1999).

More recently, scholars have looked at smaller-scale issues in organizations. In the 20th century research has originated from various fields including social sciences, psychology, economics, political theory and game theory. We will first consider politics and power in more detail before looking at conflict via the lens of game theory.

Politics

Organizations are arenas for political activity (Mintzberg, 1985). Organizational politics involves 'intentional acts of influence to enhance or protect the self -interest of individuals or groups' (Allen *et al*, 1979). The study of politics is the study of who gets most of what there is to get (Allen *et al*, 1979). Scholars are also interested in resistance to the wishes of those with power. A recent study by Starr (2011) suggests that teachers in Australia resist change. She used a longitudinal approach over three years where she compared newly appointed and experienced principals (head teachers in UK terms) whose planned changes were resisted using both formal and informal means. Resistance was often successful, which has implications for change management strategy generally. Reactions to organizational politics can also be linked to cultural differences as a recent study by Vigod (2001) showed. He carried out a cross-cultural comparison of UK and Israeli public sector workers' attitudes and found that while they shared similar views the clear differences could be best explained by culture. Resistance to change seems to be rooted in local contexts. This research also shows the benefit of taking a critical view of power as it makes managers become more sensitive to context rather than taking a 'one size fits all' approach with an overall recipe for challenging existing power relationships embedded in, for example, schools.

We should, however, be careful not to assume that every activity in organizations can be labelled political. Reciprocity – defined as a selfless act entered into without any direct benefit – may help build a mutually successful organizational climate. However, when unresolved issues emerge then political tactics (Pfeffer, 1981) may become much more noticeable. Such tactics include impression management, support building for ideas, associating with the influential and building long-term relationships. There is much anecdotal evidence for how political tactics work in practice. In 19th-century London an eminent financier was asked if he would support someone who wanted to raise money. The financier, who was Lord Rothschild, said no to direct support, but instead offered to walk across the floor of the Stock Exchange with the young man. Everyone who watched them together assumed that Lord Rothschild supported him and in consequence the offer was oversubscribed. Gialdini, 1989). That is a clear example of impression management.

From limited research we know that in organizations political activity is usually linked to the place of the executive in the organization (Allen *et al*, 1979). The sentiment is that those at the top of the organization view politics as natural and about resolving differences while front-line managers see politics as getting in the way. One view of these findings is to argue that those who are good at politics get promoted while the obverse is true. We believe that this may be linked to the difference between discretionary and nondiscretionary power where front-line managers tend to obey the decisions of top managers whereas top managers have to choose what to do and hence have to negotiate in the dominant coalition (Child, 1972). This is more akin to Machiavelli's (1999 edition) account of politics in the Renaissance court. Child's view of a dominant coalition is similar to Hambrick's view (1995) of top management teams. Here political behaviour is common and can lead to fragmentation. Researchers from Bradford carried out a study in the 1970s showing how a top management team could disintegrate into a mere constellation of senior executives pursuing their own agendas. Decisions were games of manoeuvre characterized by obstacles, power and muddle. Outside stakeholders were often called in to redress an internal power balance (Astley *et al*, 1982). The research highlighted the two factors driving strategic decision making as complexity: the variety of interests involved and politicality, ie the balance of interests. These findings have also been found in a more recent study of how an information strategy was implemented in a university over three years, a process that showed a similar pattern characterized by social dramas that seem at variance with a view of an organized change process. (Peszynski and Corbitt, 2006). So in organizations, once researchers can go more into the reality of what is happening, a richer picture of political activity emerges that is very different to what is sometimes portrayed in change management texts. Political behaviour is not irrational or perverse but rather an inevitable consequence arising from the nature of organizational life.

Politics is important in decision making. The theoretical basis for this view was first made by economists (March, 1962). March and colleagues criticized the traditional model of decision making because it assumed that there is a consistent preference for decision ordering among decision makers and that decision rules are known and accepted by everyone. In reality, decisions are taken with incomplete information. March argues that this is linked to the problem of information processing. To combat this, executives have to operate on the basis of taken for granted assumptions or schemata about their world (see Chapter 2 and 'schemas', Glossary). They also use bias and heuristics because of their need to simplify their input of data. But politics is not harmful in itself. It may lead to a more creative outcome as executives surface differences. Problems emerge when differences cannot be reconciled and conflict becomes endemic. The organization descends into civil war and this can lead to organizational breakdown (Mintzberg, 1985).

Power

Traditionally, power studies have mainly been based on the work of psychologists such as Skinner who follow a view of behaviour based on stimulus response. However, Lukes (1974) suggests that this can lead to a one- or two-dimensional view of power, which is inadequate. He argues that power exists in three dimensions. Direct power is where actor A can influence actor B to do something that actor A does not want to do. Indirect power is where actor A so influences the process that what actor B wants to discuss never gets on the agenda. Lukes' third dimension is where the overall meaning is determined. This is akin to Gramsci's hegemony argument (see Glossary) where what actor B wants to do is unthinkable – it is against the cultural norms. We will explore what hegemony means in practice when we consider the case study on page 206.

Lukes' summary of these three dimensions of power (1974) is shown in Table 7.1.

TABLE 7.1   Summary of three dimensions of power (Lukes, 1974)

One-dimensional view of power	Focus on behaviour, decision making, key issues, observable conflict, subjective interests, seen as policy preferences revealed by political participation.
Two-dimensional view of power	Qualified critique of behavioural focus. Focus on decision making and no decision making, observable conflict (overt or covert), subjective interests seen as policy preferences or grievances.
Three-dimensional view of power	Critique of behavioural focus. Focus on decision making and control over political agenda (not necessarily through decisions), issues and potential issues, observable (overt or covert) and latent conflict, subjective and real interests.

The comment on 'real interests' in the third level of power in Table 7.1 is a reference to the Marxist critique of capitalism where the real interests of the workers are hidden from the workers themselves. Hence revolutionaries may awaken the workers to their real interests by provoking the ruling class to acts of oppression. Such logic has been used to justify terrorism where to save people it is legitimate to blow them up so that they can realize what they should do to free themselves! We see here how any debate on the theory of power can lead to social action.

Traditionally OB and HRM research has been at the level of the first two levels of power that often used experiments such as the obedience tests. However, a more critical view of power has led to some very interesting case study based research into strategic change. Anthony Giddens' work is especially significant from the sociological perspective. This led to a focus on culture in strategy (Johnson, 1992). Recent studies include a study of implementation using a critical epistemology (Peszynski and Corbitt, 2006). When we assess the implications for the executive we will include how issues of meaning relate to power.

Power is usually linked to reward. Those who manage the sources of uncertainty usually have greater power and often enjoy greater rewards than others. For example Crozier (1964), in a classic study of the state-controlled French tobacco industry, found that where prices were fixed and the firm had a monopoly the only source of uncertainty was production. And the workers who mended the machines had the greatest power and so enjoyed the highest wages. We see a similar process in the airline industry where pilots have the greatest power in negotiating wages. Their shop steward in the UK in the 1960s in fact was Norman Tebbit, who as a Conservative MP was a key member in forming the government's policy to restrict union power in the 1980s. His career shows the link between interests and behaviour. When a position of power is challenged those who see their power weakening will respond. We are seeing this today in the London Underground where driverless trains will weaken the power of drivers. Their union therefore opposes the reform on the grounds of safety. A key point here for managers is that the behaviour of the drivers is predictable. This is not of course a new issue. Demarcation disputes in traditional industries have historically affected competitiveness by raising labour costs. So the debate about power is important in employee relations.

Power is sought actively by executives but their motive is not necessarily always financial but may be more about achieving organizational goals. Power is the great motivator (McClelland and Burnham, 1976).

Power is related to the position of the executives in the organization as well as to their physical position such as where their offices are located. The importance of where executives are located is clear when an office is reorganized. Location confers status as well as access to unplanned informal conversations. This is clearly non-trivial; there is normally opposition as those losing a central position often see it as a loss of power. We also know from social network analysis studies that the position of individuals is linked to how others see their personal power (Krackhardt, 1990).

Power in top teams has also been actively researched. What is of especial interest is the external links of top teams. Since the days of Adam Smith it has often been thought that when businesspeople meet then they will engage in anti-competitive behaviour (1970 edition). In the popular imagination when politicians meet businesspeople there is a fear of undue influence being exerted under the cover of a legitimate sharing of views. The external ties are also important in the role they play in decision making. Senior executives make decisions under conditions of information overload and ambiguity. They therefore tend to economize (Geletkanycz and Hambrick, 1997) on searching themselves for data and instead rely on external referents for insights into plausible alternatives. In simpler terms, they use their personal networks. We also know that weak ties or people you don't know that well are more likely to give you new information (Granovetter, 1973). So the personal networks of top managers are one of their sources of power.

The role of networks leads into a wider argument involving social mobility and stratification (see Glossary). Any academic debate about power and politics in organizations can quickly shift into a much deeper debate about the way that a society is developing. We all live and work in organizations. We are all affected by what they do. And HR managers are part of the process. There needs to be a more critical approach into how staff experience power that takes an assumption that the views of the silenced may not have been heard. We also know that any change is resisted for often good reasons and that unless those reasons can be addressed then change will be blocked.

Conflict

We can think of conflict occurring at five different levels (Deutsch, 1990): personal, interpersonal, inter-group, inter-organizational and international. In this section, we will restrict ourselves to consideration of disagreements at the interpersonal and inter-group level with occasional forays into conflicts at the inter-organizational level. In particular, we concentrate on how to handle this conflict. The boundaries between these five different levels can be a little blurred, and we will, on occasion, take examples from other levels to help illustrate our concepts.

Dictionaries generally define 'conflict' in terms of war, mental struggle and difference. The roots of the definition are Latin via Old Middle English, and mean 'fought'. We can immediately see how war refers to conflict at the international level, and mental struggle refers to conflict at the personal level. Thus, we restrict ourselves to consider conflict arising from difference, and the *Oxford English Dictionary* defines this form of conflict as: '… a serious incompatibility between two or more opinions, principles, or interests …'.

When individuals and groups disagree, these clashes can be violent, but is this always the case? Does difference always lead to disagreement, clashes and violence? Under what circumstances does this occur? Can it be handled and overcome? Can difference have positive outcomes? These are some of the questions this section seeks to answer.

Difference

We begin by investigating the nature of difference. We want to know whether difference is a good or bad thing. An example may help here.

In the 1990s, there was a series on BBC television that examined the recruitment of a variety of jobs. Each week, the programme followed the recruitment process for one vacancy. Two programmes stuck out. The first was for the chief constable for a police force in the heart of England. Recruiters were shown devising the selection criteria, and candidates were shown undergoing normal selection processes such as interviews. One process was a formal dinner of the shortlisted candidates with members of the Police Authority, the governing body of the force, where the candidates' table manners (and presumably their capacity for alcohol) were minutely examined. The second was for a creative writer in an advertising agency. A key criterion for this job was to work with others in the agency to devise creative solutions. This time, the recruitment process involved some interviews and presentations of portfolios of work, but it also involved group problem-solving simulations. These were electric events, with group members raising their voices, losing their tempers, and coming to the very edge of physically attacking each other. This extraordinary behaviour was described, admiringly, by the senior partner of the agency as 'teamworking'.

The contrast between these two examples could not be greater. Members of the Police Authority were looking for someone like them, 'one of us'. They didn't want difference. Indeed, in August 2011, the Metropolitan Police in the UK sought to recruit a replacement for their commissioner who had recently resigned following allegations of police corruption. The Prime Minister suggested that the pool of possible candidates should be widened to include overseas candidates. This was widely interpreted as meaning that an application from a strikingly successful US police commissioner should be considered. The UK Home Secretary rejected this suggestion, and the advert specifically restricted the position to UK applicants only, as reported in an article entitled 'Cameron's "supercop" blocked by Theresa May' by Tom Whitehead and Andrew Porter and published in the Telegraph (London) on 5 August 2011.

The advertising agency was determined to employ someone different, even if it led to organizational discomfort. Now stop for a moment and consider: the creative industry in the UK is hugely successful and admired worldwide; the police in the UK have been under attack from almost all quarters for the last four decades.

Is there a connection? These small examples cannot prove that there is. They don't prove that difference is necessary, but the example of the advertising agency does prove that difference is not necessarily a bad thing – it can bring major benefits. You may even think, like Handy (1993), that life is a little dull without difference.

We need different ways of looking to explore this topic further. A useful line of enquiry is systems theory (see Glossary). Organizational theory has, in its short history, borrowed concepts from science. For example, classical organizational theory uses the tools of natural science, such as physics. Based on the work of Isaac Newton, it sees the world as made of clockwork. People are cogs and wheels in this clockwork, and we can see this in the teachings of Taylor and scientific management, with the assembly line as its ultimate expression. After the First World War, attention shifted to psychology as a consequence of the Hawthorne effect (see Glossary) and the human relations movement (see Glossary). The psychological needs of people became the major focus of attention. After the Second World War, systems theory became the focus, with major contributions by Lewin (1997), Simon (1997), March (1962), and Senge (1990). Systems theory borrows ideas from the biological sciences, which see organizations as living things, organisms, rather than pieces of clockwork. They are constantly changing in ways that we cannot, generally, predict.

In its most general sense, a system is a collection of parts that are connected in some way and do something. In terms of an organization, we can think of staff in a department having a web of relationships, work and personal, that has an effect on the workings of the whole department. Perhaps the males in the department have a ritual of meeting in the pub after work on Fridays, excluding females from this arrangement. This has the potential for having a significant impact on departmental politics, decision making and promotions.

Of particular interest here is the idea of systems entropy. This has its origins in the second law of thermodynamics and refers to the tendency of systems to decay if left alone. A simple example should make this clear. Consider a student flat. Students are not well known for undertaking housekeeping or washing up of dishes. The opposite is more generally the case. As a consequence, living areas become increasingly untidy and covered by layers of dust and detritus, dirty dishes accumulate in the kitchen sink, and wise parents, when they visit, avoid the bathroom. Indeed, the kitchen sink may possibly be incubating hitherto unknown life forms. This decay has been caused by the lack of inputs – in this case, elbow grease and application. This is a general point: when there is no change of inputs, decay occurs. To stop a system decaying, there must be a change of inputs.

If we apply this idea to the two recruitment examples given earlier, we can draw some deeper conclusions. It seems very likely that the procedures for the selection of a new chief constable are designed to ensure that there is no change of inputs: those involved want to recruit 'one of us'. In the case of the advertising agency executives, they want to recruit someone with ideas, energy, and creativity: they want to encourage change of inputs. Hence, we can reasonably conclude that the system used by the police may well decay, but the advertising agency will not. It may, however, explode, as we will see.

This brings us to consideration of inputs. They can be anything that has an effect on the system. Investment, more resources, energy, passion, creativity, new people, new ideas and reorganization of resources all qualify. A suitable metaphor would be a dark, musty room, and changing the inputs as opening the windows to let the sunlight and fresh air in. Indeed, this is a metaphor widely used. We can even expand this metaphor to talk of open and closed systems. The dark, musty room is a closed system: it is closed to the outside world, the windows are shut; it doesn't interact with its environment. Opening the windows turns the room into an open system that does interact with its environment. You can see how entropy is therefore associated with closed systems. You would expect that a closed system would decay and eventually stop functioning. This is precisely what happened to the USSR. This example of a closed system, isolated from the West for many years, collapsed rapidly following the fall of the Berlin Wall in 1989.

In summary, we consider that open systems are preferable to closed ones, that they change their inputs, and that these inputs involve different ways of looking at the world. Put even more simply, we need difference to overcome the effects of systems entropy in order to survive, let alone move forward and prosper. Although we have used the term 'difference' throughout this section, we could equally have used the term 'diversity' when we talk about human inputs.

Difference can be bad

We have established that difference can be healthy and should generally be encouraged. But is this always so? Under what circumstances does difference lead to undesirable outcomes?

In an early study, Schmidt and Tannenbaum (1960) viewed disputes as passing through a number of stages starting with an initial awareness of a difference, and eventually resulting in open conflict, as shown in Table 7.2. Schmidt and Tannenbaum point out that a manager, seeking to settle this potential conflict, will have most influence at the early stages and least influence at the later stages.

The resemblance between this evolution and modern models of managing change is striking. Kanter (1992), Lewin (1997) and Pugh (1978), for example, all suggest change processes that start with gaining awareness, moving through educating those concerned of the consequences, getting participation of all affected, involving them in problem solving, searching for win–win solutions, and implementation of agreed solutions. The major learning point of this is that change is concerned with difference, and this can lead to conflict if not handled carefully.

From Figure 7.1 it is clear that difference does not have to lead to conflict. We can intervene at any stage of the process to affect the outcome. However, interventions at early stages have the greatest probability of success. Figure 7.1 provides a useful way of examining the stages of evolution. Studying this process in a little more detail, we know that

TABLE 7.2 Stages of dispute (Schmidt and Tannenbaum, 1960)

Stage 1	**Anticipation.** The manager learns of a planned event that will result in change.
Stage 2	**Conscious, unexpressed difference.** Awareness rises among the people who will be affected by the change. Tensions rise.
Stage 3	**Discussion.** Information is presented, questions are asked and differing opinions emerge openly.
Stage 4	**Open dispute.** The parties present their cases to each other and argue. Differences now sharpen into clearly defined points of view.
Stage 5	**Open conflict.** The parties are now committed to their positions. The dispute is clearly defined. The outcome can now only be described in terms of win, lose or compromise.

FIGURE 7.1 Simplified representation of Schmidt and Tannenbaum's stages of evolution (Schmidt and Tannenbaum, 1960)

From Schmidt, W H and Tannenbaum, R (1960) Management of Differences. *Harvard Business Review*, November 1960.

argument has a noble history, from the teaching of rhetoric in ancient times to the debating societies of today. In general, we consider that argument can be a good thing; it helps to clarify points, sharpen thought, encourages learning, and so on. However, argument can be a negative thing, disruptive and raising emotions to the point of anger. The consequence of this last point is that it can lead to competition and conflict. Skill is required to turn negative arguments into productive discussions.

We can think of competition as a contest between individuals and groups for territory and resources. According to the *Oxford English Dictionary*, it is: '... the activity or condition of striving to gain or win something by defeating or establishing superiority over others...'. Indeed, we frequently talk of 'win–lose' situations.

Competition has three positive effects. First, it sets standards. In competitive sport, performance standards consistently improve. In athletics, there are very few records that have stood for any length of time. Second, competition stimulates and channels energies. This is an important argument for the existence of free market economies. Resources are constantly being redirected to those areas where there is the greatest likelihood of reward, and away from those areas where there is little prospect of it. Third, competition is Darwinian. It sorts out the fit from the unfit. It is the driving force of adaptation and evolution.

However, many think that competition has negative effects. As in the case of argument, competition can be disruptive and raise emotions to the point of anger. In fact, during the 1980s there were celebrated cases of local authorities in the UK banning competitive games in schools because they felt that they fostered negative attitudes.

In summary, we can say that argument and competition are negative if they degenerate into conflict.

Possibility of competitions degenerating into conflict

It is difficult to predict whether competition will degenerate into conflict. It largely depends on whether competition is open or closed. An open competition is one where everyone can win, whereas a closed competition is one where one person wins at the expense of the others.

In negotiations, distributive bargaining is an example of closed competition. The parties fight for a share of a fixed-size 'cake'. On the other hand, integrative bargaining is an example of an open competition where the parties seek to increase the size of the cake before sharing it out.

Closed competitions are more likely to degenerate into conflict; an open competition can produce more cake to go round. The following examples should make this clear.

The supplier–customer relationship in industry has traditionally been regarded as a closed competition, but the Japanese have redefined this as an open competition where both parties act as partners. Thus, the partnerships between, say, Toyota and its suppliers have devastated the US auto industry. By 2009, the once mighty General Motors had to enter

Chapter 11 (a form of bankruptcy in the United States). Another example can be found in education: if a fixed proportion of students achieve certain grades at A level (the examination taken in the final year of school) in the UK each year, the competition is closed, but if there is scope for everyone to get a grade A, the competition is open. This last example is of great interest to a number of people. A levels were introduced in the UK in the 1950s as an admission examination for universities. Thus, since university places were restricted at that time, the competition was closed. Indeed, there were a fixed number of grades awarded. A certain number of A grades, a certain number of B grades and so on were awarded each year, regardless of the standard of the individuals concerned. In a poor year, an indifferent performer could get a grade B; in a good year, an indifferent performer might get a grade D. In the 1990s, A levels became open competitions, and the grades started to improve. Now, a large percentage of candidates achieve As and Bs. However, there are still restrictions on places at the older, more prestigious universities, and excellent performers are turned away. Thus the competition for places is closed. We now have the worst of all possible worlds – an A-level system that is an open competition in one regard and a closed competition in another.

Another example also makes this clear. In the summer of 2004 there was a major dispute in the UK civil service over pay. Traditionally, civil servants receive a pay increment each year. Lately, this had depended on performance, but all staff had the opportunity to reach the top of the scale through these increments. The civil service tried to introduce a system whereby only a proportion of the staff reach the top of the scale, depending on their performance. So, while it was possible for all staff to reach the top before, now the civil service wanted only, say, 20 per cent to reach the top. An open competition had been turned into a closed competition. The unions resisted this change strongly, claiming, quite reasonably, that it was a transparent device to save money by cutting people's pay. For open competitions to be fully productive, three conditions must be met:

- The competition must be perceived as genuinely open.
- The rules and procedures for arbitration must be seen to be fair.
- The major determinants of success must be under the control of the competitors.

If these conditions are not met, the competition will be seen to be closed.

Game theory

What is happening here? We turn to game theory for an explanation. This theory deals with games where the most profitable thing for you to do depends on what your opponent does and vice versa; it attempts to simplify the world and produce the best outcome for any particular situation. Game theory has many applications, and it is widely used in the social sciences.

It started when John von Neumann, a Hungarian genius who was possibly the greatest mathematician of the 20th century, and one of the architects of the modern computer, published a book on the theory of parlour games (1928). He collaborated with an economist, Morgenstern, to publish a later work (von Neumann and Morgenstern, 1944).

Initially, von Neumann identified the concept of the zero-sum game, where one party wins at the expense of the other. Later, von Neumann and Morgenstern invented the concept of the non-zero-sum game where it pays to collaborate and form coalitions. They were absolutely clear that non-zero-sum games could only arise through collaboration. Notice also that distributive bargaining is a zero-sum game, whereas integrative bargaining is a non-zero-sum game. These distinctions are important.

After the Second World War, John Nash arrived at Princeton University in the United States. He chose to study game theory for his doctoral thesis, and showed that non-zero-sum games could occur in competitive situations as well as collaborative ones. For this work, Nash received the Nobel Prize for Economics in 1994.

Main players in game theory

The 1960s film, *Dr Strangelove*, or *How I learned to love the bomb*, featured a deranged scientist with a crippled body and prosthetic hand, confined to a wheelchair. This was Dr Strangelove, the crazed genius, advising the US President on waging nuclear war against the USSR. Many people considered this depiction to be far-fetched, even for the purposes of satire. It was not. This was John von Neumann, the brilliant Hungarian, who developed game theory in order to win the coming conflict with the Soviet Union. He developed the modern computer to carry out the lengthy and complex calculations required. The film was directed by the masterly Stanley Kubrick and remains fresh today.

John Nash was the subject of the film *A beautiful mind*. His PhD thesis was 29 pages long.

The points made about types of bargaining, games and game states are summarized in Table 7.3.

TABLE 7.3   Summary of bargaining types, games and game states

Distributive bargaining	Zero-sum games	Win–lose, lose–win
Integrative bargaining	Non-zero-sum games	Win–win, lose–lose

Since the outcome of a game depends on the choices made by both parties (we restrict ourselves throughout this description to games involving two parties only), an equilibrium is generally reached, after which change is unlikely to occur. In practice, this means that the four states (win–lose, lose–win, win–win and lose–lose) are very stable. If a win–lose state is achieved, it is very difficult to shift, as illustrated in the box below.

Famous games in history

The prisoner's dilemma

The most famous game in history is the prisoner's dilemma. Imagine that two criminals have been caught and locked up in separate interview rooms. The crime is robbery with murder. The police offer a deal to each separately, but without the other prisoner knowing. If the prisoner is prepared to confess and tell on his mate, the police will offer a deal: that prisoner can walk away free and the other prisoner will be executed. If neither rats on the other, they can both expect five years in gaol. The rational thing to do is to tell on the other prisoner, but this will mean very heavy prison sentences if both confess. So, although mutual cooperation is in everyone's interest, self-interest tends to prevail. Generally, this is to society's disadvantage.

The Red Queen race

Another example of a famous game is the Red Queen race. This is taken from Lewis Carroll's famous children's story, *Alice Through the Looking Glass*, where the Red Queen instructs Alice to run faster in order to stay in the same place! In nature we see tropical forests where trees grow incredibly tall, all competing with neighbouring trees to reach the light. The upshot is that all the trees are tall: if they cooperated, then they would be much smaller and still receive the same amount of light as they do as tall trees.

The tragedy of the commons

This game is taken from observations of behaviour on a piece of common land near Oxford in England. Common land is land that isn't owned by anyone, but local inhabitants can use it freely: the problem is that local people graze their sheep and other livestock there, and the land becomes overgrazed and poor. It makes sense to limit grazing, but who is going to agree to that? Individuals are not going to volunteer to give up their rights to grazing: what would they gain from that? So how do we solve the problem?

This is particularly relevant at the moment in the UK fishing industry. Everyone agrees that the North Sea is over-fished, but no fisherman is prepared to give up fishing voluntarily. So the EU has to impose quotas to restrict fishing. No-one is happy, of course.

Segregation

There is one other way in which difference can lead to conflict. In the mid-1960s, Jenkins and MacRae studied intercommunity conflict in Northern Ireland between Protestants and Catholics. At that time, the two communities had started to segregate and live in different physical locations. As they segregated, social interaction between the two groups diminished. The authors predicted (Jenkins and MacRae, 1967) that as segregation increased, intercommunity tension would also increase. They were proved correct, and violent conflict erupted in the late 1960s. Even today, conflict exists in the province, although at a much lower level.

The tendency to segregate has been examined in a series of simulations. Schelling (1969) showed that total segregation could occur if people preferred neighbours who had the same colour as themselves. He used coins on graph paper to show that people would move from their existing home location to another where they would be 'happier'. This idea can be extended to include preferences for neighbours of the same type (middle class or working class, straight or gay, and so on). For each preference, segregation occurs. These simulations are now performed by computers using automata. These are simple computer programs that look like (large) chess boards. Interestingly, these automata were studied intensely by von Neumann and form part of the general study of game theory.

The implications are clear: if populations are allowed to segregate, then conflict will most probably occur in some form or other. Organizations display many forms of segregation, so that conflict is ever present. The familiar silos of bureaucratic organization are the most obvious example of such segregation. Thus, one objective of organizational development must be to minimize this segregation.

Handling conflict

The question remains: how can we use these ideas to handle conflict successfully? We have already noted that people will hold different perspectives of that conflict, and will hold different objectives. Indeed, our personal experience tells us that they may be arguing about different things, and it takes a while before the penny drops and normal service resumes. Using that idea, we can think of a process where both parties learn about each other's objectives. For example, a company can be thought of in many different ways: a place where you earn income, interact socially with others, express individual talent, a prison, a rut. When the threat of redundancy emerges, people will react differently. Some will welcome the release from the rut, the chance to retire from exhausting physical work, the opportunity to use the redundancy money to retrain for a career they have always desired, and so on. Some will react badly, viewing the loss of income or social interaction negatively.

The point of this is that, by surfacing these objectives, it may be possible to satisfy them for both parties and avoid conflict. This requires skill and subtlety on the part of practitioners, of course, but this can be learned. Surfacing objectives requires communication. The more communication there is between parties, the more chance there is of defining objectives so that they don't conflict with each other.

However, increased communication can also bring complexity and confusion, and may make things worse. It's a difficult balance to achieve. Table 7.4 represents this approach.

This is one of a number of conflict handling styles, and they seem to have many common elements. An early model was based on the managerial grid developed by Blake and Mouton (1964). A subsequent adaptation by Thomas (1976) injected a little humour. For example, it referred to the lose–lose position as a 'pair of lemmings', and the lose–win position as a 'poodle'. The above model (Kilman and Thomas, 1977) is in wide use in management development training. The key lesson is that, unlike personality traits, conflict-handling behaviours are learned and so can change. For example, young sales representatives often display a strong urge to compete while experienced managers who manage complex

TABLE 7.4   Five conflict-handling styles (based on Kilman and Thomas, 1977)

Conflict style: competitive	I win, you lose
Conflict style: avoidance	I lose, you lose
Conflict style: collaborate	I win, you win
Conflict style: surrender	I lose, you win
Conflict style: compromise	We both win partly

alliances will often show a strong tendency to avoid conflict. This observation is based on running exercises with aerospace managers over a 15-year period using this instrument.

The ideal position is win–win. This is the assertive position, and not to be confused with the win–lose position, which is aggressive and confrontational. Many assertiveness training courses use this model as their basis. In simple terms, to be assertive, you need to have high courage of your own convictions to achieve your own objectives, and high consideration for other people to identify and achieve theirs. You could summarize this by saying that, in order to achieve win–win outcomes, we cooperate effectively in pursuit of purely selfish aims. Intuitively, it also means that the parties must learn to trust each other when searching for win–win outcomes. The description of the prisoners' dilemma (above) showed that while mutual cooperation is in everyone's interest, self-interest tends to prevail. High levels of trust are needed to overcome this barrier. In the absence of trust, the only rational option for one-off games is win–lose. Axelrod (1984), however, argues that over time in a game without any end then cooperative behaviour may develop. The point here is that the time period of the game is key.

Evolutionary psychology

Game theory teaches us that handling conflict is possible, but it is a rational theory, based on logic. Conventionally, we think of humans as being irrational. Is there any truth in this, and how does it influence our study of conflict? To answer these questions, we need to explore the growing field of evolutionary psychology, or cognitive science, as it is known in the United States. Throughout history, our species has engaged in win–win activities in order to survive. The underlying theory is that our brains have not developed in the short time (150,000) years since *homo sapiens* left Africa. Thus, we have Stone Age genes and our behaviour is still dictated by our memories of the African savannah. We had the key problem of alliance formation. We lived in groups because it provided us with extra protection from predators. But, because resources were scarce (food, mates, and so on) competition became intense. Squabbles were common. So, this problem was solved by forming alliances whereby we worked together in order to compete with other alliances. This required two forms of behaviour – competition and 'reciprocal altruism'.

We can observe this behaviour directly. Children have a tendency to behave altruistically. In the ultimate bargaining game, two children play a game. One is given a pile of chocolate money – let's say ten pieces. This child has to share this pile of money with the other child. The second child can accept the coins given or reject them. If the second child rejects what has been offered, both children receive no chocolate money. If the second child accepts the offer, both children receive the chocolate coins distributed. You would think that the second child would always accept the coins offered, no matter how few, since they are getting something they would not otherwise receive, but that is not the case. In simulation after simulation, children will reject a distribution of chocolate coins that they think unfair. They will accept a fair distribution – roughly half – but not less. This has its roots in our primeval past when sharing was the most effective route to survival. It explains, to some extent, our altruistic nature. You can imagine how this might work in practice. You may be a fine hunter, but a poor maker of axes and spears. Another member of your group may well be an incompetent hunter (perhaps he or she is lame) but has a talent for axe making. It is in both your interests to divide up your efforts: you will hunt and provide the other member with meat. In return, he or she will provide you with excellent axes and spears to help you to hunt more effectively. This is a win–win solution to a real problem. But genetically, we are still highly competitive. We have to compete to survive: we compete for jobs, mates, position, you name it. Indeed, the mere fact that each one of us exists is testimony to our competitive nature. Humans have very few ancestors: in the West, the majority of people are descended from just seven women (Sykes, 2002). The other women have not been successful in passing on their genes in the competition for life.

In addition, the body also hardwires the memory of failure into the brain. There is a simple genetic reason for this: living in the Stone Age, it was important for primitive man to avoid making mistakes. Any mistake made could have been fatal, so humans had to learn quickly from their mistakes. Those humans that developed a rapid memory of previous failure (and survived) clearly had an advantage over less careful humans, and so were more likely to spread this gene through the population. We have developed to be cautious by nature. We are risk averse, and trusting others carries risk we may not wish to bear.

Points to ponder

Having considered the various theories on conflict, power and politics, what do you think are the lessons for managers?

Reflect on some of the major conflicts in your organization currently. Are they about territory? At what stage of Schmidt and Tannenbaum's stages of a dispute have they reached? What do you think will happen next?

Think and reflect on how your budget is decided. To what extent can you and do you participate? This is often a difficult process in businesses, but it illustrates well the differences between open and closed competition in negotiating.

Key learning points and conclusions

- Politics is a normal part of organizational life. If it is banned then it will be driven underground and become more dangerous. If debate is encouraged and disputes or concerns raised then a better decision is more likely.

- The use of power is part of a manager's toolkit. Managers need to be clear about what actual power they have and how it is best used. If indirect power or influence is used more – as is the case in complex organizations – then there needs to be an audit trail to follow.

- Conflict is often hardwired into organizations as well as places by history and by the nature of the game. So if the rules of the game are changed, cooperation is more or less likely.

- Senior executives are already very aware of political issues. Would it be healthier if this could be more openly acknowledged? One option is to enforce the principle of cabinet government where the rules are that open debate in cabinet is encouraged but that decisions are collective and are not challenged afterwards by opponents. This is a suitable area for management development.

- Conflict is sometimes inevitable and predictable. Managers need to plan for such conflicts but should also offer an honourable way for an opponent to accept the need to change. HR executives need to be part of that process.

- The lessons from our evolutionary past must be better understood. We have highly developed competitive and altruistic instincts; however, our risk-averse nature may make it difficult for us to trust the other parties sufficiently to overcome our competitive nature.

Case study and discussion questions

CASE STUDY   easyJet

EasyJet is a successful budget airline. Its main shareholder is its founder, Sir Stelios Haji-Ioannou (Stelios). The European budget airline sector is highly competitive where the market leader, Irish-based Ryanair, consistently delivers lower-cost flights. Actual or potential conflict exists at several levels. There is competition between the various actors, which includes competition between: individual airlines; between airports competing to attract airlines; between airlines and substitutes, such as rail for short-distance travel, London to Paris, for example. EasyJet needs to improve its main UK airport, Luton, which is owned by the local council although managed by an operating company. There are also disagreements with pressure groups for environmental change and with government ministers whose decisions on the taxation of passengers or the location of airfields or rail links can either help or hinder the aviation sector. There is also, in Marxist terms, a current crisis of global capitalism – until quite recently there were opponents in tents in the City of London. Carolyn McCall OBE, easyJet's CEO, decides to discuss the issues with her HR director. That easyJet is of professional interest to HR managers can be shown in recent articles in the *Human Resources Management Journal*.

What are the main issues from the case in terms of power, politics and conflict? What practical advice can the various theories offer her? Her first task is to decide what is outside the influence of her board or is irrelevant to the business. Her second task is to consider where cooperation with rivals may offer a better chance of success as opposed to conflict. This leaves strategic issues that are urgent and important. These are 1) reduce the tax on air travel; 2) improve the links to substitutes such as rail; 3) compete with Ryanair; 4) manage the shareholders, especially the founder Stelios. What do you think should be done? What games are being played? What sources of power are available to the board? What are the conflict handling styles of the actors? And what help does evolutionary theory and game theory offer? Firstly most of the important issues are outside the control of the board. Other issues are not so urgent and are also outside the control of the board. This leaves issues that the board can influence and that are important as well as those over which it has no direct power. This political strategy analysis is shown below.

Power	Action needed now	Action can wait
Direct or indirect power	Manage shareholders better especially Stelios. Compete with Ryanair.	Environmental strategy to reduce emissions.
Board does not have direct or indirect power	Reduce travel tax.	Substitutes such as rail. Improvement to airports such as the main UK base in Luton.
Meaning power	All airline companies need to improve their image on the environment. Perhaps a joint initiative should be funded?	In the long term, air travel within the UK will be replaced by high-speed rail. Can easyJet form an alliance with one of the train operating companies to offer a joint service?

In most cases the board lacks power and so will have to negotiate. The nature of the game is also important. Games are both open and closed. Airlines can attract as many passengers as the market will bear so the market here is open. However, airlines are limited in terms of landing rights at airports so here the market is closed. The case will be used to assess the likely future actions of the top team as well as future issues.

Finally, Carolyn needs to maintain the confidence of the board in her ability to deliver shareholder value. Here the conflict with the main shareholder is critical. Where possible she should seek to collaborate but she should not avoid conflict if the strategy is correct – such as the current plans to expand the company's operations to new areas. The make-up of the board is critical here.

What actual advice should be offered? The board faces a series of dilemmas and raising them publicly will not help solve them. So the problem of a difficult shareholder who disagrees with strategy may best be left to other shareholders to manage. PR to assist the image of aviation will help all the players so here a cooperative strategy is the best option – especially when looking at overall transport policy with the government. At the level of the actual workforce the firm seems to be doing well, although as they expand and take on more non-UK staff clear communication is important.

Discussion questions

- Using the model of conflict in the text where do you see the organization is on the dimension of conflict?
- What type of games are being played – open or closed?
- What power does the board have over the strategic issues raised in the case?
- What should the board members do next?
- What issues does the case and the in-class discussion raise for you and your own organization?
- What are the implications for HRM?

SOURCE This case study is based on open sources and a 2011 University of Bedfordshire case study written by P Davies and E Lloyd on the European Budget Airline Industry. Copies available on request.

08
Organizational culture

ELIOT LLOYD

LEARNING OBJECTIVES

- Understand the complex nature of organizational culture.
- Recognize the variety of ways in which organizational culture has been studied and interpreted.
- Understand the role that organizational culture may have as one of the sources of competitive advantage.
- Understand the dynamic nature of organizational culture and its development through the organizational life cycle.
- Understand perspectives and dimensions of organizational culture.
- Understand the difficulties of changing organizational culture and the process by which a change might be approached.

Introduction

It has become increasingly commonplace to hear and read about managers being concerned about the culture of their organizations. This may be expressed in a desire to change the culture, to embed a particularly effective culture, mesh different cultures after acquisition, merger or joint venture, or maybe to preserve the culture that has proved to be successful. In addition, as companies and economies become more global, managers seek to understand the intricate effects of local and national cultures on the firms and markets with which they interact. These concerns become more significant as the battle for competitive advantage becomes one that increasingly focuses on the 'soft' side of organizations and its role in establishing a meaningful differential. This presents a problem as managers may lack a true understanding of what culture is, how it develops and the role it plays. As a result, efforts to build or change a culture may prove to be frustratingly difficult and the effort put in may be misguided in its direction (as might the optimism about the potential outcome). This may seem a harsh observation for the concept of organizational culture is one that seems to be readily understood at a superficial level to the extent that people can easily conceptualize it as having meaning and type. This level of understanding may extend to a seeming ability to define and describe the culture of other organizations of which one has but a passing acquaintance. Organizational culture is therefore a subject that seems to be part of the *lingua franca* of organizations and yet managers (and for that matter scholars) may be forgiven for not fully grasping the intricacies of the concept, for it is also one of the most difficult subjects to define and describe with any real precision (Hatch, 1997). This difficulty stems from the intangible elements of the nature of culture and from the interpretative nature of the subject itself. As we shall see, culture and organizational culture have been studied from a variety of viewpoints, all of which have added to our understanding, but have not helped us to reach a consensus. Organizational culture has been interpreted in many ways, depending on the method and intellectual lens through which it is studied. It can be viewed from an operational or practitioner viewpoint, from an anthropological perspective or from a modern and even postmodern perspective. From the perspective of OB our desire is to understand better how culture is formed, how it evolves, its impact on the members of the organization (and vice versa) and its potential impact on organizational effectiveness. In addition we should aim to understand the issues surrounding attempts to 'grow' and shape organizational culture. The aim of this chapter, therefore, is to help you understand more about the subject and ultimately to try to make the study of organizational culture of use and interest to students as future practitioners.

Interest in organizational culture has arisen from the study of humans in society. The natural desire to understand more about our species has driven research about individual and group behaviour. This has led to a search for differences, similarities, trends, etc, resulting in intense debate that reflects the perspective of the researcher and often reflects the times in which the research was carried out. Thus more 'insular' ages will seek to find cultural differences from the accepted norm of the day (for example the 'right' culture, which is usually that of the researcher's own experience) while more 'enlightened' times emphasized the importance of studying culture for what it is and not for what it should be. Thus researchers would attempt to embed themselves in the culture of the group that they were studying and attempt through a deep immersion in the life and practices of the group to report on and understand its culture, an anthropological approach that has worked its way into organizational research.

More recently, the interest in organizational culture was heightened by the desire to find managerial tools with which to gain competitive advantage. The decline of US industry precipitated by (or at least attributed to) the supremacy of Japanese management practices led management gurus to look to Japan as a model of management and operational excellence. Firms were therefore urged to develop 'strong cultures' as a means of enhancing performance. Sadly, the research evidence concerning the culture–performance link remained unequivocal and the lack of sustainable success from the companies cited by the management gurus rather punched a hole in the argument. Nevertheless this legacy persists and practitioners and managers still look towards organizational culture as something to be leveraged in order to improve organizational output and performance.

Interest into organizational culture now has many strands. As stated, the culture–performance legacy still persists, but the managerial viewpoint has now shifted emphasis toward a more interpretative stance. The manager is encouraged to understand the cultural nuances in the organization with a view to gaining a more rounded understanding of the consequences of any managerial actions, rather than attempting to manipulate the culture with a view to improving performance. Other viewpoints focus on the study of organizational culture as a subset of the wider attempt to understand organizational life.

From an HRM and OB perspective, culture is likely to be a subject of interest with the intention of understanding the impact of people management practices (for example recruitment, training, reward and performance management) on individual and organizational effectiveness as well as their potential impact on retention and image. Postmodern studies will examine organizational culture through various lenses. This may include interpretation and emancipation with an emphasis that anyone studying culture must be doing so through his or her own interpretative bias, and that issues such as managerial control (see Glossary) must necessarily reflect manipulation of other groups in the organization.

A similar viewpoint can be extended to the study of culture from an emancipatory angle such as gender and race.

Defining organizational culture

The variety of interpretations and understanding of the concept of culture makes it a difficult subject to define. The central debate about culture is whether it is something that an organization *has* or something that an organization *is*.

The former suggests that culture is a set of deeply held assumptions that guides behaviour and that these assumptions are developed over time and are shared by members of the group. Those who view culture as something that an organization has will also view it as something that can be manipulated and used as a tool for improvement. In contrast, those who view culture as something that an organization is, suggest that processes, rules, regulations, systems, behaviour and structure, and so on, are all part of the cultural life and they will argue that culture is something that cannot be manipulated. These contrasting views have significant implications for how culture is studied, interpreted and used in a managerial sense.

Unsurprisingly, in addition to the various ways in which culture can be conceptualized, it can also be interpreted in different ways. Some researchers interpret meaning from what is manifested in the organization, for example symbols, furniture, the general surroundings in which people work and the manner in which they interact with each other. The alternative view stems from the concept of culture as being a shared set of deeply held assumptions and therefore surface level manifestations are not things that can be interpreted as revelations of those assumptions. The emphasis here is on values and beliefs of those working in a company, and although these may be discovered over time they lie very deep and may not be revealed merely by studying the physical environment of the organization. Adding to the difficulty of understanding and interpreting culture is the debate surrounding whether what is studied and interpreted as meaningful may actually be a reflection and revelation of the interpreter's own bias. Despite these conceptual and interpretive difficulties, it is nevertheless helpful to try to define the concept of organizational culture, in order to try to bring us a little closer to understanding how culture has been conceptualized and to add focus to the various debates about organizational culture.

Interpretations of organizational culture

As we have seen, culture is something about which people feel they have an intuitive understanding and many of the conceptualizations of organizational culture will have a reassuring familiarity. The simplest way of looking at organizational culture is the standard description that it is 'the way we do things around here'. This implies that there are accepted practices and norms of behaviour in an organization and that these can be passed on to newcomers and can be experienced by anybody who comes into contact with it. Indeed, it is this focus that forms the basis of much of the most widely accepted interpretation of organizational culture in the literature. Perhaps the best-known definition is that of Edgar Schein, who describes it as: 'The pattern of basic assumptions that a given group has invented, discovered, were developed in learning to cope with its problems of external adaption and internal integration, and that it works well enough to be considered valid and therefore to be taught to new members is the correct way to perceive, think, and feel in relation to these problems' (1983).

Schein's view, therefore, is that organizational culture is something that has been developed as a reaction to the external environment and, crucially, has become something that is now shared as an appropriate set of norms. In other words, 'the way we do things around here'. Many others such as Pettigrew (1979) and Martin (in her earlier work; for example 1992) also conceptualize organizational culture as something that is shared by the members. However, this view is not universally accepted as culture can also be conceptualized as being diverse or even fragmented, a concept that will be explored later in this chapter.

Earlier in this section we considered that organizational culture may be interpreted through the physical manifestations of the organization, while the above definitions seem to suggest that it is something that lies deep in the psyche of the members of the group and that it is crafted and embedded over time. Again, we can look to the work of Schein (1992) who regards culture as having elements that he categorizes as being artefacts, shared values, beliefs and attitudes, and basic assumptions. We can view these as being the layers of culture. Artefacts are the surface layer, and are represented by some of the following:

- the way people dress;
- how the office or factory space is laid out;

- symbols and rituals of behaviour and ceremonies;
- stories about heroes and villains;
- jokes.

While it may be tempting, it is dangerous to make too many strong assumptions and interpretations about the culture from these artefacts, for although they may be indicative of the values, beliefs and assumptions held by the members of the organization and thus representative of the culture, they may also be symbols reflecting how the organization would like to be perceived rather than a true expression of deeply held beliefs. Ceremonies and symbols may just as easily form the target for the value of rebelliousness that reflects an assumption that management is somehow aiming to manipulate the behaviour of staff. Nevertheless as certain authors have pointed out (Gagliardi, 1990), artefacts may truly be 'the tip of the iceberg' and may act as a powerful indicator of the values, beliefs and deeply held assumptions in the organization.

Beliefs, values and attitudes

Hofstede (2001a), defines values as being 'a broad tendency to prefer certain states of affairs over others' and these will be reflective of ethical moral and behavioural standards. Beliefs reflect what people hold to be true, and it is here that Schein's argument that time and experience are crucial in developing culture becomes critical, for successful responses to external pressures become 'truths' that in return become beliefs about what is right and wrong. And it is this learned linkage between values and beliefs that is 'attitude' (Brown, 1998).

Assumptions

Over time, values, beliefs and attitudes, unless shocked out of the system, will become so entrenched that they are no longer expressed or debated, or even discussed, but become in essence the fabric of culture. It is this very deepest layer that forms assumptions. Anyone who is felt not to share these basic assumptions will be regarded as an outsider and will quickly become ostracized by members of the group.

It is evident that beliefs, values, assumptions and attitudes are human characteristics (Brown, 1998), and they are clearly something that organizations per se cannot possess. This of course creates a problem for those who perceive that culture is something that an organization is, presuming that they also believe culture to be made up from such concepts as beliefs, assumptions and values. Nevertheless, as organizations are not just physical structures and systems but are also made up of people, we can at least characterize the groups in the organization as having human characteristics. It should also be evident that membership is made up of individuals and the above explanation and definition makes the assumption that individuals share a high degree of similarity in interpretation of events. It also makes the assumption that, over time, they have come to share values and beliefs, and therefore attitudes. Schein's framework, discussed above, takes a unitary view of culture that is one that is shared and common to all in the organization.

National culture and organizations

As pointed out by Nelson and Gopolan, there is: 'ample reason to expect some kind of relationship between national and organizational cultures' (2003) as there has been considerable research into the differences between national cultures and the socialized development of national culture. The best-known work in this area is that of Hofstede (2001a, 2001b), whose impressively broad study of national and work culture proposed four dimensions:

- Individualism versus collectivism. This reflects a preference for acting as individuals rather than as members of the group.

- Power distance. This indicates the degree to which inequality between societal and work members is regarded as normal and acceptable.

- Uncertainty avoidance. This indicates the degree to which members are comfortable or prefer structure over a lack of structure.

- Masculinity versus femininity. This indicates the relative prevalence of values such as competitiveness, assertiveness and success versus values that emphasize such things as quality of life, care for the more vulnerable members of society, togetherness and personal relationships.

Hofstede's research (conducted with members of IBM in many different countries) indicated that different countries showed significant preference across certain dimensions. Although his work is not without critics – McSweeney (2002) is particularly vocal and consistent in this regard – it has achieved a great deal of traction in the OB and HR literature.

The majority of research in this area focuses on dimensions that display a considerable amount of overlap. Terms such as 'embeddedness versus autonomy' (Sagiv and Schwartz, 2000), individualism and collectivism (Hofstede, 2001) and individualism and communitarism (Trompenaars and Hampden-Turner 1997) reflect the extent to which individuals act or expect to act as part of the group. Similarly, power distance, as described above, has parallels with the dimensional of 'hierarchy and egalitarianism' (Sagiv and Schwartz, 2000) as it describes the relationship with authority. Hofstade's dimensions of masculinity versus femininity are categorized by Sagiv and Shiraz as mastery and harmony and reflect on a continuum the degree of domination of one's environment.

The vast majority of research on international culture and work culture is based on the concept of values which, as described above, are socialized and learned as opposed to inherited and over time become deeply held assumptions. Researchers including Hofstede, Trompenaars and Hampden-Turner, and Schein are united in their view that these beliefs must be shared before they can be considered as culture.

In addressing the above, McSweeney (2002) reasonably suggests that geographical boundaries are artificial and often temporary, suggesting that these barriers are in essence false and to assign cultural differences to false boundaries is in itself unrealistic and false. He also points out that it is equally unrealistic not to expect and identify many different sub-cultures within regions, let alone nations. Nevertheless, work on national culture has received considerable effort and enjoys a good deal of credibility. If we accept, therefore, that there are national cultural differences, along the dimensions suggested above, and that these are deeply embedded then it is also reasonable to expect that organizations in those regions and countries will in some way be influenced by cultural values and norms shared not only by those in individual organizations, but also in groups of organizations. This national context may therefore become very important when attempting to work across national boundaries and with multicultural staff.

Organizational culture and performance

One of the most alluring and yet ultimately frustrating areas of research in this field is the link between culture and performance. There is a sense that culture has a significant role to play in performance and yet establishing that link has proven to be extremely difficult. In the initial phase of research on organizational culture, performance did not feature except as a passing comment that culture may have a role to play in performance. The emphasis of the research was on trying to understand the behaviour of individuals and groups in organizational systems. As has been mentioned previously, interest and research into the culture–performance link took off with the rise of Japan as an international business superpower and the relative decline of the United States. Studies into Japanese companies around the late 1970s and early 1980s suggested that their superior productivity was in many ways a result of their focus on human relations, and this focus was in contrast to their US counterparts. The natural result of these investigations, therefore, was to suggest that if the United States were to regain its pre-eminence, then its companies should follow suit and emphasize human relations as a key part of their businesses. Probably the best-known voices suggesting this focus at that time were those of Peters and Waterman. Their book on seeking excellence (1982) was an exhortation to companies to emphasize the creation of shared values that would add focus and direction to the efforts of those in the organization. Peters and Waterman claimed that, in turn, this would create a 'strong' culture that would help to create excellence. This work proved to be extremely popular and gained a great deal of traction in the business community. Unfortunately for this area of research, the arguments presented, and in particular the examples used, proved to be less than robust, for some years after Peters and Waterman's study, many of the companies who were cited as being 'excellent' had run into financial difficulties. Further research had indicated that measures used to identify strong culture revealed less than significant differences with other companies who possessed 'ordinary' cultures. While these criticisms proved to be disappointing to those who were seeking a link between culture and performance, it should be noted that this period of interest focused on attempts to criticize the notion of a culture–performance link and not on trying to investigate further whether there is indeed a link. Despite these criticisms and lack of empirical evidence, the legacy of the research remains and since the 1990s more sophisticated efforts have been made to try to isolate and measure a link between culture and performance. This body of research suffers from a great many problems among which the more obvious are as follows:

- There are inherent problems in trying to isolate any one factor as a predictor or cause of performance.

- There is lack of agreement as to what constitutes organizational performance, as there is a debate over whether this should focus on financial results or on more global stakeholder measures of performance.

- There is disagreement as to what should actually be measured in terms of culture, as there is no firm agreement as to how culture should be studied, or indeed how it should be contextualized.

- There is ambiguity as to whether it is culture that influences performance or performance that creates either strong or weak cultures.

- The familiar problem is that studies in this area tend to be of a snapshot rather than longitudinal nature.

- The majority of worthwhile studies were conducted in isolation and did not use similar instruments nor did they build on from each other.

Clearly, if any progress is to be made in this direction, measurement devices of extreme sophistication would need to be developed to isolate both national and organizational culture as drivers of organizational performance. In addition, previous research suffers from the assumption that the culture that is being measured represents that of the whole organization and is not one shared only by a relatively small cohort – this area of concern would also have to be addressed. Despite these difficulties and disappointments, culture as a driver of organizational performance remains an alluring concept and it is one that is closely linked to the resource-based view of the firm and it would appear to go some way to explaining why some firms are much more effective than others given similar circumstances. Thus the elusiveness of any provable link may well be the fault of the methods of measurement and of the ambiguous nature of culture itself and these are more to blame than the lack of a causal link between culture and performance.

The resource-based view

One of the important debates in the strategy literature centres on the issue of whether it is industry structure that determines the ability of firms to generate returns or whether it is the collection and management of resources that is the predominant factor. The former view was largely developed by Porter (1980) who argued that an industry is subject to five forces – power of suppliers, threat of new entrants, power of buyers, threat of substitutes and competitive rivalry. These forces and their comparative strength, Porter argues, is what determines the overall profitability of the industry in the long run, and is therefore the key determinant in the ability of firms to make (or fail to make) above normal rates of return. This concept became one of the most widely accepted in strategic thinking, but became the focus of criticism based on the fact that even in industries that appeared to be extremely competitive, some firms were and are able to make above normal rates of return. The logical conclusion of authors such as Jay Barney was that the success of these firms must lie in their internal manipulation of their resources and competencies, known as strategic capabilities. This argument became known as the resource-based view of the firm and it is here that culture seems to have a natural role to play in the success or otherwise of the company.

The framework of valuable, rare, inimitable, organized (VRIO)

Barney (1991, 1996) argues that in order for resources to play a role in generating competitive advantage they must be valuable, rare and hard to imitate (inimitable). They must also be coordinated (organized). Thus, in order for culture to contribute to the economic advantage of the firm:

- It must enable it to do things and to behave in ways that add economic value to the firm. Thus, it must at least be consistent with the strategic intentions of the organization.

- It must not be common to many organizations in the sector as, if all firms share a common culture they will not be able to use it to generate above normal returns.

- It must be hard to imitate. For even if the culture is rare, if it is easily copied then the rareness will not lead to sustainable performance advantage.

The 'organization' part of the VRIO framework suggests that culture is something that can be managed and maintained. This argument is central to the problem of ascribing firms with shared 'excellence' cultures (Peters and Waterman, 1982) in that if these cultures are easily shared and copied then they are not inimitable and cannot therefore be responsible for adding to above normal performance. It also follows that if an individual firm is able to manipulate its own culture to enhance its value to the firm, then its competitors are likely to be able to do the same and such manipulation is also likely to reduce the rarity and therefore the potential to enhance performance. Barney points out the dilemma: 'Only when it is not possible to manage a firm's culture in a planned way does that culture have the potential of generating expected sustained superior financial performance' (1986).

Therefore, while it may be only one of many factors that contribute to sustained performance, ironically it may be the fact that culture is difficult to describe, difficult to manipulate and difficult to identify precisely as a source of advantage that may hold its promise as a source of performance and competitive advantage.

The development of culture

The majority of later work on the development of culture takes as its central point Schein's view that culture is a shared view based on reactions to responses to the operating environment that have demonstrated themselves to be successful and robust enough to become 'truths'. In this section we will examine how culture is developed from the influence of the leader in the early life of the organization through to the embedding process. Issues surrounding attempts to change culture will also be examined.

The dynamic nature of culture

As described previously, one of the criticisms and difficulties with understanding culture and its role in relation to performance is that it is often explored as if it were a static state. However, culture should be viewed as a dynamic process that goes through several stages before it develops into the level of assumptions (Gagliardi, 1986; Schein, 1992; Hatch, 2000). A useful way to conceptualize this dynamic nature of culture is to view it through the life-cycle framework, which takes a firm through from conception to potential decline.

Schein (1983, 1992) argues that at the earliest stage where the organization is born, the founder has a crucial role to play in the development of the culture. This role will diminish as the firm progresses through its various stages and the role of the external environment and the

FIGURE 8.1 Life-cycle framework of culture

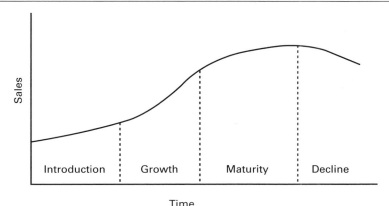

interpretation of the firm's members of their successful interaction with the environment will become more important. The developmental roles of various agents are described below:

1 **Birth and early growth.** During this phase, it is likely that the founder will have a predominant role in the development of the culture of the organization. As founder, he or she is likely to have strong views about the values that should be espoused, how the organization should be structured and how performance should be measured. In addition, the founder is likely to have a key role in appointing personnel and in designing roles and functions. It is likely at this stage that the firm will share a united culture.

2 **Growth.** As the firm grows, it is likely to develop new products, strategies and approaches towards its competitors and customers. It is also likely to be involved in geographical expansion and maybe mergers and alliances. At this stage, members of the organization are likely to be investigating appropriate strategies for dealing with environmental shifts and competitors' actions. In addition, if a company is growing it is likely to be forming subcultures. During this stage, the dominant role of the leader is likely to diminish.

3 **Maturity.** Presuming the firm has survived this long, it is likely to have developed what it believes to be a set of appropriate successful strategies for dealing with its environment. These will now become embedded in the mindsets of its members, and

will be enshrined as assumptions taken for granted. At this stage it will be extremely difficult to effect any cultural change.

4 **Decline or turnaround.** The embedded nature of the cultural assumptions mentioned above suggests that it may be extremely difficult for members of the firm to envisage any solutions to external and internal difficulties that have not been successful in the past. It is now that the influence of an external agent may be necessary to effect the turnaround.

In general, researchers of culture suggest that its development is largely one of interpretation of the organization's members. That is how they perceive the environment and their successful reaction to it is likely to become embedded and has become instrumental in the formation of the culture. Many, such as Hatch, view the members' interpretation of the actions of the leadership and the symbols of the organization as being crucial to the development of the culture. In order to understand this further it is useful to examine the four stages of development framework of Gagliardi (1986) and the dynamic view of culture offered by Hatch (2000).

Gagliardi's four stages of development

In a very similar way to the processes described above, Gagliardi argues that the founder strongly influences the early stages of how the organization is developed. The founder is likely to bring a vision and set of beliefs to the new enterprise that have been forged through previous experiences of success and failure. Any success is viewed as a cause-and-effect linkage that suggests it is the vision and the actions taken that are the cause of success and these actions will then become patterns of behaviour due to simple logic that, because success was due to previous actions then similar future actions will repeat the success. Strangely, humans do not seem to go through the same attribution process with failure. These actions, therefore, are likely to become guiding policies for future actions. At this stage, this view may not be shared by all members of the organization, but early in the organization's life the leader has the power to shape behaviour of the members in the desired direction. If the behaviour that is oriented by the beliefs of the leader becomes successful, then these actions are likely to come with what Gagliardi refers to as 'reference criteria for action' and will influence the choice of approach to future events.

Where Gagliardi goes deeper than the previous discussion is to suggest that the emphasis on interpretation shifts away at this stage, from the effect of the action to its cause. Thus members will interpret any success as being a direct result of their method. In this way, their previous interpretation of how to deal with events in the external environment becomes 'valid'. When this is challenged, the group will defend and assert the correctness of their beliefs and anyone who disagrees will be regarded as a heretic. The fourth stage is that in which these beliefs are no longer even consciously thought about and attain the level of basic assumptions – 'the way we do things round here'. Gagliardi argues that: 'Organizational values can be seen as the idealisation of a collective experience of success in the use of the skill and the emotional transfiguration of previous beliefs' (1986).

In effect, members of the group have replaced the rational with the emotional, in that they initially identified with the leader's vision because they could see the rational sense in it, later the experience of success appears to be linked to pride and self-esteem. This process clearly has significant impacts for attempts at cultural change.

Hatch's dynamic model of culture

The early role of the leader also has important influence in Hatch's dynamic model of culture. It is here that Hatch also draws heavily on the work of Schein in suggesting that artefacts, values and beliefs are heavily interpreted in the formation of culture. Unlike some researchers, Hatch places great value on the importance of artefacts that she describes as being: 'the visible, tangible, and audible results of activity grounded in values and assumptions' (Hatch in Ashkanasy, 2000).

She therefore argues that artefacts are the manifestations of the deeper lying elements of culture and they become 'real' (tangible, explicit, etc) when they express the values and beliefs that have become entrenched in the organization. This process can only truly take effect when the artefacts become symbolic, that is when they develop personal, social and emotional significance to the members of the group. The link between the symbolization of the artefact and the experiences and historical context of the organization's members is the basis of interpretation. Put rather crudely, the interpretation allows artefacts to become manifestations of what it means to be a particular group, in that artefacts will be interpreted as reflecting values, beliefs, norms of behaviour and patterns of action that been developed (following Schein) as a consequence of the interaction with the environment, and have proved themselves successful, or at least interpreted as such (Gagliardi, 1986).

As Hatch comments: 'the best way to think about these relationships is to regard artefacts and symbols as expressions of assumptions and values rather than as their outcomes' (in Ashkanasy, 2000).

The Australian cricket team provides a good example of this. Members of the team are awarded and wear a traditional green cap with the national team's emblem. The cap is a rather old-fashioned baggy design and is known by the team as 'the baggy green'. Its use has long since passed the functional and it is used by the team to symbolize what they perceive as the team's (and Australia's) virtues. These are togetherness, toughness, determination, etc. The players are required to wear this cap on the first morning of a match and no deviation from this is allowed. To Australian players it has a deep significance and to cricket followers worldwide it has meaningful cultural assertions (Croke and Harper, 2011).

As shown in Figure 8.2, there is directional flow to the process of cultural development, but it is not unidirectional. Thus interpretations are likely to be influenced by existing assumptions, which will of course be reinforced by the artefacts and their symbolization.

FIGURE 8.2   Dynamic model of culture by Hatch (taken from Ashkanasy, Wilderom and Peterson, 2000)

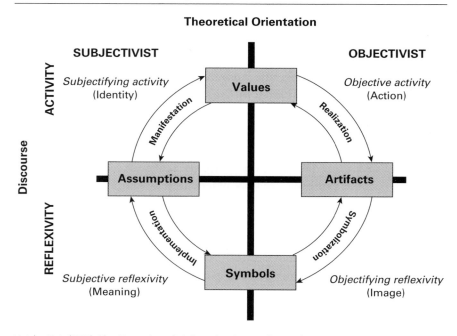

Hatch, M J (1993) The Dynamics of Culture in The Academy of Management Review, vol 18(4) pp 657–693

Multiple perspectives of culture

The discussion and examination of culture so far in this chapter has been based on the assumption that all members of the organization share the culture; therefore, it can be seen as having a single or unitary culture. This perspective is not an uncommon approach; indeed, it is shared by Schein, whose layered model of culture implies the unitary view. It is not a view, however, that is universally held by all researchers of the subject.

Organizational subcultures

An alternative to the single culture view is the belief that organizations are divided up into distinct subcultures that can be developed in the same way as previously described, but in distinct subsets of the organization, such as functional groups, geographical groups, friendship groups and hierarchical levels. Subculture has been defined by Van Maanen and Barley as: 'a subset of an organization's members who interact regularly with one another, identify themselves as a distinct group in the organization, share a set of problems commonly defined be the problems of all, and routinely take action on the basis of collective understandings unique to the group' (Hatch, 1987).

In a firm I worked in many years ago there was a distinct cultural difference between those in the administrative function and the sales team. Not only were the routines markedly different, with the sales team operating in a much more fluid attendance pattern than the administrative staff; there were also distinct differences in values and beliefs between the two groups. For example, the administrative staff were keen that organizational processes were rigidly adhered to, while the sales team believed that flexibility was important in being able to attract potential clients. Both groups were rewarded in substantially different ways, which only reinforced the differences between the two. In addition to this type of functional subculture, subcultures may also form across different organizations and in professional groups (for example medical consultants or university professors may often meet and work together as part of a distinct professional body outside the normal organization).

Much of the blame for the failure rate in mergers and acquisitions has been aimed at problems with integrating cultures of the two joining organizations. If the culture of the two organizations is developed along the lines suggested above, with a developed set of responses being attributed to the success of the organization, then it is highly likely that when they are merged there will be significant problems in integrating values and beliefs, and therefore attitudes. Even if the two firms have, at the point of merger, their own unitary culture, when merged the single organization will have two distinct subcultures. It is even more likely, however, that they will have many subcultures for the reasons stated above. Change in organizational contexts and the human impact of mergers and acquisitions are discussed further in Chapter 9.

Perspectives on the divisions of culture

The study of organizational culture can be viewed from three different perspectives: the integration perspective; the differentiation perspective and the fragmentation perspective:

- The **integration** perspective takes the view that there is an organization-wide consensus about the values and beliefs that are held common to all. From this perspective, there is a lack of ambiguity and although the views and assumptions held may not be unanimous, there is consensus.

- The **differentiation** perspective focuses on inconsistencies between behaviour and interpretation. An example might be when attendance at meetings is stated as being important and yet non-attendance is commonplace and goes unpunished. In addition, there is consensus at the subcultural level, which is that the organization is divided into subcultures and there is consensus within the subcultures, but not between them.

- The **fragmentation** perspective focuses on lack of consensus and ambiguity. As stated by Martin (2002), a perspective that focuses on ambiguity is the hardest to conceptualize. In the fragmentation perspective consensus is possible, but is likely to be temporary and issue specific: 'Fragmentation [that] focuses on multiplicity is interpretations that do not coalesce into the connectivity wide consensus characteristic of an integration view and that do not create the subcultural consensus that is the focus of the differentiation perspective. Instead, there are multiple views of most issues and those views are constantly in flux' (Martin, 2002).

A way of understanding organizational subcultures is to follow the continuum laid out by Hatch, in which she categorizes subcultures as ranging

FIGURE 8.3   Perspectives of culture (Hatch, 1997)

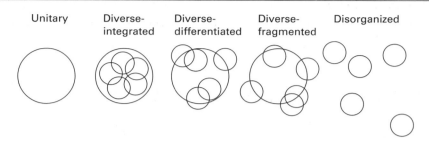

| Unitary | Diverse-integrated | Diverse-differentiated | Diverse-fragmented | Disorganized |

from unitary through to disorganized (see Figure 8.3). The unitary culture is obviously the state described by Schein when the organization shares a common culture. The closer towards this end of the continuum that the culture lays, the more closely the subcultures identify with the overall culture of the organization. Conversely, the less the subcultures identify with the espoused culture of the organization, the more fragmented the culture is. As Hatch points out, the disorganized state at the end of the continuum actually resembles several unitary cultures, and it can be seen that in this state, the subcultures are distinct from one another.

The emergence of subcultures

Subcultures are likely to emerge through personal interaction between members of the organization. Interaction may be most frequent between groups who share a common function, or are brought together for specific projects, although share a similar hierarchal level or simply share the same workspace. There is also likely to be sharing of cultures between those of the same gender, similar age and educational backgrounds. Viewed from this perspective, it would seem unlikely that an organization may possess the unitary culture but, as illustrated by Hatch, it is entirely possible for there to be a diverse integrated culture where distinct sub-cultures lie within the framework of a shared organizational culture.

The fragmentation perspective of subculture

The postmodernist view is that differentiation culture represents a false dichotomy; for example, it would represent gender as having two opposing subcultures. The postmodern view argues that there are many ways in which gender can be experienced as being different, both between the genders and within the gender groups and these perceptions and issues are constantly fluid – therefore consensus can only ever be temporary (Hatch in Askanasy, Wilderom and Peterson, 2000; Martin, 2002).

Managing organizational culture

While we hope the above discussion is useful to engage students and people management practitioners attempting to understand how culture is developed and conceptualized, it may also make depressing reading for those who are seeking to understand better how to manage culture in their organization. The real problem here is that there is no one interpretation or conceptualization of culture and therefore any recommendations about its management can be counted with a set of objections about why they may not succeed. Certainly those who view culture as being fragmented will also view attempts at managing it as being unrealistic. Those who take the unitary or even differentiated perspective may well view attempts at management as being worthwhile. This leaves us with something of a dilemma, as even attempting to make recommendations about the management of culture requires us to take a stance about which perspective we share. This section therefore will look at recommendations for the management of culture, with the assumption that it may be either unitary or differentiated, but sharing some common assumptions.

The problem of strategic drift

A common problem with organizations is that the strategy does not keep pace with changes in the environment, even when those changes are not dramatic (Johnson, Whittington and Scholes, 2011). As Gagliardi (1986) pointed out, organizations' responses to their environment may well end up repeating familiar patterns that they believe to have been successful in the past, which can easily result in a mismatch between what is actually needed and what is perceived and assumed. Particularly relevant to the discussion of strategic drift and culture is the problem whereby capabilities that have been the basis of advantage in the past are now so much part of the fabric of the organization that they rarely if ever become challenged and indeed become more and more embedded. What were once core capabilities can now be seen as core rigidities as they become extremely difficult to change and also become one of the reasons why an organization is no longer in tune with its environment.

Cultural change

Although the link between culture and performance has proved difficult to isolate and quantify, culture clearly has a significant role to play in how the organization functions and the need to prevent culture becoming an anchor on the organization is therefore extremely important. Unfortunately, change programmes in many organizations seem to take the form of 'lily padding' – that is, hopping from one new initiative to another, (often the latest managerial fad will do) – with the inevitable result that the initiatives will bounce off something as robust as culture. As Hatch has pointed out, organizational culture is dynamic in nature and while the pace of change may be relatively slow, the change is constant. Intentional change, therefore, is extremely hard to effect, as the development of culture is a product of experience, interpretation of success attempts, interaction between members and subgroups, patterns of behaviour and education, among other things. In addition to the complexity of culture, there is a tendency for those attempting to impose cultural change on an organization to fail to put in the long-term commitment that it requires. How group members make sense of their everyday experience in the organization becomes a significant factor in the development of culture and this sense-making is not something that can be easily engineered. It is therefore probably more productive to attempt to understand how culture of the organization has been formed and indeed is forming, in order to work with it. The cultural web (Johnson, Whittington and Scholes, 2011) is a method of doing this. As shown in Figure 8.4, the cultural web is made up of interlinking behavioural, physical and symbolic manifestations of culture that create the taken-for-granted assumptions known in the cultural web as the paradigm. The elements are as follows:

- The **paradigm** is the assumptions taken for granted in the organization that have been developed over time and through the interaction of members. This is the deepest level of organizational culture and it is one that is no longer discussed or debated, or even questioned. As a consequence, it is very difficult to identify exactly the nature of this paradigm.

- **Routines** are patterns of action that take place in an organization on a daily basis. And, as discussed previously, such patterns may

FIGURE 8.4   The cultural web (Johnson, Whittington and
Scholes, 2011)

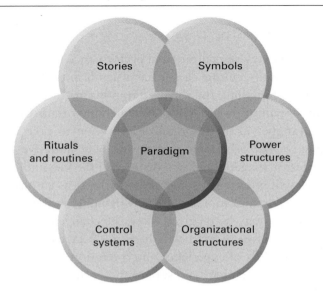

be a source of advantage but as they become increasingly routine
they may become core rigidities. The rituals of the organization
are those actions that are designed to reinforce what is believed to
be important in the culture.

- **Stories** are a way of signalling to members in the group and those
outside it what is important to the organization. Stories will often
be about heroes, villains, successes or failures and will inevitably
involve an element of attribution. These are often an important
means by which the culture of the organization is communicated
to newcomers.

- **Symbols** are objects, people, acts or events to which people attach
meaning. A typical example of this is the way in which allocation
of parking spaces becomes a symbol for status and power.

- **Power structures** are in themselves indicative of assumptions
and values and the groups in the organization that hold the most
power will, if this power has evolved over time, often have had and
continue to have a **dominant role in the development of the
paradigm.**

- **Organizational structure** is likely to reflect the power hierarchy and also reflect the dominant mindset of the organization.

- **Control systems** are designed to measure, punish and reward what is expected to be the dominant behaviour in the organization. This is again likely to be a reflection of the power structure of the organization.

The usefulness of a framework such as the cultural web lies in developing an understanding of how culture is formed in an organization. This understanding can then be used to develop methods of cultural change. Lewin's classic framework (1947, 1947a), which will also be explored further later in this chapter and in Chapter 9, suggests that change is imposed from above, with the aim being to develop a specific culture aimed at meeting the goals of the organization.

From a strategic point of view it would appear important that culture is at least aligned with organizational purpose. As we have seen, however, the process by which members may attribute success may well lead to those values and beliefs becoming embedded and the attitude becoming entrenched. Of course, the culture does not remain entirely static. New members entering the organization will have an impact and progressive successful actions, probably thought to be similar to previous actions, may have slight variants and will in turn lead to a similar process of attribution. Nevertheless, it remains evident that the external environment of the organization is likely to be evolving much more rapidly and in a much more dramatic fashion. It is really this that presents problems for culture change. Gagliardi (1986) argues that it is only the interpretation of successful events that becomes part of the cultural belief, while negative events become sources of blame and lead to identification of scapegoats. The focus of this blame is likely to be the old and now discredited culture (Brown, 1998). As a result of this, the need for wholesale cultural change may be denied by the members of the organization and may be obvious only to those outside its cultural norms (Gagliardi, 1986). Logically, therefore, change can only be affected by wholesale removal of personnel in the organization, which is likely to be both costly and traumatic. Therefore, Gagliardi argues, the only true method of cultural change must be an incremental one.

In this process, those responsible for developing responses to changing circumstances must develop and implement new approaches that are not too drastically different from the tried and trusted methods of the past. Despite the potential for resistance, if these are proved to be successful, then the idealization process, whereby group members attribute success to these new approaches, will in turn become a source of pride, self-esteem and part of the mythology of the organization. Ultimately, these will be turned into symbols, values and beliefs and deep-seated attitudes that will form new cultural norms. In this framework, change can be at best seen as incremental building on the 'logic' of the past. Gagliardi therefore argues that radical change must involve significant upheaval and is likely to be initiated by agents from outside the organization.

Lewin's three-step change process

Developed in 1947, Lewin's three-step model has become a classic in the literature of change. While this model is not explicitly about culture, it can be implied that his focus was indeed cultural change as Lewin refers to behaviours and behavioural patterns. Lewin proposes three phases of change: 'unfreezing', 'moving' and 'freezing':

- **Unfreezing.** In this stage, Lewin suggests that there must be a break with habits and well-established customs. As we have seen, this break may be extremely hard to achieve and there is often disagreement about how best to do it. The major consensus involves exposure to 'reality', which contrasts with the accepted understanding of the situation. Confronting individuals with the spectre of crisis is also seen to be a likely approach. Central to the argument here is whether it is better to target behaviour or beliefs, or indeed whether it is in fact possible to change beliefs (Sathe and Davidson in Ashkanasy, Wilderom and Peterson, 2000).

- **Moving.** In what is essentially a classic force-field approach, Lewin argues that this stage should involve increasing the forces in favour of change, pushing the attitudes, beliefs, etc to a new level. In contrast to the reality shock approach suggested above, this process is likely to be best achieved by positive reinforcement, for example by building a system to reward those who display behavioural change. Again, it must be noted that this change is relatively superficial as it does not guarantee attitudinal change.

- **Freezing.** In this phase, Lewin defines freezing as the institutionalization of the new social processes. Once again, the best approach to achieve this is a source of debate and again reflects the argument about behaviours or attitudes. As Gagliardi has suggested, as long as the processes achieve success, they will naturally become embedded in the culture of the organization. Transforming behavioural processes, on the other hand, may require implementation of motivators, although there is some argument about whether intrinsic or extrinsic motivators are more effective in this process. The psychological literature suggests that the former is likely to be the case.

Critics of Lewin's framework argue that imposition of change from above is unrealistic and is unlikely to succeed. Therefore other approaches to change have been suggested that reflect a more 'member-led' approach.

Evolutionary change

As suggested by Gagliardi, the most effective way to change the culture is to integrate new understandings and values to similar ones already existing in the organization. This approach is likely to avoid the obvious problems of perceptions of manipulation and possible resistance whereby the new values are seen as so out of line with the existing ones that they are deemed to be wrong or not worthy of implementation. The evolutionary approach is suggested by Alvesson (2002) to be developed by the members of the group, adjusting their beliefs and thinking as they interpret events, rather than being imposed from the top.

Revolutionary change

The problems created by strategic drift, as described above, may mean that drastic change of culture needs to be implemented and this is most likely to be done from above. As with all revolutions, it is not enough to change the system and hope that those in the system will commit to the changes, instead it is usually necessary to remove the personnel who offer the strongest resistance and promote or recruit those who will commit to the new ideology. This is also the case in organizations in which there is need for drastic culture change and the ability to implement it often requires external agents.

Alvesson (2002) recommends that five principles are considered when implementing organizational change:

- The first principle is to link culture to specific organizational events, situations and actions in order to enable people to identify more closely with the artefacts, values and assumptions that are present in the organization.

- Managers need to recognize that culture is not developed, and driven by a top-down process, but is a consequence of a network of interactions in the organization. This recognition will help understanding that culture is more likely to develop at a deeper level, if it is created from within rather than imposed from above.

- Managers should understand that elements of fragmentation may well exist in the organization and therefore individuals and even functional groups may have multiple roles in which their cultural understanding and interpretation may well differ.

- The fourth principle is to understand that there is no one interpretation of each cultural element, there is always individual interpretation.

- Finally, it is important to understand that power creates imbalances between groups in the organization.

The role of recruitment and selection in organizational culture

Culture is a dynamic process (Hatch, 2000), and integration of new members is important in its development. The inference is that new members to the organization will experience enculturation, and over time share the existing values and assumptions of the members. New members, however, also have a role to play in the evolution of the culture. Recruitment and selection therefore has an important role to play in either embedding or reframing the culture of the organization. If we refer back to the continuum ranging from integration to fragmentation, we can see the role of recruitment and selection along the continuum. If the purpose is integration, then methods of recruitment and selection will emphasize to potential new members what the values and beliefs of the organization are. In this way the organization attempts to attract new members who are likely to identify closely with those values and beliefs, and therefore are likely to be relatively easily absorbed into the existing culture. If evolutionary change is the aim, then new members will be attracted who broadly share the values and beliefs, but who are also aware of the important differences in the organization's environment and will bring this awareness and experience of alternative and workable solutions that may help to develop cultural shifts. When revolutionary change is important, selection and recruitment will involve identifying and attracting those who do not share the existing values, beliefs and assumptions of the organization and will be able to challenge and develop these. This process may also involve deselection.

Key learning points and conclusions

- Organizational culture is a complex phenomenon that has been studied from a variety of different perspectives and consequently has been subject to different interpretations.

- Unitary view of culture does not really acknowledge the formation of subcultures that may cause culture to lie on a continuum from 'unitary' to 'fragmentation'. This development of culture and subcultures is likely to make attempts to manage culture and impose a unitary vision a frustrating process.

- Managers are encouraged therefore to understand how culture has developed throughout the organization and to be aware of its potential to act as an 'anchor' that inhibits change.

- In particular, the misapprehension that all units in the business share a common culture may lead to attempts at change being met with resistance.

- For researchers and scholars, proper understanding and interpretation of culture may rest on their ability to recognize it as a multifaceted concept and on their awareness that there is likely to be an element of interpretive bias that influences how they conceptualize culture in the organizations they are studying.

- Organizational culture is a complex, multi-dimensional construct that is not easily manipulated, evolving as it has through interaction between the organization (or its sub-units) and its environment and interaction between organizational members. These members are likely to have developed a language and set of references for success that become embedded and expressed in a way that is likely to be hard to interpret, difficult to manipulate and resistant to change.

Discussion questions

- Using Schein and Hatch's concepts outlined in the chapter, describe the complex nature of organizational culture.
- Contrast the view of culture as something an organization has, with that of something an organization is.
- What are the problems associated with establishing a link between culture and performance?
- Explain how interpretation of successful actions become 'reference criteria for action' (Gagliardi).
- What are the differences between the 'unitary' and 'divisions' perspective of culture?
- With regard to organizational culture, what are some of the problems associated with attempting to impose change programmes?

Case study and discussion questions

CASE STUDY   The decline of Eastman Kodak

By any standards the demise of Eastman Kodak from its once mighty position to the day where it filed for bankruptcy constitutes a huge fall from grace. There have been many explanations proposed for this and it is unrealistic and overly simplistic to blame it on a single cause. From the viewpoint of this chapter, however, this brief case study will examine the role of organizational culture in this dramatic and sad story.

Founded in 1880, Eastman Kodak became one of the most successful and best-known brands in the world. Its founder, George Eastman, had spotted the potential in the commercial manufacture of dry plates for photographic imaging and with investment from local businessman Henry A Strong began to build up the business and ultimately change photography forever. It was the development of film on rolls that was able to fit the majority of plate cameras that revolutionized the industry and with it Kodak (a name invented by Eastman) became the founding father and dominant player in the industry for the next 100 years. Eastman founded his business on four principles:

- mass production at low cost;
- international distribution;
- extensive advertising;
- a focus on the customer.

He allied these principles to a strong commitment to research and development (with an emphasis on reinvestment), and on fair staff relations. It was this emphasis on low-cost mass production that really led to the development of amateur photography and as the market developed so Kodak began to spread its wings and establish an international presence, initially in London and then further afield to mainland Europe and eventually to South America and Asia.

Kodak's domination

Once Kodak had in effect democratized photography and created the amateur photography industry it quickly established pre-eminence and was able to enjoy huge profitability through its classic 'razor blade' strategy. Simply put, Kodak would manufacture and sell cameras at a relatively low profit and sell film at a very high margin in the same way that the likes of Gillette sell razors at low margin and the replaceable blades at high profit. This strategy proved to be superbly successful and it was one that Kodak repeated across many product ranges such as copiers and printers and video cameras. During this period it created many classic brands in the industry such as the Brownie and the Instamatic as well as producing quality film. Kodak pursued its strategy of aiming at the lower end of the market to great effect, leaving the specialist end to others.

Decline

Kodak's decline began in the 1980s when competitors began to eat away at its advantage in the film market. In particular, Fuji made significant inroads by offering film at either a cheaper price and in one particularly bold move gaining the rights to become one of the main sponsors of the Olympics in 1984, seizing an opportunity over which Kodak had dithered.

Ultimately, however, it was the shift from the classic rolls of film to digital technology that was the cause of Kodak's downfall. It was described by one of the people close to the company as 'the monster hurricane' that hit Kodak. The huge margins that Kodak made from its 'razor blade' strategy cannot be made with digital cameras and as in all industries there was a host of eager competitors ready and willing to take advantage of the change in the market. Even further down the line, the low end of the market that was always such a happy hunting ground for Kodak was now dominated by cameras that were integrated into Smartphones and so ultimately Kodak had nowhere to run.

Blaming Kodak's demise on competitors' pricing and a shifting business environment seems rather simplistic. Although the digitalization of film was a huge shift, Kodak was well placed to take advantage of this as it had invented the first digital camera as long ago as 1975 and Kodak executives such as Larry Mattesson had predicted in a report to the board that digital would infiltrate various parts of the market and eventually dominate (including the mass market) by 2010. Clearly, he was some years out but the report was written in 1979 and gave due warning (*Economist*, 2012).

Culture's role in Kodak's decline

There were a great many reasons for Kodak's decline and many were complex and intertwined but some of the blame must lie at the feet of the culture in the organization. George Eastman founded the business with a philosophy of continuous innovation and was focused on making the company a 'moving target' for competitors. This is a classic entrepreneurial approach and it would seem that Kodak moved away from this. Despite the initial development of a digital camera and early warnings about the change to a digital market the response of Kodak's managers seems to have been sluggish to say the least. The inventor of Kodak's digital camera, quoted in an article published in the New York Times on 5 February 2008, cites the management attitude as: 'But it was filmless photography, so management's reaction was, 'that's cute – but don't tell anyone about it.'

Kodak seems to have gone through the classic responses of the successful company when faced with threats and changes, at first denying that Fuji could possibly be a serious competitor in the US market, and then recognizing the threat of the external change but not its urgency. Kodak then fell in to the trap of what Donald Sull referred to as 'active inertia' in an article entitled 'Why good companies go bad' published in *The Financial Times* on 3 October 2005. Active inertia is where a company recognizes the need to act but the actions tend towards being 'more and more of the same'. Thus Kodak diversified into chemicals; produced hundreds of products and entered the Chinese markets. The problem with all this action is that it is based on the original successful business. In other words, Kodak was pouring most of its effort and finance into maintaining the company's hold on the traditional camera and film business (even the chemical business was directed at this) or at least a digitalized version of this whereby people would print off digital copies of their pictures.

In short, it was probably the failure of Kodak to 'cannibalize' its core business (and with the margins being made, Wall Street would not have been an encouraging voice), that was the key ingredient in Kodak's demise. It is ironic that it failed to follow its founder's determination to make itself a moving target and became stuck in the mindset that had made it so successful but was now redundant.

NOTE Some newspaper and magazine articles describing Kodak's demise are: articles by Andrew Hill in *The Financial Times* (London) entitled 'Snapshot of a humbled giant' published on 2 April 2012 and 'A victim of its own success' published on 5 April 2012; article in the *Birmingham Post* (England) entitled 'Kodak predicted the digital threat in 1979 – so how could a global giant destroy itself?' published on 26 January 2012; article by Chunka Mui in *Forbes* magazine entitled 'How Kodak failed' published on 18 January 2012; see also *Economist* (2011).

Discussion questions

- To what extent does Gagliardi's concept of 'reference criteria for success' explain Kodak Eastman's failure?

- Apply the concept of strategic drift (with an emphasis on culture) to this case.

- From the perspective of organizational culture what actions would you take to turn the company's fortunes around?

09
Managing organizational change

**FATEN BADDAR AL-HUSAN and
KONSTANTINOS KAKAVELAKIS**

LEARNING OBJECTIVES

- Understand the various facets of the change process through a critical discussion of key academic perspectives.
- Demonstrate an understanding of the nature of resistance and the causes that often underpin this phenomenon.
- Be able to comprehend and explain the role of the change agent in driving change.
- Develop an understanding and awareness of the role of the HR function as a change agent.

Introduction

During the last three decades, change management has emerged as one of the key organizational capabilities but also as a difficult challenge, especially when taking into account that usually the success rate of change initiatives is low. Indeed, research evidence shows that around 70 per cent of change initiatives fail (Miller, 2002), and that the impact of such failures to introduce effective change can also be high in terms of such things as loss of market position, loss of key employees and loss of stakeholder credibility.

Evidence shows that managing change is about managing people and that change does not occur in a vacuum as it influences and is influenced by a number of environmental and organizational aspects, particularly people aspects as the effects of change on employees can be considerable. Hence, resistance is inevitable and as expressed by one senior manager at one leading MNC: 'The employees are at the heart of organization and at any rate there will be resistance to change because change is painful.' From a managerial perspective, the questions then arise: how can change be implemented in a less painful way; and in a way that generates the desired commitment in different contexts and cultures to achieve organizational goals?

To deal with such questions and to put up with the increasing pace of change, therefore, over the years, a multitude of OB perspectives – normative as well as more critical – have emerged, aiming to explain the nature of change, the challenges of change management and how they can be addressed. The aim of the chapter is not to favour particular approaches and present those as an antidote to change management failures. Instead, our objectives are twofold.

First, at a broad level we hope that through a critical discussion of the key academic perspectives on organizational change the reader will obtain a better understanding of the change process and the key issues surrounding change initiatives, such as resistance. Second, having provided an overview of different perspectives, we proceed by examining the role of the HR function in shaping change initiatives and implementation activity and we further examine some of the key challenges of change management by looking at international mergers and acquisitions as an example of radical change.

Mergers and acquisitions have proved a popular strategy through which managers respond to exogenous pressures for achieving greater shareholder value (Thompson, 2003). Consequently, they provide a good empirical context in which change management can be examined. Over the years there has also been prolific writing on issues that concern 'the human side' of mergers and acquisitions (Buono and Bowditch, 1989). Therefore, the impact of mergers and acquisitions on the human resources of an organization has been examined, with a focus placed on the importance of communication (Schweiger and Denisi, 1991), the crucial factor of gaining employees' trust (Nikandrou, Papalexandris and Bourantas, 2000), and the influence that cultural issues can have on the integration of two companies, something that illustrates the significance of examining the factor of cultural fit (Buono, Bowditch and

Lewis, 1985; Schraeder and Self, 2003). As cultural integration and associated issues of staff integration are often seen undermining the successful implementation of mergers and acquisitions, the second part of the chapter also examines the role of HR function as a change agent.

Drivers and triggers of change

Many things cause organizational change. The environment (external and internal) is a major driver for change. The external environment can be a source of opportunities and threats, captured by organizational members who see a need for change in the organization as a result of external changes. In the internal environment (micro level), change may simply be instigated when organizational members are no longer satisfied with the performance of the organization. Examples of external and internal drivers and triggers are given below.

External drivers and triggers of organizational change include:

- challenges of growth, especially global markets;
- economic downturns and tougher trading conditions;
- technological changes;
- competitive actions and pressures, including mergers and acquisitions;
- changes in customers' demands and tastes;
- government legislation, initiatives and policies;
- political drivers and changes in government ideologies.

Internal drivers and triggers of organizational change include:

- changes in strategy;
- the need to learn new behaviour and skills;
- the arrival of new personnel or the emergence of a new outlook;
- low performance and morale;
- innovations in new products, and service design and delivery.

Different types of change

Change management refers to managing the process of renewing an organization's strategic direction or key operational aspects to enhance competitiveness. As the definition suggests, change is a permanent feature of organizational life at both the strategic and operational levels (Todnem By, 2005). In terms of time, change may be reactive when it is taking place as a response or reaction to something, and may be proactive when it is carried out in anticipation of what is expected to take place. In terms of scope or scale, change may be strategic or incremental.

To capture the full range of change initiatives from operational to strategic or small-scale, local change to radical change several typologies have been developed. For example, Whipp (2003) uses a four-fold typology incorporating the following types of change:

- retaining the status quo, which signifies no changes in current practice;
- expanded reproduction at the operational level (producing more of the same goods or services);
- evolutionary transition that requires the adoption of a new strategy that is, however, based on remixing existing capabilities (the move of book publishers into electronic formats in the 1990s);
- revolutionary transformation that requires redefining the organization's reason for existence.

Similarly, Dunphy and Stace (1994) offer a framework which distinguishes among four types of change occurring at different scales in an organization, namely:

- **Fine tuning,** which aims to ensure there is adequate operational support to the organization's strategy. It consists of small changes in anticipation of future environmental changes. Thus, at this scale, organizational change is an ongoing process marked by fine tuning of the alignment between the organization's strategy, structure, people and process, reflected in minor changes at departmental or divisional levels. Examples include refining of policies, processes and procedures; and developing staff to acquire the necessary skills for the current strategy.
- **Incremental adjustment,** which is also operational in nature and may require some changes in certain management processes, structures and corporate strategies. Examples include expanding sales areas and adjustments to organizational structures to improve product or service delivery.

- **Modular transformation**, which requires major changes that are restricted to certain departments or divisions not the whole organization, such as a major restructuring of a department or division and introduction of completely new technologies affecting the main departments.

- **Corporate transformation**, which is radical in nature and affects the organization as a whole. It includes such things as reforms in an organization's mission, strategy, structures, systems, procedures and core values across the organization; and new top management.

Having discussed the different facets of organizational change, the following parts of the chapter aim to offer an overview of how change has been conceived and understood by various perspectives.

Planned change

Models of planned change have been particularly popular with practitioners. The main focus here is on managerial action, which is viewed as the main force through which organizational change comes about. One of the most well-known frameworks on planned change that remains influential to this day is Lewin's (1947, 1951) force field analysis (see also Chapter 8). According to Lewin (1947, 1951) the status quo in an organization is a result of an equilibrium between various forces that drive change and forces that act against it. Therefore, to create a climate receptive to change, the key task for managers is identifying which forces support the change and which ones restrain it. The identification of forces for and against change leads to a framework of action consisting of three phases (see Chapter 8 for further detail). The first phase, 'unfreezing', involves the possible removal of restraining forces so that the organization is put in the appropriate condition for change. The second phase involves the implementation of change in the organization, while the last stage, 'refreezing', refers to embedding the changes, which gives rise to a new status quo. Lewin's influence is evident on subsequent models of planned change such as the ones by Beckhard and Harris (1987), where change is conceived as a process consisting of three states – present state, transition state and future state – and Dunphy and Stace (1988), where four different strategies for promoting and managing change are suggested depending on a background of contingency factors – time, support or resistance by key groups and the organization's environment.

Additionally, prescriptive writings on the ability of individual leaders to effect organizational change and innovation, such as the work by Bennis and Nanus (1985) – although not directly influenced by Lewin – still function in an individualistic perspective, which stresses the role of managerial action (Slappendel, 1996).

Some of the criticism levelled at the planned approach points to its assumptions of stability (that do not correspond with the fast-changing business environment most organizations are faced with), its depiction of change as a discrete episode in organizational life that unfolds in a rational and linear fashion and its tendency to ignore issues of politics and conflict (Todnem By, 2005). These issues have been tentatively addressed in the work of authors such as Quinn (1980) and later on, Kanter, Stein and Jick (1992) and Kotter (1996). In Quinn's work, for example, the focus is slightly removed from individual agents in order to involve factors such as an organization's operating environment, a concept already introduced in the work of contingency theorists such as Burns and Stalker (1961) and Lawrence and Lorsch (1967). According to Quinn (1980), organizational change is still a process that can be planned, but the planning and implementation should occur in small steps, following the collection, study and dissemination of information related to the organization's environment. The importance of Quinn's logical incrementalism (see Glossary) lies in the fact that he recognizes the various limits inherent in the effort of an organization to change and that he also introduces (albeit implicitly) the element of politics by stressing the need to build consensus over the content and implementation of strategic change (Pettigrew, 1985). Similar points are made by Kanter, Stein and Jick (1992) and Kotter (1996) who stress the importance of building supportive coalitions around the vision for change. However, an element of rationalism (see Glossary) is still evident in these models, as change is presented as a planned outcome to be achieved through a series of specific activities.

Emergent change

The concept of planned change has been challenged by writers who believe that it does not account for the influence of structural forces that reside outside the control of individuals and therefore they have conceived organizational change as an emergent process. This particular view has been adopted by a number of writers, most notably by the population ecology (see Glossary) writers such as Aldrich (1979, 1986).

According to the population ecology models, organizations are viewed as members of a population with similar characteristics and the requirements of the operating environment of a particular population of firms will determine the survival or demise of certain firms (Hannan and Freeman, 1989). Therefore, organizational change mainly results as a reaction to environmental pressures and as an attempt to secure a specific position in the population of organizations. Consequently, firms that operate in the same industry or sector tend to adopt similar strategies for change.

However, although this perspective acknowledges the impact of structural elements on organizational change, it is silent about the role of individual agency, providing a deterministic account of change. More recently, writers such as Orlikowski (1996) have developed accounts of emergent change that is rooted in the everyday activities of organizational actors including both managers and employees. In particular, it is argued that change can emerge out of the constant improvisations of organizational actors as they attempt to cope with the challenges of performing their work. Orlikowski's (1996) research on the customer service department of a software company showed how the practitioners' continuous experimentation with a new piece of technology for tracking customer calls led to a series of further and rather unpredictable changes in many other areas such as work distribution, performance evaluation, etc. Therefore, the key point from this situated action perspective is that since organizational rules or routines have to be put into action by practitioners, change is ongoing as it is grounded in the inherent ability of actors to amend and adjust the former (Tsoukas and Chia, 2002). Thus, change is part and parcel of the everyday organizational reality, not necessarily a planned event that follows long periods of continuity (although it is acknowledged that, at times, change can occur as a 'deliberate event with key players and substantial resources' (Orlikowski, 1996). This perspective's contribution is that it helps highlight the dynamic and emergent nature of change in a way that acknowledges the role of individual action that is obscured by the structuralist (see 'structuralism', Glossary) accounts of change mentioned earlier. However, a limitation of the situated activity perspective is that it may lose sight of the broader context in which micro-level action unfolds. Such an emphasis could help provide a more convincing explanation of the fact that in certain cases local improvisations may not necessarily lead to broader organizational changes (Fairclough, 2005).

The processual or contextual perspective

The previously discussed approaches provided a one-sided view of change, which was depicted as the outcome of either deliberate individual action or structural forces. Additionally, planned change models (indicative of the individualist approach) implicitly assumed a consensus around the course of action necessary to introduce and embed organizational changes, overlooking the issue of politics. The processual or contextual perspective developed by Pettigrew (1985) is an attempt to address these limitations by presenting an account of change that acknowledges the impact of both action and the broader context in which organizations operate. A complete framework of contextual analysis on change was presented in Pettigrew's (1985) work on strategic change in ICI, although elements of that framework were already evident in his earlier work on organizational decision making as a political process (1973) and in his work on organizational culture (1979).

A key element of the processual or contextual perspective is that in contrast to planned change models that view change as 'a single event or a set of discrete episodes somehow separate from the immediate and more distant context which gave those events form, meaning, and substance' (Pettigrew 1985), change (particularly major strategic change) is understood as a process that unfolds over lengthy periods of time. It is therefore essential to regard organizations as social systems with a past, a present and a future. Thus, to assess the success or failure of change processes, there is a need to examine how future plans play against an organization's history and current context (including both aspects of culture and structure). With regards to contextual influences, Pettigrew has stressed the importance of paying attention to both the intra-organizational context and the broader environment in which an organization operates. However, in contrast to deterministic structural analyses such as those offered by population ecology authors, context is not regarded just as a constraining force. It can equally facilitate and constrain the change process while aspects of it can be maintained or altered through action. In particular, actors can mobilize aspects of structure and context in order to achieve outcomes important to them.

This last point also pertains to an understanding of change as a political activity, as different groups try to secure outcomes in line with their particular interests. As Pettigrew (1985) remarks, such activity may take place particularly during the early discussions on deciding to promote change – as such a decision might threaten the status of certain groups and be seen as an opportunity by others to gain in prominence in the organization. The activity is also influenced, as it was implied above, by certain changes in the macro-environment of the firm. Within this political process, a key concept is that of legitimacy of certain ideas relevant to change. Legitimacy is directly connected to an activity that is defined by Pettigrew (1979) as 'the management of meaning' and it involves the construction and establishment of language, symbols and myth, so that purpose and commitment around ideas that support change can be generated while ideas that act against it can be delegitimized.

The emphasis on the interplay between context or structure and process (action), the awareness of the political aspects of organizational life and the equal attention on the role that cultural elements can play in relation to change, make processual analysis a far more sophisticated theoretical account of change in comparison to previous attempts and models. One of the criticisms levelled at the processual or contextual perspective is that it presents change as too complex a process and almost unmanageable (Buchanan and Huczynski, 2010). As a result, it is often seen as a rigorous theoretical framework that is, however, of little use to practitioners who may be more attracted to the prescriptive models such as those offered by the planned change authors. While this argument may hold some weight, it should be noted that some research undertaken from the processual perspective was concerned with the practical implications for managing change. Pettigrew and Whipp (1991), for example, have raised issues such as the need for multiple leaders at different organizational levels and the significance of revising change strategies in the light of implementation activities. However, another point that could be raised in relation to this perspective is that although it acknowledges the role of action in shaping change, this is restricted to those at the apex of organizational hierarchies, thus overlooking to an extent how action unfolding on the ground can also influence change processes. This interest in uncovering how micro-level processes can inform broad organizational change has been the motivation behind the situated activity perspective, discussed earlier.

Points to ponder

How can individual action shape change?

Is change the outcome of planned activity or spontaneous improvisation?

How does context inform change?

Resistance to change

The key challenge facing managers involved in change initiatives is that of resistance to change, ie the inability or unwillingness of individuals or groups to adopt the changes proposed. Subsequently, resistance to change has proved a popular topic of research, with the mainstream literature providing accounts of resistance that tend to maintain a view that is 'management centric'. In line with the dominant perspective on planned organizational change, the focus has often been on identifying sources of resistance either of individual (Eccles, 1994; Dirks, Cummings and Pierce, 1996; Eilam and Shamir, 2005) or organizational origin (Cameron and Quinn, 1999) and on outlining specific courses of action to deal with forces that block change (Kotter and Schlesinger, 1979; Dunphy and Stace, 1988; Geller, 2002). In summary, this literature depicts resistance as an inevitable reaction to change, which often seems threatening, suggesting, however, that resistance can be overcome provided that the right 'strategies' or 'management styles' are followed.

A similar view of resistance is also implicit in Carnall's (1990) famous model on how individuals cope with change. In particular, Carnall suggests that people usually go through a five-stage cycle when coping with change (denial, defence, discarding, adaptation, internalization). Therefore, he suggests, resistance (here in the form of defence) is considered to be a behaviour that individuals unavoidably adopt to protect themselves from the threatening nature of change but that gradually (as time passes by and with the management support) gives place to the acceptance of the new situation. The idea that resistance to change should be expected to decrease with time and as a result of management initiatives such as change communication is also evident in recent research, for example the study by Stanley, Meyer and Topolnytsky (2005) focusing on resistance to change, stemming from employees' cynicism.

More recently, the dominant view of resistance as a spontaneous response stemming from change recipients has come under criticism. For, example, Ford, Ford and D'Amelio (2008) have stressed that mainstream accounts tend to be one-sided, usually favouring change agents. Thus, they note how the latter fail to see resistance as an outcome shaped by the interaction among change agents and change recipients and not as a phenomenon that strictly resides in the latter. More specifically, Ford, Ford and D'Amelio (2008) argue that change agents' references to resistance constitute a defence mechanism that they invent to divert attention from their own failings. Additionally, the authors contend that change agents themselves often contribute to resistance in a number of ways, for example by violating trust, failing to legitimize change or mobilize action or by resisting any ideas put forward by change recipients. Ford, Ford and D'Amelio (2008) encourage change agents to use resistance as an indicator of change recipient commitment and as valuable feedback that could guide change implementation activity. Overall, it is argued that the concept of resistance should be reconstructed to include three dimensions: change recipients' action, change agents' interpretations and the interplay between the two. From this perspective, the notion of 'overcoming resistance' becomes outdated as it only highlights recipients' action while ignoring change agents' own assumptions and actions and obscures the importance of managing the agent–recipient relationship.

Finally, the scope for clear strategies of 'overcoming resistance', as discussed in the managerialist (see 'managerialism', Glossary) literature on change management, has also been debated by critical management writers such as Collinson (2000) and Knights and McCabe (2000) who have approached the issue of resistance from a slightly different angle. From their perspective, resistance is regarded as a response to managerial control (see Glossary) and therefore it is an endemic feature of organizational life. This is the case because managerial control is not as all-pervasive and rational as it appears to be (and as it is implicitly assumed by writers on planned organizational change). No matter how effective means of control are, they are not exhaustive of employee subjectivity, which can be defined as 'the way in which individuals interpret and understand their circumstances and is bound up with the sense they have of themselves (identity)' (Knights and McCabe, 2000). This focus on the notion of subjectivity questions the ability of managers to predict or anticipate specific forms of resistance on the part of employees and address those in a strategic way.

The change agent

Over the last three decades there has been a growing interest in the role and significance of change agents in organizations. The change agents' responsibility has evolved and dispersed over the years from the charismatic leaders and heroes who sought to transform corporations by destroying rigid and inflexible structures in the 1980s, to the traditional managers and functional specialists who had to embrace change attributes and actions to cope with uncertainty and risk in more dynamic environments, to the employees who were encouraged to participate and be receptive to change and technological innovation. Self-managed teams, quality circles and task groups were the main channels for this diffusion of change agency. The complexity of change operations has also instigated the increasing use of internal and external management consultants to lead or drive change to achieve results on time and within budget (Caldwell, 2003).

Thus, in many cases, and in particular in planned change, a change agent will take the responsibility to drive the change. A change agent may be defined as someone from inside or outside the organization seeking to facilitate, encourage, promote, advance, support, sponsor, initiate, implement, guide the change process or help to deliver change. The change agent can be a manager or non-manager, employees of the organization or outsider consultants. Nevertheless, it may be claimed that the trend is that change is part of every manager's role and it is involving different organizational members at all levels. To provide a more comprehensive picture of the different change agency models and variety of change agents, and based on a critical review of the literature and empirical research on change agents, Caldwell (2003) proposes a four-fold classification of change agency:

- **Leadership models:** Change agents are identified as leaders or senior executives who initiate or sponsor strategic change or transformational nature.

- **Management models:** Change agents are identified as middle level managers and functional specialists who carry out or build support for strategic change in business units or key functions.

- **Consultancy models:** Change agents are identified as internal or external consultants who operate at a strategic, operational, task or process level in an organization, and provide advice, expertise and process skills in facilitating change.

- **Team models:** Change agents are conceived as teams that may operate at different levels – strategic, operational, task or process level – in an organization and may be composed of managers, functional specialists, employees at all levels, and internal and external consultants. The popularity of this model increased over the last decade due to such factors as: the importance of team coordination at different levels as change in one area has an impact on other areas in the organization; the sheer complexity of large-scale organizational changes and associated high risk for anyone to take on individually; and the belief that change teams as units of learning can institutionalize behavioural change more deeply while encountering employee resistance. For example, teams of employees who are empowered and encouraged to participate in change initiatives in certain functions or tasks such as HR policies, represent a bottom-up task-oriented change approach that is considered to be a more effective mechanism for institutionalizing and embedding change than the top-down approach.

It must be pointed out that, as Caldwell argues, these models that represent a synthesis and re-conceptualization of the nature of change agency indicate that there is no single universal model of change agency or a single type of change agent with a fixed set of competencies. That being said, evidence shows that change agents are usually selected for their expertise in the area of change. However, under the emergent approach, rather than specialist expertise, it is advocated that change agents need to have certain competencies to manage change successfully, such as diagnostic, communication, presentation, negotiation and influencing skills.

More specifically, the change agent role can be complex and therefore there are strong suggestions that the person needs to have special skills and competencies to be able to deal with such complex situations. For example, in a survey to identify the critical competencies of effective change agents, Buchanan and Body (1992) found the following important areas:

- sensitivity to key personnel changes and their impact on goals;
- clarity in specifying goals and defining the achievable;
- flexibility in responding to change and risk taking;
- team building bringing together stakeholders and workgroups;
- networking establishing and maintaining contacts with different stakeholders;
- ambiguity tolerance able to work comfortably in uncertain environment;
- communication skills in transmitting effectively the need for change;
- interpersonal skills in effective listening, managing meetings, identifying concerns;

- personal enthusiasm in expressing plans and ideas;
- stimulating motivation and commitment in others;
- selling plans and ideas to others;
- negotiating with key players for resources and change;
- political awareness of political coalitions and conflicts;
- influence skills to gain commitment for change;
- helicopter perspective and taking a broader view of priorities.

Considering the competencies of HR in change initiatives, Ulrich and Yeung (1998) found that critical competencies related to focusing individual attention to organizational mindsets and culture; strategy implementation; and building change capability (cited in Higgs and Rowland, 2000).

The role of HR in change management

Historically, change has always been part of HR but with different degrees of engagement in the design and implementation of change over the years (Ogilvie and Stork, 2003). However, since the emergence of the literature on strategic HRM it has been argued that HR departments should play a key role in managing change (Storey, 1992; Ulrich, 1997; Caldwell, 2001). A number of writers attempted to classify the various HRM roles and argued for a new set of HR competencies. Ulrich's work has been especially influential here (Ulrich, 1997, 1998). Ulrich suggests four key HRM roles that help in building organizational capability and add value in an increasingly challenging and turbulent environment. These HRM roles are advocated as: strategic partner; administrative expert; employee champion; and change agent (Ulrich, 1997). As a change agent, Ulrich argues that the HR department should become 'an agent of continuous transformation' that is actively involved in shaping organizational processes and culture to improve an organization's capacity for change (Ulrich, 1998).

It is also argued that effective delivery of organizational change requires an alignment or fit between the organization's corporate and business strategies, its change strategies and its HRM strategy. This means that much of the HRM function's role in organizational change is in creating alignment, by developing HR strategies, policies and practices that support the organization in adapting to its environment and in meeting its change objectives (Graetz *et al*, 2006). Thus, for example, if one of the strategic objectives of a firm is to increase efficiency and competitiveness this implies a change initiative to improve the performance of individuals through the design of HRM strategies and policies to improve the way organization members behave, communicate, make decisions, reward, monitor, praise and coach, to be consistent with the new strategic directions.

In general, during the change process, it is maintained that HR professionals should assist top managers in achieving the set strategic objectives while, at the same time, maintaining employees' motivation and commitment. As an active change agent, this also entails creating a strong HR climate in which the employees understand and internalize the change initiatives through transmitting clear, consistent and consensual messages. This will contribute to curbing rumours and suspicions about the change initiatives and clarify the benefits of the change initiatives, which helps in reducing the resistance to these change initiatives. An active HR agent also works on developing adaptable and flexible HR systems and practices, enlarging the competencies of the employees, and enhancing employees' behavioural flexibility (Bowen and Ostroff, 2004; Wright and Snell, 1998). Thus, it is advocated that the HR department must promote a shared understanding of the change initiatives to be able to undertake the role of a change agent successfully. Developing social capital and good relations with line managers also becomes imperative to assist the HR department in the implementation of the change initiatives and succeed as change agent (Kim and Ryu, 2000).

Evidence shows that HR can play a central role in the effective management of organizational change. For example, the CIPD (2005) research identified seven key areas of activity associated with successful change, in each of which the HR department contributed constructively to make change happen and to build organizational capability for sustainable change. These were termed the 'seven Cs' of change (Molloy and Whittington, 2005; **www.cipd.co.uk**):

- choosing a team with the key skills such as management of organizational culture and organizational design;
- crafting the vision and the path – setting realistic and achievable objectives;
- connecting organization-wide change – coordinating 'hard' change with 'soft' people issues;

- consulting stakeholders – consulting and involving stakeholders such as unions and employees;
- communicating – providing accurate, regular and up-to-date messages throughout the organization;
- coping with change – introducing mechanisms that help people to cope with change;
- capturing learning – acquiring and disseminating knowledge and experience internally and externally.

The above shows that considering the specific content of HR's role in managing change is important. Consequently, Thornhill *et al* (2000) adopt a content-oriented approach and focus on seven relevant HR practices that HR specialists can use to support change. These are:

- **cultural change** and HR's role in influencing employees' values and beliefs;
- **recruitment** and ensuring the selection of employees whose attitudes and abilities support the change objectives;
- revision of **performance management practices** to align individual goals with new organizational goals and reward behaviour that supports the strategic change;
- **resource development** initiatives and activities to ensure the possession of the necessary skills, capabilities and knowledge to be more efficient and cope with change;
- **reward management** revision and integration with performance management to support the new strategic organizational objectives;
- **management of employee relations** and maintaining good relations with the unions and observation of legal regulations;
- **downsizing** that is closely monitored and implemented by HR.

Points to ponder

In your opinion, why is it important that HR is involved in managing change?

What will be the main challenge facing HR in the process of managing change?

Globally and within MNCs, evidence shows that HR plays a prime role in leading change (Evans *et al*, 2011). With globalization and the accelerating expansionary strategies of MNCs, particularly through mergers and acquisitions, the attention of researchers to date has been focused, for the most part, on the role that HRM plays in 'post-acquisition management', a term that has usefully been defined by Child, Faulkner and Pitkethly to encompass 'the process adopted to bring about changes in the acquired companies, the type of changes introduced and the measures taken to integrate and control the acquisition' (2001). Indeed, evidence shows that paying attention to people and cultural issues is imperative for the success of cross-border mergers and acquisitions strategies. For example, the most important factors identified in the McKinsey study of international mergers and acquisitions were all associated with HR issues and were considered to be detrimental to the success of the acquisition. In descending ranking order these were (Kay and Shelton, 2000):

- retention of key talent;
- effective communication;
- executive retention;
- cultural integration.

All mergers and acquisitions require some degree of integration. Merger or acquisition integration is a change process. Most merger or acquisition failures are linked to problems in post-merger integration – that is, in managing the change process. Cultural and people issues consistently rank among the main difficulties in executing acquisition, and therefore it is argued that the HR department should take an active role in leading and managing change. This is also particularly true in cross-border mergers and acquisitions due to the complexities arising from cultural and physical distance or more comprehensively, from psychic distance. For example, Inkpen, Sundaram and Rockwood (2000) note that the problems surrounding management styles and practices, and inadequate planning for post-merger acquisition integration are the two most commonly cited reasons for acquisition failures. The authors go on to observe that these issues are exacerbated in the cross-border setting because they embody 'questions of corporate culture, national culture and corporate governance' (Inkpen, Sundaram and Rockwood 2000). A number of studies have further suggested that these problems of cultural integration are likely to be particularly problematic where acquisitions involve the coming together of organizations from developed and emerging and developing economies. For example, Jackson (2004) has drawn attention to a number of what are seen as characteristics of 'post-colonial' management systems that can act as a barrier to such transfers. Such characteristics are seen to include an emphasis on motivation by control rather than results, the presence of high levels of bureaucracy, the use of authoritarian management practices, and promotions and appointments based on relationships and a lack of management skills. In this case, it is expected that intra-organizational variations in responses to Western management techniques can be linked to broader evidence concerning how types of workplace changes can differentially affect workers. Subcultures, more or less hostile to management change efforts, can exist in organizations, shaped by a number of factors such as professional identities, length of service, functional groupings and hierarchical positions (Harris and Ogbonna, 1998).

Al-Husan and James (2007) also found that local subsidiaries actively mobilized their resources both at the micro (organizational) and macro (national) levels to resist and influence the implementation of the changes introduced by the parent company and to undermine the institutionalization of the desired HR practices imported from the corporate headquarters of the MNC. Kostova (1999) argued that practices transferred from the parent company may be adopted only at the surface level and not internalized by the members of the subsidiaries, and therefore the success with which MNCs transfer centrally desired changes and HR policies and practices to subsidiaries needs to be evaluated in two ways: first, in terms of the extent to which they have been 'implemented' at the local level; and second, in relation to how far employees have 'internalized' them. In an empirical study that built on Kostova's argument, Al-Husan and James (2007) found that the HR reforms introduced in the subsidiary were more internalized by the staff group that was targeted by the parent company as it was accompanied by good material rewards for this group. The negative outcomes were reported to be linked to the group of workers who were adversely affected materially by the HR change introduced. This suggests that care needs to be taken not only in terms of the cultural and institutional barriers to change but also to the differential effects on the material interests of staff, and that change programmes introduced by MNCs may require the adoption of different approaches towards the management of different categories of staff.

Evans, Pucik and Björkman (2011) argue that HR should be involved in a merger and acquisition as early as during the selection and evaluation of a suitable target, ie during the 'due diligence' process, and during the planning of the post-combination integration process. This is due to the fact that the key challenges of mergers and acquisitions are HR issues and because the 'soft' people aspects, such as the assessment of culture and HR practices in the organization to be acquired, are just as important as the financial analysis. Support for this argument is provided, for example, by the recent developments in the UK amendments to the code for take-over (see Glossary) in which a strict timetable of 28 days between the identification of a bidder and the withdrawal of a bid was imposed. This change implies the involvement of the HR function into the merger and acquisition process at a much earlier stage not only to carry out all the required due diligence but also to manage the communication with employee representatives and respond to their employee-related questions (Brockett, 2011).

Key learning points and conclusions

- Change management is a multifaceted process shaped by the interplay of managerial action and broader contextual forces.

- One of the key challenges in initiating and implementing change is that of resistance.

- Mainstream management accounts restricted the locus of resistance in the actions of change recipients. However, more recent research has highlighted the nature of resistance as a phenomenon shaped by the interplay between change recipients' actions and change agents' own assumptions and interpretations of the process. More critical accounts have cast doubt on the ability of managers to manage resistance in a strategic mode.

- From an international perspective, managing change, particularly in merger and acquisition ventures, during the integration largely depends on the effective management and integration of different cultures and the workforce.

- This highlights the importance of the active involvement of the HR department in the change process and in acting as change agents and early involvement in any change process to ensure the full and effective implementation of the issues identified. This involves, as Ulrich (1998) maintains, 'replacing resistance with resolve, planning with results and fear of change with excitement about its responsibilities'.

Case study and discussion questions

CASE STUDY   Jordan Cement Factories

It is widely evident that the period since the mid-1980s has been marked by changes in the world economy that have led to profound developments in the international operations, strategies and structures of MNCs and many other organizations worldwide. Among other things, such changes consisted of the liberalization of financial markets, deregulation and privatization of state enterprises, globalization and intensification of international competition. In the face of these changes MNCs have adopted fast track expansionary strategies, such as cross-border mergers and acquisitions, and a variety of non-equity arrangements such as management contracts and licensing agreements. They have also increasingly expanded their growth into developing countries of which many were embarking on economic structural adjustment reforms and privatization programmes under the directive of the World Bank (WB) and International Monetary Fund (IMF), which led to the sale of their state-owned enterprises, and in many cases, to MNCs.

The Hashemite Kingdom of Jordan was one of the countries in the Arab world in the Middle East region that had to undertake structural adjustment programmes under the auspices of the WB and the IMF and, as a result, a number of state enterprises were privatized and sold to Western MNCs to improve their efficiency and competitiveness. The first state enterprise that was privatized was Jordan Cement Factories that was acquired by a French MNC through the purchase of equity shares. Jordan Cement Factories is a public shareholding company that was incorporated in Jordan in 1951. The main activities of the company are the manufacturing, production and trading of cement and its by-products and until 2002 it had a monopoly over the supply of cement in Jordan. The Jordanian government and its institutions had long owned around 58 per cent of the company's share capital. In November 1998, it sold 33 per cent of these shares to Lafarge, a French MNC, that subsequently increased its stake to 50.27 per cent controlling share.

The process of change

Jordan Cement became the subsidiary of Lafarge that had strategic importance to the MNC because, according to the General Manager of Jordan Cement, it was 'the first operation in the Middle East and therefore could be the basis for market access and further operations and developments in the area'. The parent company has adopted a management style known as the 'Lafarge way'. Under this the organization seeks to encourage personal initiatives and involvement of everyone in the implementation of group strategy. At the same time, the MNC was moving towards operating along global lines and as a result was attaching great importance to the issue of integration. In terms of HR, this is reflected in the implementation of company-wide HR policies in respect of a number of issues. Thus, in relations to this, the Middle East director for HR-related issues noted that:

'We apply the same HR policies on everything – on all HR related issues and on all other activities such as training and development, etc. There are company-wide policies that will apply as much as the local culture and the law allow us… we apply the same policies because the parent company has its own internal culture and we aim to achieve integration. This means doing the same everywhere in the world. It is part of our culture. Each function should have the same methods of doing things, same understanding, and same efficiency.'

Accordingly, after the acquisition, the French MNC adopted a gradual approach to change whereby it was envisaged that the change process would occur over a period of between two and three years. In this process, a 'methodological guide' is used to integrate new subsidiaries, under which teams from different functional areas are sent to the subsidiary to identify priority actions that have to be undertaken within the first 100 days. This action programme is, in turn, accompanied by the development of a longer-term, two- to three-year, programme of actions aimed at making the changes needed to integrate the new subsidiary fully. The MNC adopted a gradual approach to change due to three main considerations. First, there was a desire only to introduce the changes after an appropriate management infrastructure had been developed. Secondly, there was a recognition that cultural change is a slow process, and thirdly, there was a felt need to prepare employees adequately for change.

In addition, the company used participative change processes that encompassed the use of task groups and working parties, and a bottom-up orientation to problem solving. Consequently, and following the change project known as the JCF Horizon 2001 that was created and the HR audit that was conducted by staff at the parent company, a range of new HR policies and procedures were proposed. These policies included the establishment of a new system for career management and succession planning, the implementation of revised job descriptions and a new job evaluation scheme, and the development of improved policies in relation to performance appraisal, recruitment and selection, and training and development. This was in parallel with the implementation of a new organizational structure under which a new HR division was created. Under this new structure, the HR function gained greater strategic importance, became part of the company's overall strategic planning process and was directly linked with the operating committee that was in charge of the daily operations of the company, while previously the role of the personnel function was mainly administrative, HR had no representation at board level and its participation in planning was very weak.

Furthermore, decision-making style, which was very centralized before privatization, had to be changed after privatization. Decentralization and delegation were seen as important changes that needed to be introduced in order to create a management style that was in line with the parent company's best practice. Thus many positions were merged to reduce the number of layers of management and senior managers were encouraged to devolve greater authority to line managers. Line managers were also given more HR responsibilities in such areas as communication with employees; pay rises and promotion of subordinates; the use of performance appraisal to determine the level of bonus pay and the objectives of subordinates; recruitment and selection; training of subordinates; planning manpower requirements; communication with subordinates; paying attention to the budget and control of costs; and the dismissal and discipline of subordinates. Overall, line managers participated in making such decisions contrary to the situation in the period before the acquisition where decisions were made centrally.

Changes were also introduced in a number of other areas such as performance management, rewards, training and development. Working parties were also created to carry out the JCF Horizon 2001 project and the HR changes. These working parties or task groups comprised staff from different functions including members of the trade union. A key objective of the new management was to involve the trade union in the changes being made. Jordan Cement had a well-established and powerful union and the company's employees were members of The General Trade Union of Construction Workers. This involvement of the trade union reflected the parent company's participative culture. For example, the Middle East director for HR-related issues observed that:

> The parent company's culture is very humanistic and works with the individuals.
> It is a consensus seeking culture rather than a confrontation culture... and that
> employees are at the heart of the organization... you cannot force change...
> change must come indigenously. I mean people should be willing and should be
> participating in change... otherwise, for example, you can make the perfect
> organization on the table but you cannot implement it because the unions are
> going to resist it and because the individuals are going to resist. So you must have
> ownership and participation to change and I think the parent company is trying to
> do this and is trying to create participation to change... you cannot change the
> culture overnight. You need to convince the people that what you are bringing
> them is going to serve them better.

It must be noted that the union gained power during the privatization process due to the delicate political situation in the country and its power continued to grow after the privatization. The power of the union grew not only at the company level but also at the national level and it obtained further support from the public and the press, and from the several actions it took that threatened the stability of the company and the country. It also had international support as it was a member of other international unions such as the Union of Arab Workers. Thus, according to the union's president, during the period when the company was considering a restructuring based on the Jordanian Labour Law No. 31 article 33, which gave the firm's owner the right to terminate the services of the employees without compensating them, the union 'declared war on the company' and announced strikes and sit-ins that were widely supported in Jordanian society, and by national figures and political parties. At the same time, for the government this was a very sensitive situation since many of the company's employees came from high unemployment and low income regions and the company was considered to serve the national interest by employing these people. As a result of the growing influence of the union, it succeeded in obtaining several gains such as the distribution of 4 per cent of the company's annual profits to all company staff, pay increase on the basic salaries of all employees, and among other things, it changed the terms of the early retirement scheme and gained more favourable terms and incentives for employees. The way that the MNC dealt with the changes and the resistance if faced is illustrated in the area of remuneration below.

Remuneration

Prior to privatization, pay was determined according to the qualifications and experience of the individual and was made up of a number of elements: basic salary, various allowances, a production bonus and annual performance-based increases of between £3.00 and £4.00. Shortly after privatization, it was agreed to raise the basic salary by an average of £6.00 for every employee. In addition, the existing production bonus was doubled, and 4 per cent of the company's annual profits were distributed equally to all the company's employees as a bonus. These changes were made in response to forceful union claims and against the background of an increase in union influence stemming from the delicate political nature of the privatization and a desire on the part of both the government and the company to avoid any bad publicity during the early days of privatization. In addition, a new company-wide performance-related bonus scheme was proposed under which payments would be distributed on the basis of individual performance. Initially, the new bonus arrangements were only applied to the cadre people because of union opposition to the revised bonus arrangements. In the face of this opposition, the company therefore later decided to link only half of the bonus to individual performance. Accordingly, a decision was made to distribute 2 per cent of annual net profit equally among the 1,800 non-cadre employees, while the other 2 per cent was to be distributed according to their personal performance. In a similar vein, the union was also able, against the background of its enhanced negotiating power, to secure an increase from 75 per cent to 86 per cent in the average annual appraisal mark, as the following quote from the company's career manager illustrates: 'The main obstacle is the union. The annual appraisal is linked to the annual increase and the bonus. Thus, the unions argued that this affected the employees' incomes and demanded an increase in the average mark from 75 per cent to 86 per cent. At the end, the company had to make concessions and we reached an agreement to have an average mark of 84 per cent'.

Discussion questions

- Explain the MNC's approach to change. To what extent do you agree with it and why?

- Discuss the different factors that need to be taken into consideration to implement change successfully, particularly when operating across borders.

- What are the sources of resistance to change? To what extent do you think that the MNC was successful in dealing with resistance to change, and why?

- What are the limitations of the planned perspective on change?

- Discuss the factors that may support the argument that change is shaped by the interplay of action and context.

10
Creativity, innovation and the management of knowledge

PAULINE LOEWENBERGER

LEARNING OBJECTIVES

- Evaluate what may be regarded as new priorities in thought and action relevant to organizational behaviour and HRM.

- Draw attention to the intangible aspects of organization that point to investment of human capital in pursuit of adding value and/or developing sustainable competitive advantage through creativity, innovation, learning and knowledge management.

- Critically evaluate extant knowledge and understanding of creativity and innovation.

- Explore alternative discourses on knowledge management.

- Examine comparative emphasis and philosophies between organizational learning and knowledge management.

- Synthesize organizational creativity, innovation, learning organization, organizational learning, knowledge creation and management.

Introduction

For at least a decade, academic commentary has been drawing attention to the *intangible* aspects of organization and organizing pointing to investment in human capital in pursuit of effectiveness, renewal, transformation and sustainable competitive advantage. Knowledge creation and management, organizational learning, creativity and innovation may collectively be viewed as responsive, dynamic processes, the integration of which places people issues in the foreground. Yet, regardless of the potential contribution to theoretical understanding and practical application, most contributions in OB, HRM and HRD, at best, treat these important concepts as subsections of more traditional topics.

In this way the focus is on what may be regarded as new priorities in thought and action relevant to organizational behaviour and HRM in the global context providing a meaningful and useful application to practice. Through critical review and synthesis the merits and limitations of current argument and evidence in the fields of enquiry are assessed. First, this chapter examines how managers might overcome barriers and misunderstandings to stimulate, support and sustain organizational creativity and innovation effectively. Second, it assesses influential contributions to organizational learning, knowledge creation and management and makes explicit their links to creativity and innovation management. The overall aim is to guide you as students through the current maze of tenuous links, also drawing on the author's own research to propose how conditions necessary for creativity, innovation, organizational learning, knowledge creation, transfer and management might be interpreted and comprehended under the employment relationship through individual and group behaviour. In common with other chapters, cross-cultural perspectives are therefore assumed throughout. Case studies and vignettes demonstrate excellent and more problematic examples. Suggested questions are aimed at provoking critical analysis for individual consideration and in-class group discussion and debate.

Creativity and innovation

The essence of Schumpeter's (1934) classic reference to the gales of creative destruction that arise from disequilibrium is that all economic and social progress ultimately depends on new ideas. The basis of this argument is that competition demands creative solutions leading to innovations that fundamentally change and develop the economy, yet at the same time are necessarily destructive in contesting the inertia of the status quo. Suggestions that organizational effectiveness, competitiveness and survival in a rapidly changing, dynamic, highly competitive global business environment frequently depend on new ideas is not new (Williams and Yang, 1999). The fostering of creativity and innovation is essential in supporting creative revolutions (Gibb and Waight, 2005). The key is unlocking the potential of all employees, regardless of position and level rather than only the traditionally more creative roles (Axtell *et al*, 2000; Madjar, Oldham and Pratt, 2002; Madjar, 2005). This applies equally to the private sector in developing sustainable competitive advantage, and to the public sector where 'the demand for efficiencies and enhanced performance is continual as governments attempt to manage demands for expenditure to improve the quality of life that exceed their incomes' (Dodgson and Gann, 2010).

A UK survey suggests 84 per cent of participating companies regard innovation as critical or important (Searle and Ball, 2003). However, this is not ubiquitous. Many companies still regard innovation as an irritant that gets in the way of 'real work' (Basadur and Gelade, 2006). Realization demands raised awareness and understanding of the need for creativity and innovation and how organizational capability might be developed. Commitment and capability are often lacking (Salaman and Storey, 2002) and aspirations blocked because of perceived risk, lack of understanding of what this means, how to generate and implement creative ideas, manage the creativity and innovation processes and overcome institutionalized routines and inertia (Storey, 2000). Simply, 'It [innovation] is the theatre where the excitement of experimentation and learning meets the organizational realities of limited budgets, established routines, disrupted priorities, and constrained imagination' (Dodgson and Gann, 2010). More than a decade ago Storey (2000) observed extensive differences between managers in the same company, even among managers in the same top-level teams, about the actual meaning of the injunction to be innovative and the priority accorded to it, leading to the suggestion, 'firms are more than happy to use the concept of innovation in their advertising and corporate PR, but sustained behaviour in practice seems to present managers with a difficulty' (2000). Confusion between the rhetoric and practice remains.

Innovation calls for creative solutions. Consensus identifies key elements of creativity as novelty or originality that is useful (Taylor, Smith and

Ghiselin, 1963; Gardner 1988; Mumford and Gustafson, 1988; Amabile, 1996; Sternberg, 1999). It has been suggested that '… without creative ideas to feed the innovation pipeline so they may be promoted and developed, innovation is an engine without any fuel' (McLean, 2005). Others define creativity as the seed of innovation (Amabile *et al*, 1996) that potentially plays an important role across levels of analysis and throughout different phases of the process. Innovation is the implementation or exploitation of creative ideas shifting the focus to social validation, acceptance and viability. Not all innovations necessarily result from creative processes (Damanpour, 1990) and might include adoption of ideas imported from the external environment (Amabile, 1988; Beswick and Gallagher, 2010). Creative ideas provide greater potential for sustainable competitive advantage. Evidence is emerging in support of idea-rich environments. For example, Davis (2000) found that organizations earning more from new products and services were nurturing around 115 ideas per day, compared to 18 for an average organization. Stevens and Burley (1997) suggest it takes 3000 raw ideas to produce one substantially new and commercially successful product.

Stimulating, supporting and sustaining creativity and innovation

Creativity and innovation depends on management capability and commitment (Mumford, 2000). Scope for synergy emerges between interactive process theories (eg Van de Ven, Angle and Poole, 1989) and interactional models of creativity (Amabile, 1983; Woodman, Sawyer and Griffin, 1993; Sternberg and Lubart, 1999). All propose the need to understand the dynamic, temporal, multiplicative interaction of individual, social and organizational characteristics in overcoming cognitive blocks and organizational barriers. In the organizational setting, potential barriers and facilitators operate at the individual, group and organizational levels. Climate represents an indication of the feelings and beliefs of employees in relation to policies, practices and procedures. This demands stimulation of the generation of creative ideas including training in creative problem solving, and a work environment that is supportive of idea generation and implementation and that is sustainable through embedded processes and practices.

The individual

Notions of the lone creative genius have long given way to perspectives that emphasize everyone has the potential, yet generation of creative ideas remains uncommon (Egan, 2005). Social and educational influences interact in the interests of cognitive economy to favour reproductive thinking. Creativity demands productive thinking (Hurson, 2008) in overcoming cognitive blocks through training in creative problem solving (e.g. Osborn, 1957; Parnes, Noller and Biondi, 1971) employing structured techniques (VanGundy, 1988; De Bono, 1993; Michalko, 2006; Isaksen, Dorval and Treffinger, 2010). Evidence is emerging of positive effects of robust approaches to creativity training (Balestra, 1997; Puccio *et al*, 2006). Associations between training in creative thinking techniques and the openness to experience dimension of personality raise interesting questions concerning the direction of causality (Loewenberger, 2009).

Undoubtedly some individuals are highly creative and the importance of personality characteristics to creativity are well documented (Barron and Harrington, 1981; Mumford and Gustafson, 1988). The five-factor model of personality (Costa and McCrae, 1985) validated by organizational psychologists to feature individual differences important to workplace performance, suggests the association of openness to experience (McCrae, 1987; McCrae and Costa, 1997; Feist, 1998; Loewenberger, 2009) to creativity. Open individuals are not only more flexible in absorbing information and combining new and unrelated information but also seek out unfamiliar situations and new experiences, raising awareness of problem opportunities and increasing potential for new ideas. Alternative perspectives emphasize the complexity of associations of contrasting traits to creativity and innovation, the 'creative' individual able to operate at both polarities (Csikszentmihalyi, 1996).

Climate for creativity and innovation

That creative behaviour is easily overshadowed by an unsupportive environment leads to the significance of organizational culture and climate. Group creativity (Woodman, Sawyer and Griffin, 1993; Amabile, 1996) mediates individual creativity and organizational creativity and is a function of the outputs of component groups and contextual influences. Challenges arise in dealing with co-workers and superiors, who may not support ideas or who may wish to steal or suppress ideas for nefarious reasons (Williams and Yang, 1999). Psychological climate refers to intrapersonal perceptions, the aggregate of which represents the organizational climate (Amabile, 1996; Amabile *et al*, 1996; Isaksen, 2007a). Climate is distinct from culture in that it operates at a more accessible level and is more malleable, therefore conducive to change and improvement efforts.

Similarity exists between stimulants and obstacles identified by two of the most influential climate surveys (see Figure 10.1): the KEYS survey (Amabile, Burnside and Gryskiewicz, 1999), developed from Amabile's (1983, 1996) componential model and the situational outlook questionnaire (SOQ) (Isaksen, 2007b). Differences are also apparent. For example, the SOQ specifically incorporates idea time, playfulness and humour and separates conflict. Amabile's is the only model to include a workload pressure dimension.

FIGURE 10.1   Climate factors supporting creativity and innovation (adapted from Amabile, 1996 (inner radial) and Isaksen, 2007 (outer radial))

Amabile (1997) suggested five scales as most supportive of creativity in a large organization, four of which have been supported through multi-level investigation on small-to-medium sized organizations (Loewenberger, 2009). The resulting model supported interaction of organizational encouragement, challenging work, work group support and (lack of) organizational impediments (Amabile *et al*, 1996) with the openness to experience (Costa and McCrae, 1992) personality dimension in explaining 47 per cent variance between participating organizations. Qualitative investigation of meaning (Loewenberger, 2009) extended climate models, highlighting the communication of senior management vision leading to shared vision and shared meaning and understanding of what it means to be creative and innovative in context. Misconceptions of creativity as purely aesthetic remain common, emphasizing the significance of creative requirement (Unsworth, Wall and Carter, 2002; Unsworth and Clegg, 2010), expectation of the generation of creative ideas and creativity goals represent important components in creative behaviour. Love for one's work (Csikszentmihalyi, 1996; Amabile, 1997) was frequently offered as was the perceived freedom to voice ideas without fear of intimidation, humiliation or ridicule. Finally, is the significance of appropriate mechanisms in organizations more supportive of creativity and innovation (for example creativity champions, training in creative problem-solving techniques, creativity and innovation clubs).

Avoidance of risk represents an element of creative climate (Amabile *et al*, 1996; Isaksen, 2007a). Research evidence (Loewenberger, 2009) also emerged in respect of acceptance of risk taking which is, of course, closely related to mistake handling (Martins and Terblanche, 2003; Isaksen, 2007a). Undoubtedly, financial risk and safety must take priority. However, acceptance of failure and mistakes, provided that we learn from these, is an important part of creativity, innovation and organizational learning. A memorable example in the UK is the opening of London's Millennium Bridge in June 2000 linking the Tate Gallery and St Paul's Cathedral. Its unsteadiness when large groups of people crossed was explained as 'lateral excitation' due to the male gait. This led to new knowledge about bridge design, clearly illustrating progress in science and engineering that is built on failure (Dodgson and Gann, 2010).

Few would question the innovations of the late Steve Jobs at Apple, and Pixar, fuelled by a passion for creative thinking leading to innovative ideas and a vision and inspiration to change lives. Gallo's (2010) biography summarizes 'seven principles of breakthrough success', supported by influential contributors and research:

- Do what you love (Csikszentmihalyi, 1996; Amabile, 1997; Loewenberger, 2009; Robinson, 2009).
- Put a dent in the universe (Martins and Terblanche, 2003; Loewenberger, 2009).
- Kick start your brain (see VanGundy, 1988; Hurson, 2008).
- Sell dreams not products.
- Say no to 1000 things ('Quantity breeds quality' – see VanGundy, 1988)
- Create insanely great experiences (if employees are not having fun, your customers will not).
- Master the message (persuasion and persistence in gaining social validation of ideas).

Support for creative climate is evident through a collaborative contribution derived from an independent theoretical underpinning (Martins and Terblanche, 2003) drawing on open systems theory (see Glossary) and Schein's (1992) work on culture and leadership. The emphasis on vision and mission, supportive mechanisms, behaviours that encourage innovation, communication and leadership have much in common with the approach here.

Organizational learning and knowledge management

Since approximately the mid-1970s economies and society in general have witnessed the replacement of manufacturing with knowledge-intensive work as the main generator of wealth and the service sector representing the biggest source of employment (Bell, 1973). As the combination of energy, resources and machine technology were the transformational agencies of industrial society, knowledge and information are the strategic resource and transforming agent of the post-industrial society (see Glossary; Bell 1980). Infamous citations of this era claimed that 'the only competitive advantage the company of the future will have is its managers' ability to learn faster than their competitors' (De Geus, 1988, 1997). We have also witnessed exceptional advances in information and communications technology and systems. The internet is central to global knowledge creation and sharing, including social networking. With services innovation relevant knowledge is nearly always distributed across a range of stakeholders including, on a much greater basis than before, the customer (Dodgson, Gann and Salter, 2005). Knowledge represents a major source of sustainable competitive advantage (Nonaka, Toyama and Nagata, 2000). For example, large multinational consultancies such as Accenture make vast amounts of money from selling what is essentially an intangible product offering – knowledge. Open innovation (Chesbrough, 2006) takes advantage of increased interrelatedness and interdependency between companies; originating in the technology sector, dedicated websites have emerged (for example **www.innocentive.com**). How does knowledge creation, management and sharing in the service sector such as this lead to sustainable competitive advantage? The focus here is on developing organizational capability, demanding increased attention to knowledge creation, management, sharing and transfer to mobilize creativity, innovation, learning, knowledge creation, management and transfer.

Links with a climate for creativity and innovation are evident in theories of organizational learning (Senge, 1990; Pedler, Burgoyne and Boydell, 1996; Marsick and Watkins, 2003), knowledge creation and management (Nonaka, Toyama and Nagata, 2000). All emphasize that humans and organizations are dynamic beings that have the potential to learn and grow together. Cross-disciplinary understanding is critical to synergy between these important areas that have traditionally been neglected in mainstream OB. Theoretical development and practical application demands that links are more explicit in informing HRM, IHRM and HRD, in particular. This is central to the suggestion, '... that HRD, as a discipline and a profession seeks to identify, support and lead the creative revolutions of the 21st century workforce and workplace.' (Gibb and Waight, 2005). Innovative companies tend to be characterized as knowledge creating (Nonaka and Takeuchi, 1995) and a blurring of the boundaries between research on knowledge management and innovation has become evident in recent years. Others suggest that concepts of knowledge management and organizational learning usefully integrate with creativity by using knowledge for creative adaptation and flexibility in the 'thinking organization' (Basadur and Gelade, 2006). In this way, direct links between climates for creativity, innovation and learning become more transparent.

The learning organization and organizational learning

The idea of the learning organization has attracted much criticism since the early work (Senge, 1990; Pedler, Burgoyne and Boydell, 1996) not least because of its ideology and abstraction in terms of collective learning. Was the original notion an idea ahead of its time? New organizational forms typical of the knowledge and service economy and greater acceptance of the value of the human resource to performance place the spotlight on learning and development. Rowden's definition explicitly links learning with continuous improvement, innovation and transformation: 'a model of strategic change in which everyone is engaged in identifying and solving problems so that the organization is continuously changing, experimenting and improving, thus increasing its capacity to grow and achieve its purpose' (2001). This emphasizes an organizational culture and climate that encourages, facilitates and supports individual and group learning. This is evident in Senge's (1990) five disciplines that emphasize interactive systems thinking, changing assumptions, shared vision, team learning, synergy and the need for personal mastery that discards old ways of thinking and standard routines. Consistent with this are the action learning imperatives proposed by Marsick and Watkins (2003) that emphasize organizational and collaborative learning as essential to a learning climate.

Focusing on strategic renewal tension in organizational learning an influential contribution is the 4I framework (Crossan, Lane and White, 1999). Organizational learning is a multilevel phenomenon that must satisfy the requirements of rigorous multilevel theory. Hence, the 4I theory builds explicitly on the key principles of multilevel research. This comprises four related sub-processes linking three levels. Intuiting and interpreting occur at the individual level, interpreting and integrating at the group level and integrating and institutionalizing at the organizational level. This framework draws on competition for scarce resources between exploration and exploitation in strategic renewal evident in dynamics of transference of learning across individual, group and organizational levels such that it becomes embedded – or institutionalized – in the form of strategies, structures and procedures (Crossan, Lane and White, 1999).

Knowledge management

Variously, commentary has attempted to help codify what occurs in thinking and learning in organizational contexts, to make these phenomena amenable to management. These ideas have been grouped together as something for corporate policy and action under the popular label of knowledge management, influential to which has been Nonaka and Takeuchi's 1995 publication, differentiating modes of knowledge creation and conversion through blending of explicit and tacit knowledge. Explicit knowledge is objective and easily codified through, for example, books, journals and the internet, and shared through combination with existing knowledge and internalization leading to changes in behaviour. Tacit knowledge is more subjective and not easily codified, necessitating experiential learning through articulation and social learning, for example observation and imitation. From an ontological perspective organizations cannot create knowledge without the individuals and need to provide a supportive context. Knowledge management is concerned with sharing, collaboration and institutionalization of explicit and tacit knowledge through a cycle of creation and conversion (Nonaka, Toyama and Byosiere, 2001).

However, critical debate continues with regards to tacit and explicit knowledge. For example, drawing on Polyani, Tsoukas argues that 'tacit knowledge' has been misunderstood and misinterpreted in management studies in overlooking the essential ineffability of tacit knowledge (Tsoukas, 2005) by reducing it to what can be articulated. Undoubtedly, explicit knowledge draws on tacit knowledge, experience and context manifested in what we do. 'New knowledge comes about not when the tacit becomes explicit but when our skilled performance – our praxis – is punctuated in new ways through social interaction' (Tsoukas, 2001). Essentially explicit and tacit knowledge are interrelated in that tacit knowledge is necessary to make sense of explicit knowledge. See the case study below for an example in NHS Direct.

CASE STUDY   Creativity, innovation, learning and knowledge management in NHS Direct

NHS Direct and NHS Direct Online represented new ways of accessing healthcare to alleviate pressure on doctors and others, central to the modernization of the NHS. Staffed by registered nurses, this represents an interesting context for analysis of the management of knowledge. In contrast to the emergent paradigm of call centres as one of mass production, technologically driven, low cost and lean production the service is non-commercial and the occupational base of the workforce has not been transformed. Nurses are professionally qualified and move back and forth between face-to-face care and tele-nursing, presenting two challenges.

First, separation from the patient demands one-off interactions rather than longer-term relations. Second, technologically mediated, nurses respond as generalists rather than specialists. At the heart of this innovative software is management's attempt to standardize and control the caller–nurse relationship. NHS Direct explicitly uses three forms of knowledge: 1) a number of datasets; 2) the nurse's own experience or knowledge; and 3) the CAS software. Explicit knowledge (1 and 3) consists of facts, rules and policies that can be codified and transmitted using formal language or an electronic format. In contrast, tacit knowledge (2) is personal, context specific and harder to communicate and to share, resulting in two knowledge management strategies: codification and personalization. Codification involves a process of identifying, capturing, cataloguing and making available explicit knowledge to professionals working in a team. The strategy of personalization involves the practice of creatively solving problems through the use of tacit knowledge.

CAS is the fundamental body of knowledge on which judgements and explanations of patients' needs are based. In common with customer service representatives, nurses in NHS Direct follow a script that constrains human possibility. CAS guides questioning of callers and assesses the urgency of need and most appropriate course of action. However, nurses can deviate from this script and make alternative decisions. As knowledgeable actors, nurses can control, manipulate and create knowledge, without having their autonomy subordinated to the clinical software. This makes their work situation critically different from that of customer service representatives in a typical call centre where relevant prior professional occupational knowledge is unnecessary. However, evidence suggests that rather than technological control and subordination of CAS in limiting autonomy, nurses manipulate the system and acquire new knowledge from CAS. It is suggested that nurses internalize the knowledge given through CAS, seeing their knowledge and experience as complementary. In this way the power of the software to learning, development, knowledge creation and management was underestimated.

SOURCE Adapted from Hanlon *et al*, 2005; Smith *et al*, 2008.

Integration of cross-disciplinary literatures on creativity, innovation, organizational learning, knowledge creation, knowledge management and knowledge transfer literatures emphasize different philosophical underpinnings, not least in relation to organizational learning and knowledge management. Both share common features as management discourses concerned with improved performance and shaped by the same historical and institutional context. Organizational learning and knowledge management respectively emphasize different aspects and de-emphasize others.

For example, organizational learning emphasizes culture management and leadership as a means of socialization and internalization of explicit knowledge into the values and tacit understanding of employees. Learning also stresses links between cognition and action where tacit knowledge is embedded in organizational routines, culture and languages.

Points to ponder

Consider an organization with which you are familiar. To what extent might similarities and differences between climate models for creativity and innovation be usefully applied in practice?

How easy is it for you to make links between climate models characteristics of the learning organization and knowledge management?

Metaphor is useful in effective conversion of tacit to explicit knowledge creation in experiencing links between previously unrelated concepts. We have already experienced an effective metaphor in Dodgson and Gann's reference to the theatre. An interesting metaphor for a comprehensive theory of organizational learning emphasizes the contributions of different disciplines and philosophical perspectives: '... the image we have in mind is of a tree that can support many different branches on which there is a multiplicity of leaves. The leaves connect through their different branches back to the trunk. And the trunk is grounded in a root system that extends widely, thus ensuring a strong, stable base and providing nourishment for the entire system' (Crossan, Lane and White, 2011).

Scarbrough and Swann (2005) make effective metaphoric comparisons between organizational learning as building and knowledge management as mining. Other foci of difference include an emphasis of learning on context and culture management and for knowledge management on information systems. This emphasizes information systems as a means for the externalization of knowledge and the combination of different kinds of explicit knowledge. This has been fuelled by the exceptional developments in technology including the internet, social networking, mobile technologies, blogs, wikis, discussion forums, VoIP, video conferencing and virtual learning environments. The second generation of knowledge management calls for a more proactive approach that recognizes the significance of intangible aspects of organization and points to investment in human capital in pursuit of sustainable competitive advantage. Returning to earlier metaphors this demands, we consider, knowledge management in relation to a building metaphor alongside organizational learning, creativity and innovation – rather than the mining metaphor. This also begins to raise the need for consideration of holding on or letting go. What are the benefits of sharing tacit knowledge versus a willingness to give away knowledge that involves considerable investment of personal resources? This also raises arguments around individual or organizational ownership of knowledge, possession versus practice and, importantly, considerations surrounding managerial control of knowledge. A useful starting point draws on a comparison of epistemologies of possession and practice (Newell *et al*, 2009) which suggests Nonaka's (1994) perspective as objectivist and of possession.

Ontology and epistemology

Crossan, Lane and White's (1999) and Crossan, Maurer and White's (2011) contributions are influential in stimulating research on knowing and the close association with learning. Importantly, each of the 4I processes – intuiting, interpreting, integrating, institutionalizing – makes different assumptions about organizations and society and operates within and across different paradigms (Burrell and Morgan, 1979). Acknowledgement that not everyone agrees with the incommensurability of the paradigms and questioning of the perceived mutual exclusivity of differential philosophical underpinnings is significant. Developing a comprehensive theory of organizational learning Crossan, Lane and White (1999) and Crossan, Maurer and White (2011) demand an ontology and epistemology that transcends classic paradigms (Burrell and Morgan, 1979). The perspective here concurs with such suggestions as essential to informing, advancing and interpreting theory such that it is useful in informing managers and other practitioners how this might be achieved in practice. This is not disputing the value of differential philosophical underpinnings necessary to the academic community, but insufficient in the absence of practical interpretation congruent with increasing calls for business engagement with impact and knowledge co-production at the boundaries of different communities (Van de Ven, 2007, 2011; Pettigrew, 2011). My own multilevel research necessitated crossing disciplines and classic paradigms leading to powerful and useful insights (Loewenberger, 2009) that are relevant to the overall aim of contributions in this volume, concerned with the application and interpretation of OB to HRM. General consensus identifies two dominant epistemologies. Essentially, the objectivist perspective assumes that knowledge exists independently while the practice-based perspective emphasizes that knowledge is contextually embedded (Hislop, 2009).

Drawing on Burrell and Morgan's (1979) classic two-dimensional structure, Schultze and Stabell (2004) developed a framework suggesting four distinctive discourses. Most dominant is the neo-functionalist perspective that implies consensus in social order, as do constructivist discourses, where knowledge management is positively encouraged for the benefit of all concerned. This is the main perspective adopted here in fulfilling the aims of this book drawing on OB and HRM. However, it might be argued that this represents yet another means of managerial control and exploitation. This chapter would be incomplete without raising awareness of alternative perspectives. Rarely are the dissensus perspectives (dialogic and critical discourses) considered with regards to the extent to which knowledge management might not always be positive but involving the harsh realities of organizational life including conflict, power and politics (Hislop, 2009) as discussed in Chapter 7.

Points to ponder

Have any organizations that you have worked for developed IT-based knowledge management systems? Did they embody objectivist assumptions? How successful were these systems? Is tacit knowledge necessary for you to make sense of them?

To what extent do knowledge management initiatives create conflict of interest between senior managers and workers? Give examples based on your own experience.

Implications for HRM and HRD

Evidence suggests cultures that value innovation, human resources and collaboration are more likely to produce innovative products (Arad, Hanson and Schneider, 1997; Mumford and Simonton, 1997; Mumford,

2000) and attract talented creative people. Links with HRM and HRD increasingly attract interest (Mumford, 2000; Searle and Ball, 2003; Leede and Looise, 2005; Shipton *et al*, 2005; Shipton *et al*, 2006; Jørgensen, Laugen and Boer, 2007). At this point it is salient to remind ourselves of the need for attention to dynamic multilevel interactions (Loewenberger, 2009; Crossan and Apaydin, 2010; Crossan, Maurer and White, 2011; Loewenberger, 2011). Recent developments demonstrate the nexus between human capital, the expertise applied by knowledge workers, entrepreneurship, learning, creativity and innovation (Martins *et al*, 2010; Bornay-Barrachina *et al*, 2011). The unique contribution proposed here draws directly on climate factors supportive of creativity, innovation, organizational learning and knowledge management. Informed by influential contributors in the field and by my own research the implications for HRM and HRD are considered.

The existence of what has been referred to as the 'big idea', a clear mission underpinned by values and a culture that communicates what the organization stands for and is trying to achieve, is critical to the link between HR practices and performance (Purcell *et al*, 2003; Boxall and Purcell, 2008). Shared vision, meaning and understanding have been demonstrated as essential to organizational learning, creativity and innovation (Senge, 1990; Marsick and Watkins, 2003; Loewenberger, 2009) and depend on effective employee involvement and communication practices. Related to this is the notion of creative requirement (Shalley, Gilson and Blum, 2000; Unsworth, Wall and Carter, 2002; Unsworth and Clegg, 2010), the perception that one is expected to generate creative ideas. Tierney and Farmer (2002) extend the notion of self-efficacy (Bandura, 1977) to creative self-efficacy, the extent to which individuals believe they have the ability to produce creative outcomes. This extends to the continuous improvement and transformation of the learning organization (Senge, 1990) and points to the need to raise awareness of the desirability and necessity of creativity, innovation, organizational learning and knowledge creation that might not be obvious across all roles, functions and levels and needs to be clearly communicated. Performance management provides valuable opportunity for clarification of creative requirement (Unsworth, Wall and Carter, 2002; Unsworth and Clegg, 2010) in relation to individual and team objectives, as well as for positive and constructive feedback. The subjectivity of creativity processes and the importance of team members and others suggests the appropriateness of multisource feedback or 360-degree appraisal. Linking challenging targets to creativity can provide a basis for discussion, learning and development. Targets might relate to participation in problem-solving groups and facilitation of group sessions, rather than outcomes as externally imposed goals can inhibit creativity (Mumford, 2000). For organizations newly aspiring to be creative or innovative, in the process of transformation or needing to reignite inert aspirations, rewarding efforts to engage in the processes is likely to be perceived more fairly than judgement of outcomes. An interesting and challenging exercise might be to set staff a task to use their creativity skills to design a reward system that would be meaningful, valued and intrinsically motivational in stimulating, supporting and sustaining such processes long term in the organization, department or work group.

Competing agendas of creativity, innovation and learning add complexity to the desirability of specific knowledge, skills and abilities and present interesting challenges to recruitment and selection practices. For instance, balancing sufficient versus excessive expertise is complex in encouraging fresh perspectives from new entrants or those with diverse experiences on which to draw, while avoiding over-reliance on the status quo. The openness to experience dimension of the five-factor model of personality is linked to creativity and to learning (Costa and McCrae, 1992; McCrae and Costa, 1997) and recent evidence suggests a moderating effect on climate factors and correlation with participation in training in creative problem solving (Loewenberger, 2009). Of course, this must be balanced with individual characteristics of co-workers as it is undesirable for all members of a team to score highly on openness (Shalley, Zhou and Oldham, 2004). The significance of intellectual stimulation through challenging work and work group support for individuals very high in openness is suggested as significant to selection, motivation and retention of individuals. Broad experiences increase the pool of resources on which to draw for generation of creative ideas (Shipton *et al*, 2005; Shipton *et al*, 2006). Implications of this suggest immense value in membership of professional associations, conference attendance and networking. Work–life balance initiatives are likely to be significant in creating opportunities to pursue a wide range of interests.

Implications for supporting creative and innovative behaviour, encouraging continuous learning and knowledge creation are explored through the climate lens to consider how this might be achieved in practice. Organizational encouragement (Amabile *et al*, 1996) represents a culture that encourages creativity through the fair, constructive judgement of ideas, rewards and recognition for creative work, mechanisms for developing new ideas, an active flow of ideas, and a shared vision of what the organization is trying to do. Various of Isaksen's (2007a) dimensions might be comprised within this scale, for example, trust or openness, idea support, idea time, playfulness and humour. From the perspective of the learning organization (Marsick and Watkins, 2003) this would also incorporate the inquiry and dialogue dimension, which is concerned with productive thinking skills to express their views, the capacity to listen and enquire into the views of others and a climate that supports questioning, feedback and experimentation. Support for creativity, innovation and learning draws heavily on intrinsic motivation. If this is to be sustainable it is suggested that reward and recognition are based on participation in the process of learning rather than outcomes, on the basis that not all ideas can be implemented, at least in the early stages of climate change. From a learning perspective this relates to continuous learning, enquiry and dialogue (Marsick and Watkins, 2003). While intrinsic elements of reward and recognition systems are more likely to be sustainable in the longer term, financial rewards might not be precluded. For example, these might take the form of bonuses for achieving creative targets, incentives for creative work or for ongoing learning and knowledge development. Cafeteria reward systems might also be appropriate. Recognition for creative work might also take the form of career progression, which is often based on management skills rather than creativity, yet recognition of creative work provides valuable feedback and supports personal and organizational development and transformation.

The significance of two elements of climate, mechanisms to support idea generation and the fair, constructive judgement of ideas, were exemplified and substantially extended through recent qualitative investigation (Loewenberger, 2009). Individuals were passionate about the importance of a work environment where they would feel free to say anything knowing they would be listened to. Freedom to voice ideas characterizes an absence of hierarchy facilitating an open climate where individuals feel the freedom to contribute to a lively flow of ideas, where all ideas are valued and where there is no intimidation, humiliation or ridicule. Evaluation and fear of evaluation (Egan, 2005) are important to creativity from a number of perspectives. All individuals have potential to make valuable contributions. Perceived freedom and trust are significant, particularly as historical portrayal of the lone genius implies introversion. Does the absence of hierarchy and climate exist such that all employees feel free to voice their ideas without immediate or subsequent, direct or indirect fear of intimidation or humiliation? Can organizations honestly say that all ideas are listened to regardless of employees' status? Or do power and influence preside over which ideas receive a fair hearing?

Of course, postponement of evaluation is an important part of the generation of creative ideas that is difficult to achieve in practice, failure of which often limits the effectiveness of 'brainstorming' sessions. Therefore, this is critical for a supportive climate for companies aspiring towards creativity. Such aspects are often also referred to in terms of evaluation, such as avoidance of premature evaluation and deferred judgment that in practice so often prevent effective generation of creative ideas through early termination of the creativity process (Osborn, 1957; Simonton, 2003). Sustainability is again critical here. Having not been respected, listened to, shot down, intimidated, humiliated or dismissed, how likely is it that individuals will feel free to contribute what might ultimately turn out to be **the** big idea with potential for organizational transformation.

Supportive mechanisms represent an important climate dimension where significant overlap exists between creativity, innovation and learning where the need for a champion is advocated (Marsick and Watkins, 2003; Loewenberger, 2009). Champions will either possess or be prepared to develop skills in creative problem-solving techniques and to share these through regular group staff development activities such that they become embedded. Creative problem-solving techniques, of course, represent one of the more familiar and popular mechanisms claimed as supportive of creativity. Evidence is emerging of positive effects of robust approaches to creativity training (Balestra, 1997; Puccio *et al*, 2006). Some organizations achieve this through internal creativity and innovation clubs that meet regularly and to which employees are encouraged to bring actual problems. An integral part of these clubs is practice in the application of creative problem-solving techniques such that these eventually become part of employees' repertoire of skills. Such training will directly challenge staff capabilities, for example in taking responsibility for management of small projects or a single problem. Development of idea management systems for future application contributes to the sustainability of organizational creativity.

Challenging work (Amabile *et al*, 1996; Isaksen, 2007a; Loewenberger, 2009) represents a sense of having to work hard on challenging tasks and important projects. HR models identify challenge as significant to effective performance (Purcell *et al*, 2003). Intellectual stimulation is presented by creative and innovative work and is developmental. Work might be made more challenging by assigning responsibility to an individual or group in relation to a project, task or client account, for example, starting with responsibility for a small project, perhaps, and building gradually in scale and demands. This might take the form of self-managed teams where an individual with the most relevant knowledge and/or expertise would lead. Empowerment, variously termed autonomy or freedom (not to be confused with freedom to voice ideas – above) feature in all models (Amabile *et al*, 1996; Marsick and Watkins, 2003; Isaksen, 2007a).

Work group support represents a diversely skilled work group, in which people communicate well, are open to new ideas, constructively challenge each other's work, trust and help each other and feel committed to the work they are doing. This also comprises Isaksen's (2007a) debate dimension. Of course, team working is central to models of HRM such as that of Purcell *et al* (2003) and to team learning (Marsick and Watkins, 2003). Diversity of skills in a group is likely to promote idea generation, sparking ideas in others, stimulating associational relationships and building on others' ideas. In this way this contributes to knowledge sharing, creation and management as well as to learning and development. Collaborative performance objectives and targets (although with individual recognition) and cross-functional teams, for example, might provide the diversity of knowledge and skills necessary for creativity and to allow for greater integration between teams or departments. Some individuals may be better at generating ideas while others might be more effective in securing their implementation (Puccio, Treffinger and Talbot, 1995). Mechanisms such as creativity and innovation clubs can also enhance effective team work. Organizational impediments (Amabile *et al*, 1996) represent obstacles in the work environment that impede creativity through internal political problems, harsh criticism of new ideas, destructive internal competition, an avoidance of risk, and an over-emphasis on the status quo. Control and conflict (Isaksen, 2007a) negatively influence intrinsic motivation.

Comparative emphasis and philosophies between organizational learning and knowledge management highlight the emphasis on culture management for the former and information systems for the latter. This is particularly evident with reference to the suggestion of mining as a metaphor for knowledge management. However, this de-emphasizes the necessary people-management focus and overlooks the significance of tacit knowledge to meaningful understanding and interpretation of explicit knowledge. The so-called resource-based view (see Glossary) of the firm in the strategy literature (Barney, 1991) has served as an interdisciplinary check on the early annexing of the knowledge management field by information systems and econometric commentators, emphasizing the significance of human and social capital (Wright, McMahan and McWilliams, 1994; Wright, Dunford and Snell, 2001; Morris, Snell and Wright, 2006). The building metaphor of organizational learning has far greater relevance to a proactive second generation of knowledge management that recognizes the significance of intangible aspects of organization and points to investment in human capital in pursuit of sustainable competitive advantage.

Exploration of alternative discourses on knowledge management leads us to question whether creativity, innovation, learning and knowledge management are always positive. Is this emancipation or exploitation? Early theories such as Taylor's scientific management were concerned with managing or limiting the knowledge of workers. Fordism (see Glossary) was literally about hired hands, separation of head and hands (Newell *et al*, 2009). These questions arise:

- Are 21st-century approaches attempting the same thing as early theories such as Fordism by harnessing knowledge of workers and the expropriation of knowledge?

- Is learning always positive and beneficial to all concerned?

- Learning demands considerable personal investment. Who benefits?

- Can we assume that all workers are willing to learn and develop? As the demand of learning often impairs performance temporarily there might also be implications for performance, particularly if this is directly linked to pay. Exploration of alternative discourses also highlights consensus as opposed to dissensus in social order where issues of conflict, power and politics intervene. Much of the approach to investment in people suggested here is underpinned by intrinsic motivation of workers to enhance performance and gain commitment and engagement. Intrinsic motivation is unlikely to be effective in social dissent where such negative influences on creativity, innovation, learning and knowledge management preside.

We end the chapter as we started with input from Schumpeter, who suggested that innovation 'offers the carrot of spectacular reward or the stick of destitution' (Schumpeter, cited in Dodgson and Gann, 2010). There is potential for both positive and negative outcomes. There is risk, but surely the risk of inaction is greater.

Key learning points and conclusions

- This chapter has synthesized creativity, innovation, organizational learning and knowledge management from the perspective of people management. Evaluation of new priorities in thought and action relevant to organizational behaviour and HRM draw attention to the intangible aspects of organization that point to investment of human capital in pursuit of sustainable competitive advantage through creativity, innovation, learning and knowledge management.

- Extant knowledge and understanding of creativity and innovation have been critically evaluated with an emphasis on interactional perspectives leading to a focus on climate that is more accessible and malleable than organizational culture.

- Evaluation of the learning organization and organizational learning highlight direct links with interactional models of creativity and innovation such that similarities between climates for creativity, innovation and learning become transparent. The learning organization continuously transforms itself by developing the skills of its entire people. Organizational systems must be designed to value, manage and enhance skills and career development for continuous transformation such that the learning capability of the organization is harnessed.

- There is much in common between a climate supportive of learning and a climate supportive of creativity and innovation such that synthesis directly informs our focus in this volume on practice. This makes an important contribution to our knowledge and understanding of how such processes can be supported through HRM and HRD by highlighting specific implications for practice of this theoretical and research-informed synthesis.

Discussion questions

- To what extent might a synthesis of creativity, innovation, organizational learning and the management of knowledge, such as that presented in this chapter, overcome competing perspectives? For example, consider knowledge as possession versus practice or the building metaphor of organizational learning versus the mining metaphor of knowledge management.

- What are your views on the so-called knowledge society? What is the evidence in the country where you live?

- Scientific management (Taylor) limited the knowledge of workers. Similarly, Fordism was literally concerned with hired hands. This raises important issues around knowledge as power and influence and of possession versus practice. Discuss fully the issue already raised of whether 21st-century approaches to knowledge management are attempting the same thing by harnessing knowledge of workers.

- The critical and dialogical discourses raise the idea that knowledge management initiatives may not always be in the best interests of all. To what extent do knowledge management initiatives create conflict of interest between senior managers and workers? Give examples based on your own experience.

- Does the use of IT as a knowledge management system always indicate an objectivist perspective? Is tacit knowledge necessary to make sense of these systems?

Case study and discussion questions

CASE STUDY   CoCre8 – enhancing creativity, innovation, learning and knowledge management

CoCre8 is a provider of business improvement and innovative services and solutions including communication and motivation, performance, incentive programmes and events management. Previously an independent small business, the company was acquired in 1999 by a large US group employing more than 1,000 associates worldwide and is now part of a large MNC. The UK office employs approximately 120 associates, mostly knowledge workers, servicing clients in Europe and operating autonomously from the US headquarters and operations in other countries. Organizational structure is headed by the leadership team made up of the MD, the HR director and the finance director. The HR director and MD have both been in post for approximately the last two years, prior to which the company was managed by its founders in very much a command and control style. Members of the leadership team are very committed to new ways of organizing and doing business. To achieve organizational effectiveness and competitiveness in a rapidly changing business environment the challenge is getting the very best from their staff – differentiation based on its people. The company is committed to a culture where staff are kept informed and where knowledge is shared through communication and involvement.

From the perspective of the leadership team, creativity is the very basis of the work of the company and certainly not just of the aesthetic variety, in providing creative solutions for clients. To enhance creative and innovative capability further this has recently been introduced as a major strand of the company's current strategy. Creativity and innovation are highly desired and valued, given high priority and expected. The HR director believes that some have greater potential for creativity while realizing the need exists across all levels, functions and roles in all areas of the organization. Here creativity and innovation mean fun, bringing fresh perspectives, challenging conceptions, involving clients in the development of fresh and exciting ideas and, above all, exceeding clients' expectations, views which appear to be shared by the majority of associates.

However, sharing a common language of what it means to be creative and innovative is very different from knowing that creativity is a requirement for all functions, levels and roles throughout the organization. It cannot be assumed that associates realize the need to be creative, nor understand how they might develop the necessary skills in their day-to-day work, nor that they possess the necessary skills. The misconception might be that creativity refers only to the aesthetics of the design studio rather than a skill that can be applied to improve most areas of the project work across all departments.

Through a largely bottom-up process, the HR director and the MD are jointly transforming the culture of the company to one where associates are empowered and, providing it is for the benefit of the company, 'expect that they are free to do or say anything and that they will not be shot down'.

Mechanisms are in place to stimulate and support creativity for associates. For example, the MD and client services director are involved in training in different 'brainstorming techniques', and have built a creative room with toys, gadgets, gismos and whiteboards. Training tends to be ad hoc as dictated by projects rather than to develop a repertoire of creative thinking skills. Innovation is not necessarily only dependent on creativity. A book club encourages introduction of new ideas and a business intelligence group trawls the outside world for new ideas. A floor to ceiling Perspex display allows insertion of obscure pictures or collages for associates to work out. Two teams of associates were asked to explore new ideas for employee benefits schemes. One team suggested an excellent scheme personalized to employees' lifestyles via the web with the aim of enhancing work–life balance. However, the financial risk was unacceptable. The idea taken forward involved a reward system aimed at companies with large numbers of people doing standard jobs, often of a transient population (for example retail) where turnover is high. Rather than reward positive behaviour with, say, a £10 bonus that is of little value after deductions, the company gives employees a scratch card that could be a meal for two, cinema tickets or electrical goods, for example. Because it is immediate and unknown it is more highly valued.

There are two main departments, events and client services; other areas include the design studio, the technology team and the recently developed food service rewards. However, there is some evidence of fragmentation and a lack of integration, collaboration and cooperation between the various specialist departments rather than a more holistic approach to addressing clients' needs creatively and innovatively. Some associates clearly perceive structures and procedures as too rigid.

Client services team

As head of this team the client services director's perceptions of creativity and innovation are somewhat lower than those of the HR director, suggesting it is not that the business does not rate creativity highly or give it high priority, rather that 'we operate at 150 mph all the time'. Associates tend not to prioritize creativity and rather than allowing time for the creative process 'they're just expecting it to happen'. The potential problem of having a design studio raises concerns that some associates view creativity as aesthetical and, therefore, residing only in this department. Explaining the meaning of creativity and innovation in context: 'It's about creating the right environment, getting a broad mix of people involved, canvassing everyone's views, getting them to think freely, getting rid of the hierarchy in the room and actually express themselves and to come up with lots of ideas... they're not looking for the idea but should come up with lots of ideas, and then filter those ideas down into what's right for our clients.'

Although training in creative problem solving is not a regular occurrence at an organizational level, the client services director initiates sessions with his team and clients, emphasizing that 'fun' is high on the agenda. Associates who have successfully employed such approaches are invited to share and celebrate successes through presentation to others. The client services director believes that given the right environment everyone has the potential to be more creative and innovative and strongly agrees that this should apply in all departments and job functions and across all levels. To support this the intention is to set up further mechanisms such as creativity and innovation clubs to which associates present actual problems for generation of creative ideas using structured techniques. Indeed, the client services director is now championing creativity and innovation and is working with a member of the design studio.

Design studio

Associates in the design studio comprise graphic designers and a copywriter responsible for the visuals. An example of 'Mini mayhem in Marrakech' indicates how the design team worked with associates owning the project to design all the pictures, logos and strap lines. A sense of frustration is clear among members of the design team in not being able to use their creativity as often and as freely as they would like, particularly as their involvement is often in the later stages of the process, which allows them little or no input into the planning but also means their input has to be rushed. Clearly, this is inhibiting highly creative individuals.

Data analytics

The data analytics manager presents an interesting perception of CoCre8 as not very creative compared to previous experience with 'professional radicals' in a company voted the 'Most creative agency of the decade', a perspective that he claims is shared by clients and underpins the recent emphasis on the need to enhance creativity, innovation, learning and the management of knowledge. Some of the approaches with his previous company included virtual teams, a paperless office, structured knowledge management techniques and a database of staff areas of interest and expertise so that the right people could be matched to appropriate projects. 'Hot-desking' encouraged staff to mix with different people and the social side of the organization was described as phenomenal – everyone bonded as a team inside and outside work.

HR management

Internal examples of HR practices demonstrate the commitment to creativity and for 'going over the top' in supporting knowledge creation, learning and development. For example, in recognition of the national 'Learning at work' day, the company has a 'Learning at work' *week*, which involves the members of the leadership team swapping roles, for example, and 'fantasy boss' where associates make suggestions resulting in a memorable visit for one of them to meet their 'fantasy boss'.

Creative behaviour is also reinforced through reward and recognition. Staff involvement and enthusiasm is carefully nurtured with formal and informal techniques including performance reviews and a bonus scheme. One manager specifically spoke about the recent introduction of a new pay and performance system comprising four performance ratings (outstanding, very good, good, poor), noting the absence of 'satisfactory'. Examples of creativity include the introduction of personal development vouchers for staff to spend as they wish on learning and developing new knowledge and skills, not necessarily directly relevant to work (for example they might take piano or guitar lessons or a nutritional course).

Assessing the climate for creativity (KEYS, Amabile *et al*, 1996)

The leadership team recently undertook diagnostic assessment of the climate for creativity and innovation leading to five categorizations from 'very high' to 'very low'. Rather surprisingly, given the significance of creativity and innovation in this organization, results suggested most stimulant scales in the mid-range as given below:

- organizational encouragement (very high);
- work group support (mid-range);
- challenging work (low);
- supervisory encouragement (mid-range);
- (lack of) organizational impediments (high);
- productivity (high);
- creativity (mid-range).

SOURCE Adapted from Loewenberger, 2009.

Discussion questions

- Why do CoCre8 need to enhance creativity, innovation, learning and knowledge management?

- How important was the appointment of the new directors to increasing support for creativity and innovation?

- How is creativity and innovation stimulated, supported and sustained? Give examples. What obstacles are evident? Give examples. Based on models of climate for creativity and innovation what recommendations would you make to assist CoCre8 in enhancing creativity and innovation?

- Give examples from the CoCre8 case study of how effectively learning, knowledge creation and knowledge management are supported. How could these be improved?

PART FIVE
Summation and reflection

11
Coda: HRM and OB – accenting the social

STEPHEN PERKINS and
RAISA ARVINEN-MUONDO

The chapters in this book in various ways explore questions about bringing order to what people do and how they behave in organizational settings. The authors draw attention to ways of reflecting on the social process of interaction between people employed to work in organizations, impediments to purposeful management, and how theorists have suggested identifying, interpreting and addressing these phenomena. Ideas from the HRM literature about how to enjoin the workforce in achieving managerial goals are brought into a dialogue with commentary from the wider management and social sciences, to help in contextualizing the possibilities of HRM-informed choices and working out the likely consequences.

In many senses, we have responded to the invitation extended by Ackers (2002) to recognize on the one hand the centrality of the employment relationship in capitalist society, but on the other hand to address the problem of ordering the relationship mindful of the role of organizations as social institutions. Given that our aim in this volume has been to encourage engagement between HRM and OB as a way of ordering the employment relationship, the intention has not been to limit analysis to what takes place in the work place. Analysis in this sense also requires consideration of contemporary society and social theory derived from our particular reading and exposition of the OB canon. We hope that in doing so, for those engaging in business and management education at advanced levels, the commentary presented in the previous 10 chapters will stimulate suitably sophisticated reflection and discussion.

In this final brief chapter, we flag social trends that are shaping the contexts for OB and HRM, but which have not yet been subjected to extensive in-depth analytical scrutiny in those disciplines' research literatures. Two socio-economic meta-level factors in particular can be seen as constituting the environment for ordering relations in work organizations, in turn being influenced by the outcomes of organizational behaviour: economic crisis interacting with notions of social justice; and technology enabled new social media. Each of these phenomena prompt questions that students of OB and HRM may usefully raise and debate with their tutors and peers in the classroom related to each of the topics covered in the preceding chapters. Consider the impact on how diverse employees develop and express a sense of identity and seek a warrant from other social actors to enact particular roles in organizations (Chapter 1); how talented individuals and occupational groups (Chapter 6) perceive their interaction with organizations (Chapter 2) and organizational leaders (Chapter 5), and their motivation to cooperate creatively or to place limits on willingness to innovate (Chapters 3 and 10), releasing discretionary effort to meet corporate ambitions, under performance management arrangements (Chapter 4). Considerations of social justice principles and media enabling contemporary social interaction also prompt careful reflection on power in and beyond work organizations and the potential for conflict and the legitimacy of particular institutions to channel and resolve it (Chapter 7). They stand at the forefront of debates also around cultural dynamics (Chapter 8) and change (Chapter 9) and the opportunities for and threats to influencing the outcomes of these social phenomena through management interventions.

It is widely accepted that the developed world – and the Eurozone in particular – is in the grip of a crisis of proportions not witnessed since the first third of the 20th century, with the political and social dislocations that followed the Great Depression era in the United States and wartime decimation of people and places in Europe and the Pacific. Economic developments since the autumn of 2008 have been accompanied by an emergence of social movements around the world. The emergence of such movements is evident not only in Europe and the United States, but also including what has been referred to as an 'Arab Spring' as well as early signs of strategic bias among a new generation of leaders in the economic powerhouse of China, with its distinctive centrally controlled embrace of capitalist expansion. Social movements have been animated by a common sense of grievance against the economic orthodoxy established during the 20th century's final decades, sometimes referred to as market fundamentalism.

Deregulated economic activities – offered to society as promising a 'trickle down' of benefits to all – have been seen instead as having been associated with an exponentially growing gap between the so-called 1 per cent at the pinnacle of advanced Western political economies and the rest. Elites have been forced on to the defensive as a social justice narrative has taken a grip in the popular imagination – even if former institutions (such as the trade unions and the political parties they sponsored) have lost once held strength in numbers to focus grievances into a common ideology and its translation into collective action. Government sponsored re-regulation efforts at the national and supranational level – in particular related to questions of corporate governance – equally appear as yet to be falling short in restoring a sense of legitimacy. Ad hoc actions, whether in the form of consumerist looting sprees in urban concentrations or continuing acts perpetuated by only loosely coordinated terrorist cells merely at the extremes of social expression in the heterodox space, set the context for how people and organizations interact through the medium of employment. And this is not to forget that the direct or vicarious experience of growing levels of unemployment is adding to the socialization influences on work and employment orientations to those still in employment relationships, and the next generation preparing to enter the world of work.

To anchor discussion prompted by these considerations, a definition of social justice embraces equality of rights for all peoples and the possibility for human beings without discrimination to benefit from economic and social progress everywhere (ILO, 2011). The definition also includes dignity, attention to rights, and voice for working women and men as well as their empowerment as economic and political citizens – factors for consideration by organizational leaders and managers setting future HRM priorities.

Informed by contemporary developments in economics and politics, although promoting the principle of 'decent work' as a pillar of social justice in social institutions, such as corporations and workplaces, the International Labour Organization (ILO) has highlighted the 'severe challenges' its founding goal of achieving 'social justice for all' faces, given 'the worst global economic crisis in more than six decades' (ILO, 2011). People currently leading organizations, and those such as the readers of this book being developed to lead them in the future, are challenged to avoid falling back on narrowly instrumental management practice if they are to engage people to meet the purposes set for employing organizations despite the severity of the environmental challenge, and to overcome what the ILO describes as 'growing concerns over high levels of social dissatisfaction and the potential for long-term social dislocation'. Exemplifying this at the time of writing – early summer 2012 – there is economic turmoil in peripheral Eurozone countries such as Greece and assaults on the tenure of incumbent elites in government and at the top of major corporations over apparently unjustified self-reward. This is happening in both developed and emerging jurisdictions and provides the backcloth to understanding and managing organizational behaviour in the second decade of the 21st century. Movements bringing into the foreground challengers for office espousing extremely regressive views about ordering socio-economic relations have accompanied such challenges.

A second major influence, as yet unexplored in detail but apparently reshaping the ways in which people interact within and outside employment in organizational settings, is the new medium of online social networking. It is well documented that throughout the eras of human society, new technologies have been created before people have worked out exactly how to use them taking into account social and behavioural norms. This brings new opportunities as well as questions as to whether socio-economic relationships including the employment relationship will be rendered stronger or be placed at risk. Mark Zuckerberg, the founder of Facebook, the most prominent online social networking organization that achieved its initial public offering on stock markets in May 2012, has been reported as saying that he wants to push the boundaries of what people will share, making the world more transparent (Dembosky, 2012). This raises questions about the implications for underlying values and probity of action by individuals and the institutions able to capture and use such shared, highly personal intelligence. For example, the attitudes employees bring to the workplace as to the boundaries perceived legitimate about what organizations may expect from them at the public–private interface may become more permeable. What consequences will this have? What, in turn, may individuals and groups expect from leaders of organizations in sharing intelligence that may have both tangible and intangible economic and political value? In particular, if employees perceive their relationship to the organizations that employ them as ever more ephemeral and virtual, this will have consequences for what they regard as legitimate use of proprietary knowledge to advance their interests.

In conclusion, this book is intended to prepare those interested in a managerial career by helping them understand how to approach the people dimension of organizational settings and activities. In summarizing and commenting on debates in the HRM and OB literature, accenting the social, however, the volume's authors encourage taking thought into practice that is more than solely instrumental. An important goal is to enable prospective managers to reflect on the alternatives for action open to them, guided by values that go beyond over-simplified models of economic rationality, and beyond exclusively micro-level psychological behavioural measurement scales, so as to recognize and actively embrace consideration of the socially constructed character of managerial aspirations and behaviour.

GLOSSARY

bureaucratic leaders The bureaucratic leadership style was one of three leadership styles described by Weber (1947), along with the charismatic leadership and traditional leadership styles. The bureaucratic leadership style is based on following normative rules, and adhering to lines of authority. Leaders are empowered via the position they hold. They impose strict and systematic discipline on the followers and demand businesslike conduct in the workplace. Followers are promoted based on their ability to conform to the rules of the office.

challenging work A creative climate stimulant scale concerned with the perception of working hard on challenging tasks that are important but not overwhelming, and developmental. A positive pressure.

consumerist society A term referring to the high value that is placed on material goods and ownership of material wealth.

contextualism An increasingly popular collection of views in philosophy that emphasizes the context in which an action, utterance, or expression occurs, and argues that, in some important respect, the action, utterance, or expression can only be understood relative to that context (Price, 2008).

corporate governance 'The system by which companies are directed and controlled' (Cadbury Committee, 1992). It involves a set of relationships between a company's management, its board, its shareholders and other stakeholders; it deals with prevention or mitigation of the conflict of interests of stakeholders (Goergen, 2012).

corporatist settlement The modus vivendi between labour and management, here with respect to aspects of the employment relationship, such as job security, often referred to as the 'old psychological contract'.

creative problem solving Osborn-Parnes' six-stage process. Each stage comprises a divergent and a convergent phase useful as a training process for creative thinking incorporating structured techniques at the stages of problem redefinition and idea generation.

creative requirement Expectation of the generation of creative ideas and creativity goals important to creative behaviour.

creativity champion An individual tasked with the responsibility for stimulating, supporting and sustaining organizational creativity and innovation.

creativity New ideas that are novel or original and useful. These ideas are at the front end of innovation and potentially important throughout different phases of the creative process.

employee engagement CIPD definition: 'a combination of commitment to the organization and its values and a willingness to help out colleagues (organizational citizenship). It goes beyond job satisfaction and is not simply motivation. Engagement is something the employee has to offer: it cannot be "required" as part of the employment contract' (CIPD, 2011c).

employee–organization relationship A relationship concerned with micro factors such as the psychological contract and perceived organizational support as well as macro factors such as the employment relationship (Coyle-Shapiro and Shore, 2007).

employer branding CIPD definition: 'promotes the attributes and qualities, often intangible, that make an organization distinctive, promise a particular kind of employment experience and appeal to those who will thrive and perform best in its culture' (CIPD, 2010a).

employment relationship The relationship between employer and employee. According to the International Labour Organization (ILO) it is through this relationship that 'reciprocal rights and obligations' are created between the two parties.

essentialism One of the central modes of representation in philosophy. This refers to the belief that people and/or phenomenon have an underlying and unchanging 'essence'.

Fordism The unique contribution of Henry Ford in adapting Taylorist principles of scientific management to the assembly line in the mass production of standardized products. Emphasis is on linear work sequencing, interdependence of tasks, rigidity, standardization, dedicated machinery and tools later transferred to new industries such as engineering and chemicals.

freedom A climate scale that refers to autonomy, ownership, responsibility and choice.

freedom to voice ideas Perception of a safe and trusting work environment where there is an absence of hierarchy and where ideas can be freely offered without fear of intimidation, humiliation or ridicule.

Hawthorne effect A series of experiments were carried out by Elton Mayo at the Hawthorne Works of Western Electric just outside Chicago in the period 1924–32 in an attempt to improve productivity using Taylorist principles. Mayo discovered that much of the improvement obtained could be explained by group dynamics rather than by scientific management. This was an early move in the direction of systems thinking.

hegemony A term from the radical political philosopher Gramsci (1891–1937). 'Hegemon' is the Greek word for a dominant power. In practice hegemony means the dominant global culture, which is currently capitalism. It is literally unthinkable to challenge hegemony.

human relations movement Disillusioned with the negative side effects of Taylorism and scientific management, researchers made use of the social sciences, such as sociology and psychology, to investigate the workplace. In contrast to scientific management, which saw workers as cogs in a machine, the human relations movement saw workers as human beings and looked at the relation between such aspects as motivation and job satisfaction with productivity.

innovation The implementation or exploitation of creative ideas. Focus is on social validation, acceptance and viability.

knowledge management Formal control and management of knowledge in an organization for facilitating creation, access and use aimed at achieving its objectives. The process of creating, capturing and using knowledge to enhance performance. Organizational capability to value, distribute and use knowledge.

labour flexibility Either the ability of the workforce to undertake different tasks or to employment approaches that enable organizations to access and deploy labour resources flexibly, such as via the use of a contingent (non-permanent) workforce. A company with high labour flexibility is assumed to be able to respond to changes in the market more quickly than less-flexible competitors.

learning organization   An organization that encourages and facilitates learning and development for individuals at all levels and continuously transforms itself.

locus of control   A concept coined by John Rotter (1966). It may be considered a significant aspect of personality. Locus of control is about how individuals perceive to be in control of events in their lives. Individuals who have an internal locus of control essentially believe they have the ability to influence events and therefore outcomes. Individuals with an external locus of control believe that events in their lives are outwith their control and they have little control of outcomes.

logical incrementalism   A perspective according to which strategy is not formulated through formal planning. It is the outcome of an experiential process that unfolds over time and proceeds incrementally as managers learn more about the operating environment and also from implementing small steps of a given strategy.

managerial control   A range of processes aiming to align employee behaviour with organizational objectives.

managerialism   This has been characterized in a variety of ways, for instance as a 'set of beliefs and practices, (that) will prove an effective solvent for… economic and social ills' (Pollitt, 1990). It is generally held to refer to the adoption by public sector organizations of the organizational forms, technologies, management practices and values more commonly found in the private business sector (Deem, 1998).

multilevel   Interdependent interactions between individual, group and organizational level factors.

neo-liberalism   A return to (Victorian) liberal ideology in political economy thinking. It is a label for the market-driven approach to economic and social policy based on neo-classical theories of economics that stress the efficiency of private enterprise, liberalized trade and relatively open markets, and therefore it seeks to maximize the role of the private sector in determining the political and economic priorities of the state. It has also come into wide use in cultural studies to describe an internationally prevailing ideological paradigm that leads to social, cultural and political practices and policies that use the language of markets, efficiency, consumer choice, transactional thinking and individual autonomy to shift risk from governments and corporations onto individuals and to extend this kind of market logic into the realm of social and affective relationships. The term is typically used by opponents of the policy and rarely by supporters (Wikipedia). Key proponents of neo-liberalism include Milton Friedman and the 'Chicago School' of economists.

(The) New Right   New Right ideas were developed in the early 1980s and took a distinctive view of elements of society such as family, education, crime and deviance. In the UK, the term 'New Right' more specifically refers to a strand of Conservatism influenced by Margaret Thatcher and in the United States by Ronald Reagan. Thatcher and Reagan were ideologically committed to neo-liberalism as well as being socially conservative. Key policies included deregulation of business, a dismantling of the welfare state, privatization of nationalized industries and restructuring of the national workforce in order to increase industrial and economic flexibility in an increasingly global market. Similar policies were continued by the subsequent Conservative government and by the New Labour governments, first under Tony Blair, then Gordon Brown.

ontology A range of views about what exists, involving these principal questions: What can be said to exist?; Into what categories, if any, can we sort existing things?; What are the meanings of being?; What are the various modes of being of entities?

open systems theory The organization is regarded as an open system representing a holistic approach that recognizes the interdependence of different sub-systems in an organisation. Complex interactions between individuals and groups, with other organizations and with the external environment determine organizational behaviour.

openness to experience A dimension of the five-factor model of personality. Comprises characteristics that include being imaginative, intellectually curious, cultured, original and broad minded. Different manifestations depend on the focus. Openness to fantasy refers to a willingness to explore one's inner world and to let one's mind wander; openness to aesthetics refers to an appreciation for artistic expression; openness to feelings involves a willingness to accept one's emotions, both positive and negative; openness to actions refers to willingness to try new activities; openness to ideas is intellectual curiosity and willingness to consider new ideas; openness to values refers to a willingness to examine the fundamental values on which one bases one's life.

organizational climate Psychological perceptions of members, the aggregate of which gives an indication of the feelings and beliefs of employees in relation to policies, practices and procedures.

organizational culture Collective values, beliefs, attitudes and norms that influence how employees think, feel and behave.

organizational encouragement A scale of stimulation of a creative climate, representing perceived value and support for creativity and innovation from the top to the bottom of the organization. For example, this may be in encouraging generation of creative ideas through training in creative thinking, encouragement of risk taking, reward, recognition and collaboration.

organizational impediments A scale of obstacles to a creative climate, representing perceptions of excessively formal structures and procedures, destructive competition and destructive criticism of new ideas.

panopiticism A noun constructed to describe the effect on people of not knowing whether they are constantly being watched or not. Derived from the design of the panopticon, a building designed by Jeremy Batnahm to make those in it feel watched, and therefore to behave accordingly.

perception A mental process that involves selecting, receiving, attending to, organizing, structuring, interpreting and storing information in order to make sense of the world that surrounds us.

perceptual process How we make sense of the environment external to us, events that occur in it and the behaviour of other social actors that occupy the space with us. First we select, receive and attend to stimuli (a thing or an event that evokes a specific reaction), then we organize and interpret the stimuli in a way that is meaningful to us. Finally, we store our interpretations so that they can be retrieved later as the basis of new perceptions. Perceptions are inherently interpretations we make about what we see, hear, taste, smell and touch – a subjective reality, rather than an objective one that could be interpreted in the same way by all social actors.

population ecology A management perspective that contends that the key criterion of organizational survival pertains to the ability of organizations to adapt to the changes occurring in the operating environment.

post-Fordism Definitions of the nature and scope of post-Fordism vary considerably and are a matter of debate among scholars. As a labour process post-Fordism can be defined as a flexible production process based on flexible systems and an appropriately flexible workforce since the late 20th century. It is contrasted with Fordism, the system formulated in Henry Ford's automotive factories, in which workers work on a production line, performing specialized tasks repetitively. Post-Fordism's crucial machinery is information and communication technologies. Key tenets include the dominance of a flexible and permanently innovative pattern of accumulation, flexible production, rising incomes for polyvalent skilled workers and the service class and increased profits based on technological and other innovations (Sources: Bob Jessop, Lancaster University, Wikipedia).

post-industrial society Transformation in the economic base from manufacturing to services. The result is increasing numbers employed in the delivery of services and increased consumption of services. This leads to an increase in information handling, requiring higher levels of education and training and specialist knowledge.

principal agency theory A part of game theory (how people interact) that describes the problem that all individuals act in self-interest. For example, if you work for a company, your actions will not be entirely in the interest of the company, but will be affected by your self-interests.

psychological contract There are two main definitions. The first, which is described by Herriot and Pemberton (1995) as the 'classic' definition, derives from the work of Argyris (1960) and Schein (1978). This refers to the perceptions of mutual obligations to each other, held by the two parties in the employment relationship, the employer and the employee (Herriot *et al*, 1997). The second definition which is based on the work of Rousseau (1995), asserts that the psychological contract is formulated only in the mind of the employee and is therefore about 'individual beliefs, shaped by the organization, regarding terms of an exchange between individuals and their organization'. However, in terms of underlying constructs there remains no overall accepted definition of the psychological contract and this exchange relationship is very complex and dynamic, with a wide range of factors shaping employees' perceptions of how they experience the deal. Consequently, the construct of the psychological contract has been regarded as difficult to grasp.

rationalism In strategic management the rationalist approach contends that strategy is the outcome of long-term planning based on objective analysis.

relationship-focused culture In relationship-focused cultures emphasis is placed on building and maintaining relationships with other social actors as a basis of interaction. In such cultures familiarity and trust are often prioritized over task performance. In relationship-focused cultures emphasis on communication and interaction is considered contextual.

resource-based view Focus on strategic management of resources, including the human resource, in creating uniqueness and competitive advantage through value, rarity, difficulty in copying or substitution.

schemas Information about underlying values and beliefs that individuals hold that form the basis of interpretations of the world and value systems, for example self-schemas, person schemas, social schemas, script schemas and role schemas (Clegg, Kornberger and Pitsis, 2008).

social constructivist An approach (ontological stance) to social science that takes the view that all meaning is interpreted and therefore constructed and validated by groups of humans, and therefore nothing is innately right or wrong; this can change in time through societal influences.

social exchange   Exchanges of benefits in which both employer and employee 'understand and abide by "the rules of engagement"'. Social exchange is premised on the notion that 'the bestowing of a benefit creates an obligation to reciprocate' (Coyle-Shapiro and Shore; 2007)

stratification   A term from sociology that considers how individuals are organized into various groups by income and age, for example we know that in the UK there is a lack of social mobility as the children of graduates tend to go to university and then to well-paid employment.

structuralism   A perspective on sociology and management theory according to which social structures (markets, sectors, national business systems etc) are the main source of action as they possess properties that cannot be reduced to the individual agents that constitute these entities.

succession managament   A strategic and deliberate approach to the development of talent to ensure that key positions are filled from within the organization.

succession planning   The process of identifying successors for key positions in the organization and developing and deploying such individuals accordingly.

supervisory encouragement   A scale of stimulation of a creative climate that refers to perceived clarity of goals and communication.

supportive mechanisms   Methods, systems and procedures put in place to stimulate and support creativity and innovation.

systems theory   A system is made up of a collection of elements that are connected in some way. Systems change when elements leave or join. In systems involving people, it is often very difficult, if not impossible, to know how the elements are connected. Systems are self-regulating; they have their own goals. In a mechanical system, these goals are designed in. In systems involving people, these goals develop over time and can be extremely difficult to alter. This is why management of change can be so difficult. If the system has many elements, it is known as a complex system. If the elements of the system can act independently and make decisions, these elements are known as agents, and the system is capable of adapting itself. This is known as a complex adaptive system. Large organizations are complex adaptive systems.

takeover   The purchase of one company (the target) by another (the acquirer, or bidder). The takeover can be hostile or friendly. In a hostile takeover the board of the target company rejects the offer or it takes place against the wish of the existing shareholders. In a friendly takeover the board of the target company accepts the offer as it feels it serves the shareholder better.

Taylorism   (Also known as Fordism.) Taylorism and its modern equivalent, neo-Taylorism, is the dominant management paradigm today. It is named after F W Taylor, an US engineer who invented 'scientific management' principles that were first applied in manufacturing environments such as the Ford Motor Corporation factories in the 1920s. These include practices such as management by objectives and time and motion studies to control the work process. By separating conception from execution, it was thought that work could be more cost-effectively and efficiently carried out, and (craft) workers better controlled.

transactional culture   In transactional cultures emphasis is placed on task performance and communication and interaction is content driven rather than contextual. What is of interest in transactional relationships is the transaction as opposed to the trust or familiarity in the relationship between the interacting individuals.

war for talent   Coined by management consultants McKinsey & Company, this
term refers to the ever intensifying competition for talented individuals with
global acumen, multicultural fluency, entrepreneurial skills and the excellent
ability to manage organizations.

welfare capitalism   Either the combination of a capitalist economic system with a
welfare state or, in the US context, the practice of businesses providing welfare-
like services to employees. This industrial paternalism was centred in industries
that employed skilled labour and peaked around the mid-20th century.

work group support   A scale of stimulation of a creative climate referring to group
diversity, openness to ideas, constructive challenge and shared commitment of
team members.

workload pressure   A scale of obstacles to creative climate concerned with the
negative effects of excessive time or workload demands on creativity and
innovation. While some pressure is desirable, excess can kill creative behaviour.

REFERENCES

Ackers, P (2002) Reframing employment relations: the case for neo-pluralism, *Industrial Relations Journal*, **33** (1), pp 2–19

Adams, J S (1963) Towards an understanding of inequity, *Journal of Abnormal and Social Psychology*, **69**, pp 334–345

Adigun, I O and Stephenson, G M (1992) Sources of job motivation and satisfaction among British and Nigerian employees, *Journal of Social Psychology*, **132**, pp 369–376

Adler, N (2002) *International Dimensions of Organizational Behavior*, South-Western Thomson Learning, Canada

Alderfer, C (1972) *Existence, Relatedness and Growth: Human needs in organizational settings*, Free Press, New York

Aldrich, H E (1979) *Organizations and Environments*, Prentice-Hall, Englewood Cliffs

Aldrich, H E (1986) *Population Perspectives on Organizations*, Acta Universitatis Upsaliensis, Uppsala

Al-Husan, F B and James, P (2007) Multinational HRM in privatized Jordanian enterprises: An exploration of the influence of political contingencies, Thunderbird International, *Business Review*, **49** (6), pp 637–653

Al-Lamki, S M (1998) Barriers to Omanization in the private sector: the perceptions of Omani graduates, *The International Journal of Human Resource Management*, **9** (2), pp 377–400

Allen, R W, Madison, D L, Porter, L W, Renwick, P A and Mayes, B T (1979) Organizational politics: tactics and characteristics of its actors, *California Management Review*, **22** (1), pp 77–83

Alvesson, M (2002) *Understanding Organizational Culture*, Sage, London

Alvesson, M and Deetz, S (1996) Critical theory and postmodernism approaches to organizational studies, in *Handbook of Organizational Studies* eds S R Clegg, C Hardy and W R Nord, Sage, London, pp 191–217

Alvesson, M and Deetz, S (2005) Critical theory and post-modernism: approaches to organization studies, in *Critical Management Studies*, eds H Willmott and C Grey, pp 60–106, Oxford University Press, Oxford

Amabile, T M (1983) *The Social Psychology of Creativity*, Springer-Verlag, New York

Amabile, T M (1988) A model of creativity and innovation, in *Organisations in Research in Organisational Behaviour*, eds B M Staw and L L Cummings, pp 123–167, JAI Press, Greenwich, CT

Amabile, T M (1993) Motivation synergy: Towards new conceptualizations of intrinsic and extrinsic motivation in the workplace, *Human Resource Management Review*, **3** (3), pp 185–202

Amabile, T M (1996) *Creativity in Context*, Westview Press, Oxford

Amabile, T M (1997) Motivating creativity in organizations: On doing what you love and loving what you do, *California Management Review*, **40** (1), pp 39–58

Amabile, T M *et al* (1996) Assessing the work environment for creativity, *Academy of Management Journal*, **39** (5), pp 1154–1185

Amabile, T M, Burnside, R M and Gryskiewicz, N (1999) *User's Manual for KEYS: Assessing the climate for creativity: A survey from the Centre for Creative Leadership*, CCL, Greensboro, North Carolina

Antonakis, J, Avolio, B J and Sivasubramaniam, N (2003) Context and leadership: An examination of the nine-factor full-range leadership theory using the multifactor leadership questionnaire, *Leadership Quarterly*, **14**, pp 261–295

Arad, S M, Hanson, A and Schneider, R J (1997) A framework for the study of relationships between organizational characteristics and innovation, *Journal of Creative Behaviour*, **31**, pp 42–58

Argyris, C (1960) *Understanding Organisational Behaviour*, The Dorsey Press, Homewood, Illinois

Armstrong, M (2006) *Performance Management: Key strategies and practical guidelines*, Kogan Page, London

Armstrong, M (2009) *Armstrong's Handbook of Human Resource Management Practice*, Kogan Page, London

Armstrong, M and Baron, A (1998) *Performance Management: The new realities*, Chartered Institute of Personnel and Development, London

Aronson, E, Wilson, T D and Akert, R M (1994) *Social Psychology*, Harper Collins, New York

Ashkanasy, N M, Wilderom, C P M and Peterson, M F (2000) *Handbook of Organizational Culture and Climate*, Sage, Thousand Oaks, CA

Astley, W G, Axelsson, R, Butler, R J, Hickson, D J and Wilson, D C (1982) Complexity and cleavage: dual explanations of strategic decision making, *Journal of Management Studies*, **19** (4), pp 357–375

Aston, C and Morton, L (2005) Managing talent competitive advantage, *Strategic HR Management Review*, **4**, pp 28–31

Augier, M and Teece, D J (2005) Reflections on (Schumpeterian) leadership: A report on a seminar on leadership and management education, *California Management Review*, **47** (2), pp 114–136

Axelrod, R (1984) *The Evolution of Co-operation*, Basic Books, New York

Axtell, C M *et al* (2000) Shopfloor innovation: facilitating the suggestion and implementation of ideas, *Journal of Occupational & Organizational Psychology*, **73** (3), pp 265–385

Aycan, Z *et al* (2000) Impact of culture on human resource management practices: a 10-country comparison, *Applied Psychology: An International Review*, **49** (1), pp 192–221

Balestra, I (1997) The Osborn-Parnes CPS model: empowering corporate assets, in *Complex Creativity*, ed K Rajah, University of Greenwich Press, London

Bandura, A (1977) *Social Learning Theory*, Prentice Hall, Englewood Cliffs, NJ

Bandura, A (1986) *Social Foundations of Thought and Action: A social cognitive theory*, Prentice Hall, Englewood Cliffs, NJ

Bandura, A and Walters, R H (1963) *Social Learning and Personality Development*, Holt, Rinehart and Winston, Austin, TX

Barker, J (1993) Tightening the iron cage: concertive control in self managing teams, *Administrative Science Quarterly*, **38**, pp 408–37

Barlow, L (2006) Talent development: The new imperative?, *Development and Learning in Organizations: An International Journal*, **20** (3), pp 6–9

Barney, J B (1986) Organizational culture: can it be a source of sustained competitive advantage?*Academy of Management Review*, **11** (3), pp 656–665

Barney, J B (1991) Firm resources and sustained competitive advantage, *Journal of Management*, **17** (1), pp 99–120

Barney, J B (1996) The resource based theory of the firm, *Organization Science*, September/October (7), p 469

Barney, J, Wright, M and Ketchen, D J Jr (2001) The resource-based view of the firm: ten years after 1991, *Journal of Management*, **27**, pp 625–641

Barron, F and Harrington, D M (1981) Creativity, intelligence and personality, *Annual Review of Psychology*, **32**, pp 439–476

Basadur, M and Gelade, G A (2006) The role of knowledge management in the innovation process, *Creativity & Innovation Management*, **15** (1), pp 45–62

Bass, B M (1985) *Leadership and Performance beyond Expectations*, Free Press, New York

Beckhard, R and Harris, R T (1987) *Organizational Transitions: Managing complex change*, 2nd edn, Addison-Wesley, Reading, MA

Beer, M *et al* (1984) *Managing Human Assets*, Free Press, New York

Bell, D (1973) *The Coming of Post-Industrial Society*, Basic Books, New York

Bell, D (1980) The social framework of the information society, in *The Microelectronics Revolution*, ed T Forester, Blackwell, Oxford

Bennett, M and Bell, A (2004) *Leadership and talent in Asia*, Wiley, Singapore

Bennis, W G and Nanus, B (1985) *Leaders: The strategies for taking charge*, Harper and Row, New York

Berry, M (2007) [accessed 18 July 2012] Talent management tops European challenges list, *Perspective Today*, June 19, p 8 [Online] http://connection. ebscohost.com/c/articles/26274200/talent-management-tops-european-challenges-list

Beswick, C and Gallagher, D (2010) *The Road to Innovation...* Let's Think Beyond Publishing, Hitchin

Bhatnagar, J (2007) Talent management strategy of employee engagement in Indian ITES employees: key to retention, *Employee Relations*, **29** (6), pp 640–663

Billington, R, Hockey, J and Strawbridge, S (1998) *Exploring Self and Society*, Macmillan Press, London

Bjerke, J O *et al* (2004) *Private Sector Development Study: Angola (final report)*, Norwegian Agency for Development Cooperation (NORAD), Oslo

Björkman, I and Lu, Y (1999) The management of human resources in Chinese-Western joint ventures, *Journal of World Business*, **34**, pp 306–324

Black, I S, Mendenhall, M and Oddou, G (1991) Toward a comprehensive model of international adjustment: an integration of multiple theoretical perspectives, *Academy of Management Review*, **16** (2), pp 291–317

Blake, R and Mouton, J (1964) *The Managerial Grid: The key to leadership excellence*, Gulf Publishing Co, Houston, TX

Block, P (1996) *Stewardship*, Berrett-Koehler, San Francisco

Boje, D (2000) [accessed 18 July 2012] *The Isles Leadership: The voyage of the behaviorists*, The Leadership Box (Northern Michigan State University) [Online] http://business.nmsu.edu/~dboje/teaching/338/behaviors.htm#katz_michigan

Bolman, L G and Deal, T E (2008) *Reframing Organizations: Artistry, Choice and Leadership*, Jossey-Bass, San Francisco

Bornay-Barrachina, M *et al* (2011) Employment relationships and firm innovation: the double role of human capital, *British Journal of Management*, **23** (2), pp 223–240

Boselie, P and Van der Wiele, T (2002) Employee perceptions of HRM and TQM and the effects on satisfaction and intention to leave, *Managing Service Quality*, **12** (3), pp 165–72

Boswell, W R and Boudreau, J W (2002) Separating the developmental and evaluative performance appraisal uses, *Journal of Business and Psychology*, **16**, pp 391–412

Boudreau, J W and Ramstad, P M (2005) Talentship, talent segmentation, and sustainability: a new HR decision science paradigm for a new strategy definition, *Human Resource Management*, **44** (2), pp 129–136

Bowen, D E and Ostroff, C (2004) Understanding HRM-firm performance linkages: the role of 'strength' of the HRM system, *Academy of Management Review*, **29**, pp 203–221

Boxall, P and Purcell, J (2008) *Strategy and Human Resource Management*, 2nd edn, Palgrave MacMillan, Basingstoke

Boyzatis, R (1982) *The Competent Manager: A model of effective performance*, Wiley and Sons, New York

Branine, M (2011) *Managing Across Cultures: Concepts, policies and practices*, Sage, London

Braverman, H (1974) *Labor and Monopoly Capitalism: The degradation of work in the twentieth century*, Monthly Review Press, New York

Brewster, B, Sparrow, P and Harris, H (2005) Towards a new model of globalizing HRM, *International Journal of Human Resource Management*, **16** (6), pp 949–970

Brewster, C (2007) Comparative HRM: European views and perspectives, *International Journal of Human Resource Management*, **18** (5), pp 769–787

Brewster, C and Pickard, J (1994) Evaluating expatriate experience, *International Studies of Management and Organizations*, **24** (3), pp 18–35

Briscoe, D B and Claus, L M (2008) Employee performance management: policies and practices in multinational enterprises, in *Performance Management Systems: A global perspective*, eds A Varma, P S Budwar and A Denisi, pp 15–39, Routledge, Abingdon

Briscoe, D R and Schuler, R S (2004) *International Human Resource Management*, 2nd edn, Routledge, New York

Brockett, J (2011) *Takeover code changes will increase HR workload*, www.peoplemanagement.co.uk

Brown, A (1998) *Organizational Culture*, 2nd edn, FT Pitman Publishing, London

Bryant, M (2003) Cross-cultural perspectives on school leadership: lessons from Native US interviews, in *Effective Educational Leadership*, eds N Bennett, M Crawford and M Cartwright, pp 216–228, Open University Press, Milton Keynes

Buchanan, D A and Huczynski, A A (2010) *Organizational Behaviour*, 7th edn, Pearson Education, Oxford

Buchanan, D and Body, D (1992) *The Expertise of the Change Agent*, Prentice Hall, London

Buckingham, M and Clifton, D O (2001) *Now, Discover Your Strengths*, Free Press, New York

Buckingham, M and Vosburgh, R M (2001) The 21st century human resources function. It's the talent, stupid!, *Human Resource Planning*, **24**, pp 17–23

Buckley, P and Casson, M (2001) Strategic complexity in international business, in *The Oxford Handbook of International Business*, eds A M Rugman and T L Brewer, pp 88–126, Oxford University Press, Oxford

Buono, A F and Bowditch, J L (1989) *The Human Side of Mergers and Acquisitions*, Jossey-Bass, San Francisco, CA

Buono, A F, Bowditch, J L and Lewis, J W III (1985) When cultures collide: the anatomy of a merger, *Human Relations*, 38 (5), pp 477–500

Burns, J M (1978) *Leadership*, Harper & Row, New York

Burns, T and Stalker, G M (1961) *The Management of Innovation*, Tavistock Publications, London

Burr, V (2003) *Social Constructionism*, 2nd edn, Routledge, London

Burrell, G and Morgan, G (1979) *Sociological Paradigms and Organizational Analysis: Elements of the sociology of corporate life*, Heinemann Educational, London

Cadbury Committee (1992) *The financial aspects of corporate governance*, Professional Publishing, London

Calas, M B and Smircich (1996) The woman's point of view: feminist approaches to organization studies, in *Handbook of Organization Studies*, eds S R Clegg, C Hardy and W R Nord, pp 218–257, Sage, London

Caldwell, R (2001) Champions, adapters, consultants and synergists: the new change agents in HRM, *Human Resource Management Journal*, 11 (3), pp 39–52

Caldwell, R (2003) Models of change agency: a fourfold classification, *British Journal of Management*, 14, pp 131–142

Caligiuri, P (2000) The big five personality characteristics as predictors of expatriate success, *Personnel Psychology*, 53 (1), pp 67–88

Caligiuri, P and Tarique, I (2006) International assignee selection and cross-cultural training and development, in *Handbook of Research in International Human Resource Management*, eds G K Stahl and I Björkman, pp 302–326, Edward Elgar, Northampton, MA

Cameron, K S and Quinn, R E (1999) *Diagnosing and Changing Organisational Culture*. Addison-Wesley, Reading, MA

Cappelli, P (2008) Talent management for the twenty-first century, *Harvard Business Review*, 86 (3), pp 74–81

Carnall, C A (1990) *Managing Change in Organizations*, Prentice-Hall, Englewood Cliffs

Carnegie, D (1936) *How to Win Friends and Influence People*, Simon & Schuster, New York

Cascio, W F (1998) *Applied Psychology in Human Resource Management*, Prentice-Hall, Upper Saddle River, NJ

Chang, E (1999) Career commitment as a complex moderator of organizational commitment and turnover intention, *Human Relations*, 52, pp 1257–1278

Chang, E (2006) Individual pay for performance and commitment HR practices in South Korea, *Journal of World Business*, 41, pp 368–381

Chang, E (2011) Motivational effects of pay for performance: A multilevel analysis of a Korean case, *The International Journal of Human Resource Management*, 22 (18), pp 3929–3948

Chen, H and Chiu, Y (2009) The influence of psychological contracts on the adjustment and organisational commitment among expatriates: an empirical study in Taiwan, *International Journal of Manpower*, 30 (8), pp 797–814

Chesbrough, H (2006) *Open Business Models: How to thrive in the new innovation landscape*, Harvard Business School Press, Cambridge, MA

Child, J (1997) Strategic choice in the analysis of action, structure, organizations and environment: retrospect and prospect, *Organizations Studies*, **18** (1), pp 43–76

Child, J (1972) Organizational structure, environment and performance: the role of strategic choice, *Sociology*, **6**, pp 1–21

Child, J, Faulkner, D and Pitkethly, R (2001) *The Management of International Acquisitions*, Oxford University Press, Oxford

Chua, A (2004) *World on Fire: How exporting free market democracy breeds ethnic hatred and global instability*, Arrow Books, London

Chuai, X, Preece, D and Iles, P (2008) Is talent management just 'old wine in new bottles'?: the case of multinational companies in Beijing, *Management Research News*, **31** (12), pp 901–911

Churchard, C (2011) [accessed 18 July 2012] Employers urged to address talent timebomb, *People Management*, Chartered Institute of Personnel and Development, London, 4 August [Online] www.peoplemanagement.co.uk/pm/articles/2011/08/employers-urged-to-address-talent-timebomb.htm

CIPD (2005) *Change Management, Chartered Institute of Personnel and Development*, Chartered Institute of Personnel and Development, London

CIPD (2009a) Fact sheet: Performance management in action: current trends and practice, Chartered Institute of Personnel and Development, London

CIPD (2009b) Fact sheet: Talent management, Chartered Institute of Personnel and Development, London

CIPD (2010a) Fact sheet: Employer branding, Chartered Institute of Personnel and Development, London

CIPD (2010b) Fact sheet: Learning and talent development, Chartered Institute of Personnel and Development, London

CIPD (2011a) Fact sheet: Competence and competency frameworks, Chartered Institute of Personnel and Development, London

CIPD (2011b) Fact sheet: Talent management: an overview, Chartered Institute of Personnel and Development, London

CIPD (2011c) Fact sheet: Employee engagement, Chartered Institute of Personnel and Development, London

CIPD (2011d) Fact sheet: The psychological contract, Chartered Institute of Personnel and Development, London

CIPD (2012) Work audit: Counting the cost of the jobs recession, Chartered Institute of Personnel and Development, London

Clausewitz, K (1968) *On War*, edited and with an introduction by A Rapoport, Penguin, London

Clegg, S, Kornberger, M and Pitsis, T (2008) *Managing & Organizations*, Sage, London

Collier, J and Esteban, R (2007) Corporate social responsibility and employee commitment, *Business Ethics: A European Review*, **16** (1), pp 19–33

Collings, D and Mellahi, K (2009) Strategic talent management: a review and research agenda, *Human Resource Management Review*, **19**, pp 304–313

Collins, J C (2001) *Good to Great: Why some companies make the leap... and others don't*, Harper Collins, London

Collinson, D L (2000) Strategies of resistance: power, knowledge and subjectivity in the workplace, in *Work and Society: A Reader*, ed K Grint, Polity Press, Cambridge, pp 163–198

Combs, J *et al* (2006) How much do high-performance work practices matter? A meta-analysis of their effects on organizational performance, *Personnel Psychology*, **59**, pp 501–528

Costa, P and McCrae, R R (1985) *The NEO Personality Inventory Manual*, Psychological Assessment Resources, Odessa, FL

Costa, P and McCrae, R R (1992) *Revised NEO Personality Inventory (NEO PI-R) and NEO Five-Factor Inventory (NEOFFI) Professional Manual*, Psychological Assessment Resources, Odessa, FL

Coyle-Shapiro, J and Shore, L (2007) The employee–organisation relationship: where do we go from here?, *Human Resource Management Review*, **17**, pp 166–179

Craib, I (1998) *Experiencing Identity*, Sage, London

Croke, C and Harper, M (2011) The rise of the baggy green as an Australian symbol: the modern invention of an age old tradition, *Sport in Society*, **14** (5), pp 685–700

Crossan, M M and Apaydin, M (2010) A multi-dimensional framework of organizational innovation: a systematic review of the literature, *Journal of Management Studies*, **47** (6), pp 1154–1191

Crossan, M M, Lane, H W and White, R E (1999) An organizational learning framework: From intuition to institution, *Academy of Management Review*, **24** (3), pp 522–537

Crossan, M M, Maurer, C C and White, R E (2011) Reflections on the 2009 AMR Decade Award: do we have a theory of organizational learning?, *Academy of Management Review*, **36** (3), pp 446–460

Crozier, M (1964) *The Bureaucratic Phenomenon*, Tavistock, London

Csikszentmihalyi, M (1996) *Creativity: Flow and the psychology of discovery and invention*, Harper Collins, New York

Cully, M *et al* (1999) *Britain at Work: As depicted by the 1998 Workplace Employee Relations Survey*, Routledge, London

Daft, R L and Marcic, D (2004) *Understanding Management*, 4th edn, Thomson South-Western, Mason, OH

Damanpour, F (1990) Innovation effectiveness, adoption and organizational performance, in *Innovation and Creativity at Work: Psychological and organizational strategies*, M A West and J L Farr, Wiley, Chichester

Dansereau, F, Graen, G B and Haga, W (1975) A vertical dyad linkage approach to leadership in formal organizations, *Organizational Behavior and Human Performance*, **13**, pp 46–78

Davis, T (2000) *Innovation and Growth: A global perspective*, London, Pricewaterhouse Coopers

D'Costa, A P (2008) The international mobility of technical talent: trends and development implications, in *International Mobility of Talent: Types, causes, and development impact*, ed A Solimano, pp 44–83, Oxford University Press, Oxford

De Bono, E (1993) *Serious Creativity: Using the power of lateral thinking to create new ideas*, Harper Collins, London

De Cieri, H and Dowling, P J (2006) Strategic international human resource management in multinational enterprises: Developments and directions, in *Handbook of Research in International Human Resource Management*, eds G K Stahl and I Björkman, pp 15–35, Edward Elgar, Northampton, MA

De Geus, A (1988) Planning as learning, *Harvard Business Review*, March–April, pp 70–74

De Geus, A (1997) *The Living Company: Growth, learning and longevity in business*, Nicholas Brealey, London

De Oliveira, R S (2007) Business success, Angola-style: postcolonial politics and the rise of Sonangol, *Journal of Modern African Studies*, **45** (4), pp 595–619

Deci, E L (1975) *Intrinsic Motivation*, Plenum, New York

Deci, E L, Connell, J P and Ryan, R M (1989) Self-determination in a work organization, *Journal of Applied Psychology*, **74**, pp 580–90

Deci, E L and Ryan, R M (1985) *Intrinsic Motivation and Self-determination in Human Behavior*, Plenum, New York

Deem, R (1998) 'New managerialism' and higher education: the management of performances and cultures in universities in the United Kingdom, *International Studies in Sociology of Education*, **1** (1) pp 47–70

Deetz, S (1992) *Democracy in an Age of Corporate Colonization: Developments in communication and the politics of everyday life*, University of New York, Albany

Delbridge, R (2007) HRM and contemporary manufacturing, in *The Oxford Handbook of Human Resource Management*, eds P F Boxall, J Purcell and P Wright, Oxford University Press, Oxford

Delery, J E and Doty, D H (1996) Modes of theorizing in strategic human resource management: tests of universalistic, contingency, and configurational performance predictions, *Academy of Management Journal*, **39** (4), pp 802–835

Dembosky, A (2012) [Accessed 18 July 2012] With friends like these... , *Financial Times*, ft.com, 19 May 2012 [Online] www.ft.com/cms/s/2/42d2acb2-9fb3-11e1-8b84-00144feabdc0.html#axzz20xxUVLSt

Deutsch, M (1990) Sixty years of conflict, *The International Journal of Conflict Management*, **1** (3), pp 237–263

DiMaggio, P J and Powell, W (1983) The iron cage revisited: institutional isomorphism and collective rationality in organizational fields, *American Sociological Review*, **48**, pp 147–60

Dirks, K T, Cummings, L L and Pierce, J L (1996) Psychological ownership in organizations: conditions under which individuals promote and resist change, in *Research in Organizational Behavior*, **9**, eds R W Woodman and W A Pasmore, pp 1–23, JAI, Greenwich, CT

Dive, B (2008) *The Accountable Leader*, Kogan Page, London

Dodgson, M and Gann, D (2010) *Innovation: A very short introduction*, Oxford University Press, New York

Dodgson, M, Gann, D and Salter, A (2005) *Think, Play, Do: Technology, innovation and organization*, Oxford University Press, Oxford

Dubin, R (1956) Industrial worker's world: A study of central life interests in industrial workers, *Social Problems*, **3**, pp 131–42

Dulewicz, C, Young, M and Dulewicz, V (2005) The relevance of emotional leadership for leadership performance, *Journal of General Management*, **30** (3), pp 71–86

Dunphy, C and Stace, D (1988) Transformational and coercive strategies for planned organisational change, *Organizational Studies*, **9** (3), pp 317–34

Dunphy, C and Stace, D (1994) *Beyond The Boundaries*, McGraw-Hill, Roseville, NSW

Earley, P C and Peterson, R S (2004) The elusive cultural chameleon: Cultural intelligence as a new approach to intercultural training for the global manager, *Academy of Management Learning and Education*, **3** (1), pp 100–115

Eccles, T (1994) *Succeeding with Change: Implementing action-driven strategies*, McGraw Hill, Maidenhead

Economist (2012) [accessed 17 July 2012] The Last Kodak moment? 14 January 2012 [Online] www.economist.com/node/21542796

Edwards, J (1987) *Positive Discrimination, Social Justice and Social Policy*, Tavistock, London

Egan, T M (2005) Factors influencing individual creativity in the workplace: an examination of quantitative empirical research, *Advances in Developing Human Resources*, **7** (2), pp 160–181

Eilam, G and Shamir, B (2005) Organizational change and self-concept threats: A theoretical perspective and a case study, *Journal of Applied Behavioral Science*, **41** (4), pp 399–421

Elashmawi, F (2000) [accessed 8 July 2012] How to manage people across cultures, *People Management*, 30 March 2000 [Online] www.peoplemanagement.co.uk/pm/articles/2000/03/2668.htm

Erez, M (2010) Culture and job design, *Journal of Organizational Behaviour*, **31**, pp 389–400

Ernst & Young (2004) [accessed 10 July 2012] Jose Patricio, president of BP Angola talks about building a diverse local business in Angola, [Online] www.bp.com/liveassets/bp.../Africa_Jose_Patricio_ANgola_2004.pdf

Evans, P, Pucik, V and Björkman, I (2011) *The Global Challenge: International human resource management*, 2nd edn, McGraw-Hill, New York

Fairclough, N (2005) Discourse analysis in organization studies: the case for critical realism, *Organization Studies*, **26** (2), pp 915–39

Feist, G J (1998) A meta-analysis of personality in scientific and artistic creativity, *Personality and Social Psychology Review*, **2** (4), pp 290–309

Fiedler, F E (1994) *Leadership Experience and Leadership Performance*, US Army Research Institute for the Behavioral and Social Sciences, Alexandria, VA

Fischer, R and Smith, P (2004) Values and organizational justice: performance and seniority based allocation criteria in the United Kingdom and Germany, *Journal of Cross-Cultural Psychology*, **35** (6), pp 669–688

Fletcher, C (2001) Performance appraisal and management: the developing research agenda, *Journal of Occupational and Organizational Psychology*, **74** (4), pp 473–487

Ford, K *et al* (1997) *Improving Training Effectiveness in Work Organizations*, Erlbaum, Mahwah, NJ

Ford, J D, Ford, L W and D'Amelio, A (2008) Resistance to change: the rest of the story, *Academy of Management Review*, **33** (2), pp 362–77

Foucault, M (1975) *Discipline and Punish: The birth of the prison*, Penguin, London

Foucault, M (1976) *The History of Sexuality: 1 – The will to knowledge*, Penguin, London

Foucault, M (1984a) *The History of Sexuality: 2 – The use of pleasure*, Penguin, London

Foucault, M (1984b) *The History of Sexuality: 3 – The care of self*, Penguin, London

Francis, H, Holbeche, L S and Reddington, M (2012) *People and Organisation Development: A new agenda for organisational effectiveness*, CIPD, London

Freeman, C (2003) Recruiting for diversity, *Women in Management Review*, **18** (1), pp 68–76

Frost, P J (2004) Handling toxic emotion: new challenges for leaders and their organization, *Organizational Dynamics*, 33 (2), pp 111–127

Gagliardi, P (1986) The creation and change of organizational cultures: a conceptual framework, *Organization Studies*, 7 (2), pp 117–134

Gagliardi, P (1990) *Symbols and Artifacts: Views of the corporate landscape*, Aldine De Gruyter, Hawthorne, NY

Galagan, P (2010) Bridging the skills gap: new factors compound the growing skills shortage, *Training and Development* (February) American Society for Training and Development, Alexandria, VA

Gallo, C (2010) [accessed 18 July 2012] *Innovate the Steve Jobs way: 7 insanely different principles for breakthrough success* [Online] www.slideshare.net/E-M-3/innovate-the-steve-jobs-way

Gamble, A (2009) *The Spectre at the Feast: Capitalist crisis and the politics of recession*, Palgrave Macmillan, London

Gardner, H (1988) Creative lives and creative works: a synthetic scientific approach, in *The Nature of Creativity*, R J Sternberg, Cambridge University Press, Cambridge

Gardner, W L and Schermerhorn, J R Jr (2004) Unleashing individual potential: performance gains through positive organizational behaviour and authentic leadership, *Organizational Dynamics*, 33 (3), pp 270–28

Garrow, V (2008) Talent management: issues of focus and fit, *Public Personnel Management*, 37 (4) (Special issue)

Gattiker, U E and Larwood, L (1989) Career success, mobility and extrinsic satisfaction of corporate managers, *Social Science Journal*, 26, pp 75–92

Gattiker, U E and Larwood, L (1990) Predictors for career achievement in the corporate hierarchy, *Human Relations*, 43, pp 703–726

Geletkanycz, M A and Hambrick, D C (1997) The external ties of top executives: implications for strategic choice and performance, *Administrative Science Quarterly* 42, pp 654–681

Geller, S E (2002) Leadership to overcome resistance to change: it takes more than consequence control, *Journal of Organizational Behavior Management*, 22 (3), pp 29–49

Gialdini, R B (1989) Indirect tactics of impression management, in eds R A Giacalone and P Rosenfield, *Impression Management in the Organization*, pp 45–56, Lawrence Erlbaum, Hillsdale, NJ

Gibb, S and Waight, C L (2005) Connecting HRD and creativity: from fragmentary insights to strategic significance, *Advances in Developing Human Resources*, 7 (2), pp 271–286

Goergen, M (2012) *International Corporate Governance*, Prentice Hall, Harlow

Goffee, R and Jones, G (2005) Managing authenticity, the paradox of great leadership, *Harvard Business Review*, December

Goffman, E (1959) *Presentation of Self in Everyday Life*, Penguin, London

Goleman, D (1996) *Emotional Intelligence: Why it can matter more than IQ*, Bloomsbury Publishing, London

Gollan and Perkins (2010) Employee voice and value during a period of economic turbulence, *Human Resource Management Journal*, 20 (4), pp 440–443

Graetz, F (2000) Strategic change leadership, *Management Decision*, 38 (8), pp 550–562

Graetz, F et al (2006) *Managing Organisational Change*, 2nd edn, Wiley, Maldon, MA

Granovetter, M (1973) The strength of weak ties, *American Journal of Sociology*, 8 (6), pp 1360–1381

Granovetter, M S (1995) *Getting a job: a study of contacts and careers* (2nd ed) The University of Chicago Press, Chicago

Greenleaf, R K (2002) *Servant Leadership 25th Anniversary*, Paulist Press, New York

Grint, K (1993) What's wrong with performance appraisal? A critique and a suggestion, *Human Resource Management Journal*, Spring, pp 61–77

Gronn, P (2002) Distributed leadership, in *Second International Handbook of Educational Leadership and Administration*, eds K Leithwood *et al*, Kluwer Academic Publishers, Dordrecht, Netherlands

Guerrero, S and Sire, B (2001) Motivation to train from the workers' perspective: example of French companies, *International Journal of Human Resource Management*, 12 (6), pp 988–1004

Guest, D (1987) Human resource management and industrial relations, *Journal of Management Studies*, 24, pp 503–521

Guest, D (1999) Human resource management – the workers' verdict, *Human Resource Management Journal*, 9 (3), pp 5–25

Guest, D (2001) Human resource management: when research confronts theory, *International Journal of Human Resource Management*, 12 (7), pp 1092–1106

Guest, D and Conway, N (2002) *Pressure at Work and the Psychological Contract*, CIPD, London

Guest, D and Conway, N (2004) *Employee Well-being and the Psychological Contract*, CIPD, London

Guest, D, Isaksson, K and De Witte, H (2010) Introduction, in *Employment Contracts, Psychological Contracts and Employee Well-Being: An international study*, Guest, Isaksson and De Witte, pp 1–24, Oxford University Press, Oxford

Gupta, N and Shaw, J (1998) Let the evidence speak: financial incentives are effective!, *Compensation and Benefits Review*, March–April, pp 26–32

Hackman, J R and Oldham, G R (1976) Motivation through the design of work: test of a theory, *Organizational Behavior and Human Performance*, 16, pp 250–79

Haines, V Y, Saba, T and Choquette, E (2008) Intrinsic motivation for an international assignment, *International Journal of Manpower*, 29 (5), pp 443–461

Hall, E (1990) *Understanding Cultural Difference: Germans, French and Americans*, Intercultural Press Inc, Boston, MA

Hambrick, D C (1995) Fragmentation and other problems CEOs have with top management teams, *California Management Review*, 37 (3), Spring

Hamel, G and Breen, B (2007) *The Future of Management*, Harvard Business School Press, Boston, MA

Handy, C (1993) *Understanding Organisations*, Oxford University Press, New York

Hanlon, G *et al* (2005) Knowledge, technology and nursing: the case of NHS Direct, *Human Relations*, 58 (2), pp 147–171

Hannan, M T and Freeman, J (1989) *Organizational Ecology*, Harvard University Press, Cambridge, MA

Harris, L and Ogbonna, E (1998) Employee responses to culture change efforts, *Human Resource Management Journal*, 8 (2), pp 78–92

Hatch, M J (1993) The Dynamics of Culture, *The Academy of Management Review*, pp 657–693

Hatch, M J (1997) *Organization Theory, Modern Symbolic and Postmodern Perspectives*, Oxford University Press, Oxford

Hatch, M J (2000) The cultural dynamic of organizing and change in N M Ashkanasy, C P Wilderom and M F Peterson, *Handbook of Organizational Culture and Climate*, Sage, London

Heger, B K (2007) Linking the employment value proposition (EVP) to employee engagement and business outcomes: preliminary findings from a linkage research pilot study, *Organization Development Journal*, 25 (2), Spring, pp 121–131

Heider, F (1958) *The Psychology of Interpersonal Relations*, Wiley, New York

Heintzman, R and Marson, B (2006) *People, Service and Trust: Links in the public service value chain*, Canadian Government Executive

Hendry, C and Pettigrew, A (1990) Human resource management: An agenda for the 1990s, *International Journal of Human Resource Management*, 1 (1), pp 17–43

Herriot, P, Manning, W E and Kidd, J M (1997) The content of psychological contract, *British Journal of Management*, 8, pp 151–162

Herriot, P and Pemberton, C (1995) *New Deals: The revolution in managerial careers*, Wiley, Chichester

Hersey, P and Blanchard, K H (1988) *Situational Leadership: A summary*, University Associates, San Diego, CA

Herzberg, F (1987) One more time how do you motivate employees?, *Harvard Business Review*, 46 (1), pp 109–131

Herzberg, F, Mausner, B and Snyderman, B B (1959) *The motivation to work*, Wiley, New York

Higgs, M and Rowland, D (2000) Building change leadership capability: The quest for change competent, *Journal of Change Management*, 1 (2), pp 116–130

Hislop, D (2009) *Knowledge Management in Organizations*, 2nd edn, Oxford University Press, Oxford

Hocking, B J, Brown, M and Harzing, A W (2004) A knowledge transfer perspective of strategic assignment purposes and their path-dependent outcomes, *International Journal of Human Resource Management*, 15 (3), pp 565–586

Hodges, T (2004) *Angola: Anatomy of an oil state*, Fridtjof Nansen Institute, Norway

Hofstede, G H (1980) Motivation, leadership, organization: do American theories apply abroad?, in *Organization Theory*, ed D Pugh, pp 223–249, Penguin, London

Hofstede, G H (1991) *Cultures and Organizations: Software of the mind*, McGraw-Hill, London

Hofstede, G H (2001a) *Culture's Consequences: Comparing values, behaviors, institutions and organizations across nations*, Sage, Thousand Oaks, CA

Hofstede, G H (2001b) *Culture's Consequences: International differences in work-related values*, Sage, London

HR Focus (2008) [accessed 12 July 2012] Google's lessons for employers: put your employees first, 1 September [Online] http://business.highbeam.com/4710/article-1G1-191316755/google-lessons-employers-put-your-employees-first

HR Review (2011) [accessed 13 July 2012] Employers should consider 'growing their own talent', 22 September, Symposium Events Ltd, London [Online] www.hrreview.co.uk/hrreview-articles/recruitment/employers-should-consider-%E2%80%98growing-their-own-talent%E2%80%99/31653

Huang, X and Van de Vliert, E V (2003) Where intrinsic job satisfaction fails to work: national moderators of intrinsic motivation, *Journal of Organizational Behavior*, **24**, pp 159–179

Huczynski, A and Buchanan, D (2007) *Organisational Behaviour: An introductory text*, 6th edn, Pearson Education, Harlow

Hurley-Hanson, A E and Giannantonio, C M (2006) Recruiters' perceptions of appearance: the stigma of image norms, *Equal Opportunities International*, **25** (6), pp 450–463

Hurson, T (2008) *Think Better: An innovator's guide to productive thinking*, McGraw Hill, London

Huselid, M A (1995) The impact of human resource management practices on turnover, productivity, and corporate financial performance, *Academy of Management Journal*, **38**, pp 635–672

Huselid, M A, Beatty, R W and Becker, B E (2005) A players or A positions: the strategic logic of workforce management, *Harvard Business Review*, December, pp 110–117

Hutton, W (2010) *Them and Us: Politics, greed and inequality – why we need a fair society*, Little, Brown & Company, London

Iles, P, Chuai, X and Preece, D (2010) Talent management and HRM in multinational companies in Beijing: definitions, differences and drivers, *Journal of World Business*, **45** (2), pp 179–189

ILO (2011) [Accessed 18 July 2012] *The International Labour Organisation and Social Justice*, [Online] www.ilo.org/socialjustice

Ingham, J (2006) Closing the talent management gap, *Strategic HR Review*, **5** (3), pp 20–23

Inglehart, R (1997) *Modernization and Postmodernization: Cultural, economic and political change in 43 societies*, Princeton University Press, Princeton, NJ

Inkpen, A, Sundaram, A K and Rockwood, K (2000) Cross-border acquisitions of US technology assets, *California Management Review*, **42**, pp 50–71

Institute of Personnel Management (1992) *Performance management in the UK: an analysis of the issues*. IPM, London

Ireland, D R and Hitt, M (1999) Achieving and maintaining strategic competitiveness in the 21st century: the role of strategic leadership, *Academy of Management Executive*, **13** (1), p 43

Isaksen, S G (2007a) The climate for transformation: lessons for leaders, *Creativity and Innovation Management*, **16** (1), pp 3–15

Isaksen, S G (2007b) The situational outlook questionnaire: assessing the context for change, *Psychological Reports*, **100** (2), pp 455–466

Isaksen, S G, Dorval, K B and Treffinger, D J (2010) *Creative Approaches to Problem Solving: A framework for innovation and change*, Sage, London

Jackson, T (2004) HRM in developing countries, in *International Human Resource Management*, 2nd edn, eds A W Harzing and J V Ruysseveldt, pp 221–248, Sage, London

Jenkins, R (1996) *Social Identity*, Routledge, London

Jenkins, R and MacRae, J (1967) Religion, conflict and polarisation in Northern Ireland, Unpublished maunscript, Peace Research Centre, Lancaster

Jenner, S, and Taylor, S eds (2007) *Employer branding: The latest fad or the future for HR?*, CIPD, London

Johnson, G (1992) Managing strategic change: strategy, culture and action, *Long Range Planning*, **25** (1), pp 28–36

Johnson, G and Gill, J (1993) *Management Control and Organizational Behaviour*, Paul Chapman, London

Johnson, G, Whittington, K and Scholes, K (2011) *Exploring Strategy*, 9th edn, Harlow, FT Prentice Hall

Joni, S A N (2004) The geography of trust, *Harvard Business Review*, **82** (3), pp 82–88

Jørgensen, F, Laugen, B T and Boer, H (2007) Human resource management for continuous improvement, *Creativity & Innovation Management*, **16** (4), pp 363–375

Julius, D A and Butler, J (1998) [accessed 18 July 2012] Inflation and growth in a service economy, The Bank of England Quarterly Bulletin, **38** (4) [Online] www.bankofengland.co.uk/publications/quarterlybulletin/service.pdf

Kandola, R and Fullerton, J (2003) *Diversity in Action: Managing the mosaic*, CIPD, London

Kanter, R M (1992) *The Change Masters, Routledge*, London and New York

Kanter, R M, Stein, B A and Jick, T D (1992) *The Challenge of Organizational Change*, The Free Press, New York

Kanungo, R N (1990) Work alienation in developing countries: western models and eastern realities, in *Management in Developing Countries*, eds A M Jaeger and R N Kanungo, pp 193–208, Routledge, London

Kaplan, R and Kaiser, R (2006) *The Versatile Leader*, John Wiley & Sons, New York

Kay, I T and Shelton, M (2000) The people problems in mergers, *McKinsey Quarterly*, **4**, pp 29–37

Kearns, D K (2005) *Team of Rivals: The political genius of Abraham Lincoln*, Simon & Schuster, New York

Kelman, H (1961) The process of opinion change, *Public Opinion*, **25**, pp 57–78

Kets de Vries, M (1999) High performance teams: lessons from the pygmies, *Organizational Dynamics*, **27** (3), pp 66–77

Kets de Vries, M and Korotov, K (2005) The future of an illusion: in search of the new European business leader, *Organizational Dynamics*, **34** (3), pp 218–230

Keys, J and Miller, T (1994) The Japanese management theory jungle-revisited, *Journal of Management*, **20**, pp 373–402

Kilman, R H and Thomas, K W (1977) Developing a forced choice measure of conflict handling behaviour, *Educational and Psychological Measurement*, **37** (2), pp 309–325

Kim, K, Park, H and Suzuki, N (1990) Reward allocations in the United States, Japan, and Korea: a comparison of individualistic and collectivistic countries, *Academy of Management Journal*, **33**, pp 188–198

Kirton, G and Green, A M (2005) *The Dynamics of Managing Diversity: A critical approach*, Butterworth Heinemann, Oxford

Knights, D and McCabe, D (2000) Ain't misbehaving? Opportunities for resistance under new forms of 'quality' management, *Sociology*, **3**, pp 421–36

Knights, D and Willmott, H (2007) *Introducing Organizational Behaviour and Management*, Thomson Learning, London

Kobrin, S J (1988) Expatriate reduction and strategic control in American multinational corporations, *Human Resource Management*, **27**, pp 63–75

Kochan, T A, Katz, H C and McKersie, R B (1994) *The Transformation of American Industrial Relations*, Cornell University Press, Ithaca

Kock, R and Burke, M (2008) Managing talent in the South African public service, *Public Personnel Management*, **37** (4), pp 457–470

Konopaske, R and Werner, S (2005) US managers' willingness to accept a global assignment: do expatriate benefits and assignment length make a difference?, *International Journal of Human Resource Management*, **16** (7), pp 1159–1175

Kostova, T (1999) Transnational transfer of strategic organizational practices: a contextual perspective, *Academy of Management Review*, **24** (2), pp 308–324

Kotter, J P (1996) *Leading Change*, Harvard Business School Press, Boston, MA

Kotter, J P and Schlesinger, L A (1979) Choosing strategies for change, *Harvard Business Review*, **57** (2), pp 106–14

Kouzes, J M and Posner, B Z (2003) *Credibility: How leaders gain and lose it, why people demand it*, revised edn, Jossey-Bass, San Francisco

Kovach, K (1987) What motivates employees? Workers and supervisors give different answers, *Business Horizons*, **30**, pp 58–65

Krackhardt, D (1990) Assessing the political landscape: structure, cognition and power in organisations, *Administrative Science Quarterly*, **35** (2), pp 342–369

Kreeft, G (2009) [accessed 18 July 2012] Eyeing natural promise, *Redefining the Africa Investor*, 1 May 2009 [Online] www.africainvestor.com/article.asp?id=4980

Kupka *et al* (2009) The intercultural communication motivation scale: An instrument to assess motivational training needs of candidates for international assignments, *Human Resource Management*, **48** (5), pp 717–744

Kuvaas, B (2006) Performance appraisal satisfaction and employee outcomes: Mediating and moderating roles of work motivation, *International Journal of Human Resource Management*, **17** (3), pp 504–522

Kuvaas, B (2008) An exploration of how the employee-organization relationship affects the linkage between perception of developmental human resource practices and employee outcomes, *Journal of Management Studies*, **45**, pp 1–25

Kuvaas, B and Dysvik, A (2010) Does best practice HRM only work for intrinsically motivated employees?, *The International Journal of Human Resource Management*, **21** (13), pp 2339–2357

Kim, S and Ryu, S (2011) Social capital of the HR department, HR's change agent role and HR effectiveness evidence from South Korean firms, *The International Journal of Human Resource Management*, **22** (8), pp 1638–1653

Latham, G P (2003) Goal setting: a five-step approach to behavior change, *Organizational Dynamics*, **32**, pp 309–18

Latham, G P (2007) *Work Motivation: History, theory, research, and practice*, Sage, Thousand Oaks, CA

Lau, V P and Shaffer, M A (1999) [accessed 18 July 2012] Career success: the effects of personality, *Career Development* [Online] http://ecampus.hsmc.edu.hk/moodle/file.php/445/CourseMaterials/BUS1002_1112Sem2_Tutorial02_Personality_Reading.pdf

Lave, J and Wenger, E (1991) Situated learning: legitimate peripheral participation, *Cambridge University Press International*, **4** (4), pp 225–231

Lawler, E E (2005) From human resource management to organizational effectiveness, *Human Resource Management*, **44** (2), pp 165–169

Lawrence, P R and Lorsch, J W (1967) *Organization and Environment*, Cambridge, Graduate School of Business Administration, Harvard University, MA

Leede, J D and Looise, J K (2005) Innovation and HRM: Towards an integrated framework, *Creativity & Innovation Management*, **14** (2), pp 108–117

Lewin, K (1947) Frontiers in group dynamics, *Human Relations*, **1** (1), pp 5–41

Lewin, K (1947a) Frontiers in group dynamics, in ed D Cartwright, *Field Theory in Social Science*, Social Science Paperbacks, London

Lewin, K (1951) *Field Theory in Social Science*, Harper and Row, New York

Lewin, K (1997) *Resolving Social Conflicts and Field Theory in Social Science*, American Psychological Association (APA), Washington, DC

Lewis, R J and Heckman, R J (2006) Talent management: a critical review, *Human Resource Management*, **16**, pp 139–154

Liff, S (1997) Two routes to managing diversity: individual differences or social group characteristics, *Employee Relations*, **19** (1), pp 11–26

Linstead, S, Fulop, L and Lilley, S (2009) *Management and Organization: A critical text*, 2nd edn, Palgrave Macmillan, London

Locke, E A (1968) Toward a theory of task motivation and incentives, *Organizational Behavior and Human Decision Processes*, 3, pp 157–189

Locke, E A (1976) Nature and causes of job satisfaction, in *Handbook of Industrial and Organisational Psychology*, ed M D Dunnette, pp 1297–1349, Rand McNally, Chicago, ILL

Locke, E A and Latham, G P (1990) Work motivation and satisfaction: light at the end of the tunnel, *Psychological Science*, **1**, pp 240–246

Loehlin, C (1992) *Genes and Environment in Personality Development*, Sage, Thousand Oaks, CA

Loewenberger, P (2009) Facilitating organizational creativity: exploring psychological, social and organizational factors, unpublished PhD thesis, University of Bedfordshire

Loewenberger, P A (2011) Facilitating creativity and innovation: what does it mean in practice?, *British Academy of Management Conference*, 13–15 September 2011, Aston University, Birmingham, UK

Lorenzi, P (2004) Managing for the common good: Prosocial leadership, *Organizational Dynamics*, **33** (3), pp 282–291

Lukes, S (1974) *Power: A radical view*, Palgrave MacMillan, London

Luthans, F (2002) The need for and meaning of positive organizational behaviour, *Journal of Organizational Behavior*, **23**, pp 695–706

Luthans, B and Avolio, F (2005) *The High Impact Leader*, McGraw-Hill, New York

MacDuffie, J P (1995) Human resource bundles and manufacturing performance, *Industrial and Labor Relations Review*, **48** (2), pp 197–221

MacLeod, D and Clarke, N (2009) [accessed 13 July 2012] *Engaging for Success: Enhancing performance through employee engagement*, Office of Public Sector Information, London [Online] www.bis.gov.uk/files/file52215.pdf

Machiavelli, N (1999) *The Prince*, Penguin, London

Madjar, N (2005) The contributions of different groups of individuals to employees' creativity, *Advances in Developing Human Resources*, **7** (2), pp 182–206

Madjar, N, Oldham, G R and Pratt, M G (2002) There's no place like home? The contributions of work and non-work creativity support to employees' creative performance, *Academy of Management Journal*, **45** (4), pp 757–767

March, J G (1962) The business firm as a political coalition, *Journal of Politics*, **24**, pp 662–678

Marchington, M (1999) Teamworking and employee involvement: terminology, evaluation and context in *Teamworking: Issues, concepts, and problems*, eds S Procter and F Mueller, Blackwell, London

Marchington, M and Wilkinson, A (2009) *Human Resource Management at Work*, 4th edn, CIPD, London

Marsick, V J and Watkins, K E (2003) Demonstrating the value of an organization's learning culture: the dimensions of the learning organization questionnaire, *Advances in Developing Human Resources*, 5 (2) p 132

Martin, J (1992) *Cultures in Organizations*, Oxford University Press, New York

Martin, J (2002) *Organizational Culture, Mapping the Terrain*, Sage, London

Martins, A *et al* (2010) Entrepreneurship and human capital: A framework for organizational creativity and innovation, *The International Journal of Learning*, 17, pp 15–26

Martins, E C and Terblanche, F (2003) Building organizational culture that stimulates creativity and innovation, *European Journal of Innovation Management*, 6 (1), pp 64–74

Maslow, A H (1943) A theory of human motivation, *Psychological Review*, 50, pp 370–396

Maslow, A H (1970) *Motivation and Personality*, 2nd edn, Harper & Row, New York

Mason, D (2003) *Explaining Ethnic Differences: Changing patterns of discrimination in Britain*, Policy Press, Bristol

Mayo, A J and Nohria, N (2009) Zeitgeist leadership, *Harvard Business Review*, 87 (10), pp 123–159

McSweeney, B (2002) Hofstede's model of national cultural differences and their consequences: A triumph of faith – a failure of analysis, *Human Relations*, 55 (1): 89–118

McCartney, C (2010) The talent perspective: What does it feel like to be talent-managed? Survey report no. 5262 CIPD, London

McClelland, D C (1961) *The Achieving Society*, Van Nostrand, Princeton, NJ

McClelland, D C and Burnham, D H (1976) Power is the great motivator, *Harvard Business Review*, 54 (2) pp 100–110

McCrae, R R (1987) Creativity, divergent thinking and openness to experience, *Journal of Personality and Social Psychology*, 52, pp 1258–1265

McCrae, R R and Costa, P T (1997) Conceptions and correlates of openness to experience, in *Handbook of Personality Psychology*, R Hogan, J Johnson and S Briggs, pp 825–847, Academic Press, San Diego, CA

McGee, L (2006) CEOs' influence on talent management, *Strategic HR Review*, 6 (1), p 3

McGregor, D M (1957) The human side of the enterprise, *Management Review*, 46, pp 22–28

McKenna, R B and Yost, P R (2004) The differentiated leader: specific strategies for handling today's adverse situations, *Organizational Dynamics*, 33 (3), pp 292–306

McKinsey & Company (2001) The war for talent, *Organization and Leadership Practice*, April, pp 1–9

McLean, G N (2009) Anthropology: a foundation for human resource development, in *The Cultural Context of Human Resource Development*, eds C D Hansen and Y-T Lee, pp 3–37, Palgrave Macmillan, London

McLean, L D (2005) Organizational culture's influence on creativity and innovation: a review of the literature and implications for human resource development, *Advances in Developing Human Resources*, 7 (2), pp 226–246

McQuade, E *et al* (2007) Will you miss me when I'm gone?: a study of the potential loss of company knowledge and expertise as employees retire, *Journal of European Industrial Training*, 31 (9), pp 758–768

Michalko, M (2006) *Thinkertoys: A handbook of creative-thinking techniques*, Ten Speed Press, Berkeley, CA

Milgram, S (1973) *Obedience to Authority*, Tavistock, London

Miller, D (2002) Successful change leaders: what makes them? What do they do that is different?, *Journal of Change Management*, 2 (4), pp 359–368

Milliken, F J and Martins, L L (1996) Searching for common threads: understanding the multiple effects of diversity in organizational groups, *Academy of Management Review*, 21 (2), pp 402–433

Mills, C W (1959) *The Sociological Imagination*, 4th edn, Oxford University Press, New York

Mills, C W and Wolfe, A (1999, 1959) *The Power Elite*, Oxford University Press, New York

Mintzberg, H (1985) The organization as political arena, *Journal of Management Studies*, 22 (2), pp 133–154

Mintzberg, H (2009) *Managing*, Berrett-Koehler, San Francisco

Mohrman, A M and Mohrman, S A (1995) Performance management is 'running the business', *Compensation & Benefits Review*, July–August, pp 69–75

Molloy, E and Whittington, R (2005) *HR: Making change happen, executive briefing*, CIPD, London

Moorhead, G and Griffin, R W (1995) *Organizational behavior: Managing people and organizations*, 4th edn, Houghton Mifflin, Boston, MA

Morris, S S, Snell, S A and Wright, P M (2006) A resource-based view of international human resources: toward a framework of integrative and creative capabilities, in *Handbook of Research in International Human Resource Management*, G K Stahl and I Björkman, pp 433–448, Edward Elgar Publishing, Northampton, MA

Morton, L (2004) *Integrated and integrative talent management: A strategic HR framework*, The Conference Board, New York

Mosley, D C, Pietri, P H and Megginson, L C (1996) *Management: Leadership in action*, 5th edn, Harper Collins College Publisher, New York

Mullins, L (2010) *Management and Organizational Behaviour*, FT Prentice Hall, London

Mumford, M D (2000) Managing creative people: strategies and tactics for innovation, *Human Resource Management Review*, 10 (3), pp 313–351

Mumford, M D and Gustafson, S B (1988) Creativity syndrome: integration, application, and innovation, *Psychological Bulletin*, 103 (1) pp 27–43

Mumford, M D and Simonton, D K (1997) Creativity in the workplace: people, problems and structures, *Journal of Creative Behaviour*, 31, pp 1–7

Nelson, R E and Gopalan, S (2003) Do organizational cultures replicate national cultures? Isomorphism, rejection and reciprocal opposition in the corporate values of three countries, *Organization Studies*, 24 (7): pp 1115–1151

Newell, S *et al* (2009) *Managing Knowledge Work and Innovation*, 2nd edn, Palgrave Macmillan, Basingstoke

Nikandrou, I, Papalexandris, N and Bourantas, D (2000) Gaining employee trust after acquisition: implications for managerial action, *Employee Relations*, 22 (4/5), pp 334–355

Noda, T (2004), In focus/the leadership journey: leadership begins with leading oneself, *Leadership in Action*, 24 (5), pp 17–18

Nonaka, I (1994) A dynamic theory of organizational knowledge creation, *Organization Science*, 5 (1), pp 14–37

Nonaka, I and Takeuchi, H (1995) *The Knowledge Creating Company: How Japanese companies create the dynamics of innovation*, Oxford Press, New York

Nonaka, I, Toyama, R and Byosiere, P (2001) A theory of organizational knowledge creation: Understanding the dynamic process of creating knowledge, in *Handbook of Organizational Learning and Knowledge*, eds M Dierkes *et al*, Oxford University Press, Oxford

Nonaka, I, Toyama, R and Nagata, A (2000) A firm as a knowledge-creating entity: a new perspective on the theory of the firm, *Industrial & Corporate Change*, 9 (1), pp 1–10

Norman, S, Luthans, B and Luthans, K (2005) The proposed contagion effect of hopeful leaders on the resiliency of employees and organizations, *Journal of Leadership and Organizational Studies*, 12 (2), pp 55–64

Oakes, K and Galagan, P (2011) *The Executive Guide to Integrated Talent Management*, ASTD, Alexandria, VA

ORC International (2011): *Global Perspectives Survey*, ORC International, London

Ogilvie, J and Stork, D (2003) Starting the HR and change conversation with history, *Journal of Organizational Change Management*, 16 (3), pp 254–271

Ohio State University Leader Behavior Description Questionnaire (LBDQ) (1957–62) [Accessed 17 July 2012] Fisher College of Business, Ohio [Online] http://fisher.osu.edu/research/lbdq/

Orlikowski, W (1996) Improvising organizational transformation over time: a situated change perspective, *Information Systems Research*, 7 (1), pp 63–92

Orr, B and McVerry, B (2007) Talent management challenge in the oil and gas industry, *Natural Gas & Electricity*, December, pp 18–23

Osborn, A F (1957) *Applied Imagination: Principles and procedures of creative thinking*, Scribner, New York

Owen Jones, M (1996) *Studying Organizational Symbolism: What, how, why?*, Sage, London

Oyebade, A (2007) *Culture and Customs of Angola*, Greenwood Press, Westport, CT

Parker, M (2002) *Against Management: Organization in the age of managerialism*, Polity Press, Cambridge, UK

Parnes, S J, Noller, R B and Biondi, A M (1971) *Guide to Creative Action*, Charles Scribner's Sons, New York

Patten, D M (2005) An analysis of the impact of locus-of-control on internal auditor job performance and satisfaction, *Managerial Auditing Journal*, 20 (9), pp 1016–1029

Paulo, M (2006) [accessed 18 July 2012] Angolanisation: A hindrance in the development of Angola?, *Pambazuka News: Weekly Forum for Social Justice in Africa*, 20 April 2006 [Online] www.pambazuka.org/en/category/comment/37716

Pearce, C L (2004) The future of leadership: Combining vertical and share leadership to transform knowledge work, *Academy of Management Executive*, **19** (1), pp 47–59

Pearce, C L and Conger, J A (2003) *Shared Leadership: Reframing the hows and whys of leadership*, Sage, London

Pedler, M, Burgoyne, J and Boydell, T (1996) *The Learning Company: A strategy for sustainable development*, McGraw Hill, New York

Penrose, E T (1959) *The Theory of the Growth of the Firm*, John Wiley, New York

Peppas, S C (2006) Diversity in the workplace: Hispanic perceptions of the hiring decision, *Employee Relations*, **28** (2), pp 119–129

Personnel Today (2010) [accessed 8 July 2012] Landmark disability discrimination case: woman wins payout, 22 April 2010 [Online] www.personneltoday.com/articles/2010/04/22/55310/landmark-disability-discrimination-case-woman-wins-payout.html

Peszynski, K J and Corbitt, B J (2006) Politics, complexity and systems implementation: critically exposing power, *Social Science Computer Review*, **24** (3) pp 326–341

Peters, T and Waterman, R (1982) *In Search of Excellence: Lessons from America's Best Run Companies*, Harper & Row, New York

Pettigrew, A M (1973) *The Politics of Organizational Decision-Making*, Tavistock Publications, London

Pettigrew, A M (1979) On studying organizational cultures, *Administrative Science Quarterly*, **24** (4), pp 570–581

Pettigrew, A M (1985) *The Awakening Giant: Continuity and change in imperial chemical industries*, Blackwell, Oxford

Pettigrew, A (2011) Building capacity for business engagement with impact, AIM capacity building workshop, Woburn House Conference Centre, 23 May 2011, Tavistock Square, London

Pettigrew, A M and Whipp, R (1991) *Managing Change for Competitive Success*, Blackwell, Oxford

Pfeffer, J (1981) *Power in Organizations*, Pitman, Marshfield, MA

Pfeffer, J (1998) *The Human Equation: Building profits by putting people first*, Harvard Business School Press, Boston

Pfeffer, J and Salancik, G R (1974) Organisational decision making as a political process, *Administrative Science Quarterly*, **19**, pp 135–151

Phillips, L (2007) Managers prefer thinner workers, *People Management*, 3 January, CIPD, London

Pianmsoongnern, O and Anurit, P (2010) Talent management: Quantitative and qualitative studies of HR practitioners, *The International Journal of Organizational Innovation*, **3** (1), pp 28–302

Pollitt, C (1990) *Managerialism and the Public Service: The Anglo-American experience*, Blackwell, Oxford

Poole, M E, Langan-Fox, J and Omodei, M (1990) Sex differences in subjective career success, *Genetic, Social, and General Psychology Monographs*, **117**, pp 175–202

Porter, L W and Lawler, E E (1968) *Managerial attitude & performance*, Irwin, Homewood, ILL

Porter, M E (1980) *Competitive Strategy: Techniques for analysing industries and competitors*, The Free Press, New York

Prahalad, C K (2009) *The Fortune at the Bottom of the Pyramid*, Pearson Education, Upper Saddle River, NJ

Price, A W (2008) *Contextuality in Practical Reason*, Oxford University Press, Oxford

Pritchard, R D (1969) Equity theory: a review and critique, *Organizational Behavior & Human Performance*, **4**, pp 176–211

Puccio, G J *et al* (2006) A review of the effectiveness of CPS training: a focus on workplace issues, *Creativity and Innovation Management*, **15** (1), pp 19–33

Puccio, G J, Treffinger, D J and Talbot, R J (1995) Explanatory examination of the relationship between creative styles and creative products, *Creative Research Journal*, **8**, pp 157–172

Pugh, D S (1978) Understanding and managing organizational change, *London Business School Journal*, **3** (2), pp 29–34

Purcell, J (1999) Best practice and best fit: chimera or cul-de-sac?, *Human Resource Management Journal*, **9** (3), pp 26–41

Purcell, J *et al* (2003) *Understanding the People and Performance Link: Unlocking the black box*, CIPD, London

Quinn, J B (1980) *Strategies for Change: Logical incrementalism*, Irwin, Homewood, ILL

Raelin, J A (2005) We the leaders: In order to form a leaderful organization, *Journal of Leadership and Organizational Studies*, **12** (2), pp 18–30

Ralston, D A (2008) The crossvergence perspective: Reflections and projections, *Journal of International Business Studies*, **39**, pp 27–40

Rath, T and Conchie, B (2008) *Strengths-Based Leadership: Great leaders, teams, and why people follow*, Gallup Press, New York

Reilly, P (2008) Identifying the right course for talent management, *Public Personnel Management*, **37** [Online] www.questia.com/PM.qst?a=o&d=5034445483

Resolution Foundation Commission on Living Standards (2011) [accessed 8 July 2012] [Online] www.resolutionfoundation.org/us/current-work/commission/

Robbins, S P (2005) Motivation: concepts to application, in *OM 8004: Managing and Organizing People*, ed C University, pp 163–193, Pearson, Boston, MA

Roberts, G E and Reed, T (1996) Performance appraisal participation, Goal setting and feedback, *Review of Public Personnel Administration*, **16**, p 29

Robertson, A and Abbey, G (2003) *Managing Talented People: Getting on with and getting the best from top talent*, Pearson Education, London

Robinson, K (2009) *The Element: How finding your passion changes everything*, Allen Lane, London

Rogers, C (1947) Some observations of the organisation of personality, *American Psychologist*, **2**, pp 358–68

Rosenthal, R and Jacobson, L (1992) *Pygmalion in the Classroom: Teacher expectation and pupils' intellectual development*, Irvington Publishers, New York

Rotter, J B (1966) Generalized expectancies of internal versus external control of reinforcements, *Psychological Monographs*, **80**, p 609

Rousseau, D (1995) *Psychological contracts in organizations: understanding written and unwritten agreements*, Sage, Thousand Oaks, CA

Rousseau, D M (2005) Developing psychological contract theory, in *Great Minds in Management: The process of theory development*, eds M Smith and M Hitt, pp 190–214, Oxford University Press, Oxford

Rowden, W (2001) The Learning Organization & Strategic Change, *SAM Advanced Management Journal*, **66** (3), pp 11–23

Roy, D (1952) Quota restriction and gold bricking in a machine shop, *American Journal of Sociology*, **57** (5), pp 430–431

Rubery, G and Grimshaw, D (2003) *The Organization of Employment: An international perspective*, Palgrave MacMillan, Basingstoke

Ryan, R and Deci, E (2000) Self-determination theory and the facilitation of intrinsic motivation, social development, and well-being, *American Psychologist*, **55**, pp 68–78

Ryckman, R M (1997) *Theories of Personality*, Brooks/Cole, Pacific Cove, CA

Sagiv, L and Schwartz, S H (2000) in *Handbook of Organizational Culture and Climate*, N M Ashkanasy, C P Wilderom, and M F Peterson, Sage, London

Said, E (1978) *Orientalism*, Routledge and Kegan Paul, London

Salaman, G and Storey, J (2002) Managers' theories about the process of innovation, *Journal of Management Studies*, **39** (2), pp 147–165

Sathe, V and Davidson, E J (2000) Toward a new conceptualization of culture change, in *Handbook of Organizational Culture and Climate*, N M Ashkanasy, C P Wilderom, and M F Peterson, Sage, London

Scarbrough, H and Swann, J (2005) Discourses of knowledge management and the learning organization: Their production and consumption, in *Handbook of Organizational Learning and Knowledge Management*, M Easterby-Smith and M Lyles, Blackwell, Oxford

Schein, E H (1978) *Career Dynamics: Matching Individual and Organizational Needs*, Addison-Wesley, Michigan

Schein, E H (1983) The role of the founder in creating organizational culture, *Organizational Dynamics*, Summer, pp 13–28

Schein, E H (1992) *Organizational Culture and Leadership*, 2nd edn, Jossey-Bass, San Francisco

Schein, E H (2008) *Organizational Culture and Leadership*, 3rd edn, Jossey-Bass, San Francisco

Schelling, T C (1969) Models of segregation, *American Economic Review*, **59** (2) pp 488–93

Schmidt, W H and Tannenbaum, R (1960) The management of differences, *Harvard Business Review*, November

Schraeder, M and Self, D R (2003) Enhancing the success of mergers and acquisitions: an organizational culture perspective, *Management Decision*, **41** (5/6), pp 511–522

Schultze, U and C Stabell (2004) Knowing what you don't know? Discourses and contradictions in knowledge management research, *Journal of Management Studies*, **41**, pp 549–573, in *Knowledge Management in Organizations*, D Hislop (2009) Oxford University Press, Oxford

Schumpeter, J A (1934) *The Theory of Economic Development: An inquiry into profits, capital, credit, interest and the business cycle*, Harvard University Press, Cambridge, MA

Schwabenland, C (2012 forthcoming) *Metaphor and Dialectic in Managing Diversity*, Palgrave, Basingstoke

Schweiger, D M and Denisi, A S (1991) Communication with employees following a merger: a longitudinal field experiment, *Academy of Management Journal*, **34** (1), pp 110–135

Scullion, H and Brewster, C (2001) The management of expatriates: messages from Europe?, *Journal of World Business*, **36** (4), pp 346–365

Scullion, H and Collings, D G (2011) Global talent management, in *Global Talent Management*, eds H Scullion and D G Collings, pp 3–16, Routledge, Abingdon

Searle, R H and Ball, K S (2003) Supporting innovation through HR policy: evidence from the UK, *Creativity and Innovation Management*, **12** (1), pp 50–62

Sears, L (2011) A new way of seeing: insight-led HR, *People Management*, 30 March 2011, Chartered Institute of Personnel Management, London

Selart, M (2005) Understanding the role of locus of control in consultative decision-making: a case study, *Management Decision*, **43** (3), pp 397–412

Senge, P M (1990) *The Fifth Discipline: The art & practice of the learning organization*, Random House, London

Sennett, R (2006) *The Culture of the New Capitalism*, Yale University Press, London

Shalley, C E, Gilson, L L and Blum, T C (2000) Matching creativity requirements and the work environment: effects on satisfaction and intentions to leave, *Academy of Management Journal*, **43** (2), pp 215–223

Shalley, C E, Zhou, J and Oldham, G R (2004) The effects of personal and contextual characteristics on creativity: Where should we go from here?, *Journal of Management*, **30** (6), pp 933–958

Shields, J (2007) *Managing Employee Performance and Reward*, Cambridge University Press, New York

Shipton, H *et al* (2005) Managing people to promote innovation, *Creativity & Innovation Management*, **14** (2), pp 118–128

Shipton, H *et al* (2006) HRM as a predictor of innovation, *Human Resource Management Journal*, **16** (1), pp 3–27

Shumba, T (2010) *Worklife*, RedDog Books, Pittsburg, PA

Sibson, S (2006) Rewards of work study, The Segal Group, Sibson Consulting, October

Simon, H A (1997) Administrative Behavior: A Study of Decision-Making Processes in *Administrative Organizations*, ed H Simon (1997) 4th edn, The Free Press, New York

Simonton, D (2003) Creativity as variation and selection: Some critical constraints, in *Critical Creative Processes*, ed M A Runco, Hampton Press, Cresskill, NJ

Slappendel, C (1996) Perspectives on innovation in organization, *Organization Studies*, **17** (1), pp 107–129

Smedley, T (2011) Nampak Plastics: A lot of bottle, *People Management*, 30 March 2011, Chartered Institute of Personnel Management, London

Smith, A (1970) *The Wealth of Nations*, Penguin, London

Smith, C *et al* (2008) Knowledge and the discourse of labour process transformation: nurses and the case of NHS Direct for England, *Work Employment and Society*, **22**, pp 581–599

Solimano, A (2008) *The International Mobility of Talent: Types, causes, and development impact*, Oxford University Press, Oxford

Spears, L C (2004) Practicing Servant-Leadership, *Leader to Leader*, Autumn (34), pp 7–11

Spicer, A, Alvesson, M and Karreman, D (2010) Critical performativity: the unfinished business of critical management studies, *Human Relations*, **62** (4), pp 537–560

Spillane, J P (2006): *Distributed Leadership*, San Francisco: Jossey-Bass

Stanley, D J, Meyer, J P and Topolnytsky, L (2005) Employee cynicism and resistance to organizational change, *Journal of Business and Psychology*, **19** (4), pp 429–459

Starr, K (2011) Principals and the politics of, and resistance, to change, *Educational Management Administration and Leadership*, **39** (6), pp 646–660

Sternberg, R J (1999) *Handbook of Creativity*, Cambridge University Press, Cambridge

Sternberg, R J and Lubart, T I (1999) The concept of creativity: prospects and paradigms, in *Handbook of Creativity*, ed R J Sternberg, Cambridge University Press, Cambridge

Stevens, G A and Burley, J (1997) 3000 raw ideas = 1 commercial success, *Research Technology Management*, **40**, 16–27

Storey, J (1992) *Developments in the Management of Human Resources*, Blackwell, Oxford

Storey, J (2000) The management of innovation problem, *International Journal of Innovation Management*, **4** (3), pp 347–369

Strauss, G (2001) HRM in the USA: correcting some British impressions, *International Journal of Human Resource Management*, **13** (6), pp 873–897

Syed, J and Ozbilgin, M (2009) A relational framework for international transfer of diversity management practices, *International Journal of Human Resource Management*, **20** (12), pp 2435–2453

Sykes, B (2002) *The Seven Daughters of Eve: The science that reveals our genetic ancestry*, W W Norton & Company, New York

Tansley, C *et al* (2006) *Talent Management: Understanding the dimensions*, (no. 3832), CIPD, London

Tate, W (2009) *The Search for Leadership: An organizational perspective*, Triarchy Press, Axminster, UK

Taylor, C W, Smith, W R and Ghiselin, B (1963) The creative and other contributions of one sample of research scientists, in *Scientific Creativity: Its recognition and development*, eds C W Taylor and F Barron, Wiley, New York

Taylor, F (1911) *Principles of Scientific Management*, Harper and Row, New York

Taylor, F (1947) *Scientific Management*, Harper and Row, New York

Taylor, S (2010) *Resourcing and Talent Management*, 5th edn, CIPD, London

Thomas, K W (1976) Conflict and conflict management, in ed M D Dunette *Handbook of Industrial and Organisational Psychology*, Rand McNally, Chicago, ILL

Thompson, P (2003) Disconnected capitalism: Or why employers can't keep their side of the bargain, *Work, Employment and Society*, **17** (2), pp 359–378

Thorndike, E (1920) A constant error in psychological ratings, *Journal of Applied Psychology*, **4**, pp 469–477

Thornhill, A *et al* (2000) *Managing Change: A human resource strategy approach*, Prentice Hall, London

Tierney, P and Farmer, S M (2002) Creative self-efficacy: its potential antecedents and relationship to creative performance, *Academy of Management Journal*, **45** (6), pp 1137–1148

Todnem By, R (2005) Organisational change management: a critical review, *Journal of Change Management*, **5** (4), pp 369–80

Tomlinson, F and Schwabenland, C (2010) Reconciling competing discourses of diversity? The UK non-profit sector between social justice and the business case, *Organization*, **17** (1), pp 101–121

Townley, B (1989) Selection and appraisal: reconstituting 'social relations'?, in ed J Storey, *New Developments in Human Resource Management*, Routledge, London

Tregaskis, O and Brewster, C (2006) Converging or diverging? A comparative analysis of trends in contingent employment practice across Europe over a decade, *Journal of International Business Studies*, **37** (1), pp 111–126

Trompenaars, F and Hampden-Turner, C (1997) *Riding the Waves of Culture: Understanding cultural diveristy in business*, 2nd edn, Nicholas Brealey Publishing, London

Tsoukas, H (2001) Where does new organizational knowledge come from? Keynote address at the International Conference, Managing knowledge: conversations and critiques, Leicester University, 10–11 April 2011

Tsoukas, H (2005) Do we really understand tacit knowledge?, in *Handbook of Organizational Learning and Knowledge Management*, eds M Easterby-Smith and M Lyles, Blackwell Publishing, Oxford

Tsoukas, H and Chia, R (2002) On organizational becoming: rethinking organizational change, *Organization Science*, **13** (5), pp 567–82

Tubbs, S L and Schulz, E (2006) Exploring a taxonomy of global leadership competencies and meta-competencies, *Journal of US Academy of Business*, **8** (2), pp 29–34

Tung, R L (1998) American expatriates abroad: from neophytes to cosmopolitans, *Journal of World Business*, **33**, pp 125–44

Tung, R L (2002) Building effective networks, *Journal of Management Inquiry*, **11** (2), pp 94–101

Turnbull James, K (2011), *Leadership in Context*, The Kings Fund, London

Ulrich, D (1997) *Human Resource Champions*, Harvard Business School Press, Boston, MA

Ulrich, D (1998) A new mandate for human resources, *Harvard Business Review*, January–February, pp 125–130

Ulrich, D (2001) Alignment of HR strategies and the impact on business performance, in *Strategic Human Resource Management*, 2nd edn, eds R Schuler and S E Jackson, (2007) pp 124–137, Blackwell Publishing, Oxford

Unsworth, K and Clegg, S R (2010) Why do employees undertake creative action?, *Journal of Occupational and Organizational Psychology*, **83**, pp 77–99

Unsworth, K L, Wall, T D and Carter, A (2002) Creative requirement: A neglected construct in the study of employee creativity?, XIth European congress of work and occupational psychology, May, Lisbon, Portugal

Van de Ven, A H (2007) *Engaged Scholarship: A guide for organizational and social research*, Oxford University Press, Oxford

Van de Ven, A H (2011) Engaged business research for impact, AIM capacity building workshop, Woburn House Conference Centre, 23 May 2011, Tavistock Square, London

Van de Ven, A H, Angle, H L and Poole, M (1989) *Research of the Management of Innovation: the Minnesota studies*, Harper Row, New York

VanGundy, J A B (1988) *Techniques of Structured Problem Solving*, 2nd edn, Van Nostrand Reinhold, New York

Van Maanen, J and Barley, S R (1985) Fragments of a Theory, in *Organizational Culture, Beverley Hills*, eds P Frost, M Moore, M Louis, C Lundberg and J Martin, Sage, London; cited in *Organization Theory, Modern, Symbolic and Postmodern Perspectives*, Hatch, M J (1987) Oxford University Press, Oxford

Van Vugt, M, Hogan, R and Kaiser, R B (2008): Leadership, followership, and evolution: some lessons from the past, *American Psychologist*, **63** (3), April, pp 182–196

Verbeke, W (1994) Personality characteristics that predict effective performance of salespeople, *Scandinavian Journal of Management*, **10**, pp 49–57

Vigod, E (2001) Reactions to organizational politics: a cross-cultural examination in Israel and Britain, *Human Relations*, **54** (11), pp 1483–1518

von Neumann, J (1928) Zur Theorie der Gesellschaftsspiele, *Mathematische Annalen*, **100**, pp 295–300

von Neumann, J and Morgenstern, O (1944) *The Theory of Games and Economic Behaviour*, Princeton University Press, Princeton, NJ

Vroom, V H (1964) *Work Motivation*, John Wiley & Sons, New York

Walton, R (1985) From control to commitment in the workplace, *Harvard Business Review*, **63**, March–April, pp 76–84

Walton, R E (1985) Toward a strategy of eliciting employee commitment based on policies of mutuality, in *Human Resource Management: Trends and challenges*, eds R E Walton and P R Lawrence, Harvard Business School Press, Boston, MA

Watson, T (2002) *Organising and Managing Work*, Prentice Hall, Harlow

Watson, T (2006) *Organising and Managing Work*, 2nd edn, Pearson Longman, Edinburgh

Watson, T J (2010) Critical social science, pragmatism and the realities of HRM, *The International Journal of Human Resource Management*, **26** (6), pp 915–931

Weber, M (1947) *Theory of Social and Economic Organization* (chapter 3: The nature of charismatic authority and its routinization, translated by A R Anderson and Talcott Parsons). Originally published in 1922 in German under the title *Wirtschaft und Gesellschaft*

Weber, M (1978) Economy and society, in *Economy and Society: an outline of interpretive sociology, two volumes*, eds G Roth and C Wittich, University of California Press, Berkeley, CA

Weiss, J W (1996) *Organizational Behaviour and Change: Managing diversity, cross-cultural dynamics and ethics*, West Publishing Company, New York

Whipp, R (2003) Managing strategic change, in *The Oxford Handbook of Strategy Vol 2: A strategy overview and competitive strategy*, eds D Faulkner and A Campbell, pp 237–66, Oxford University Press, Oxford

Wiley, C (1997) *What motivates employees according to over 40 years of motivation surveys?*, International Journal of Manpower, **18** (3), pp 263–281

Williams, W M and Yang, L T (1999) Organizational creativity, in *Handbook of Creativity*, R J Sternberg, Cambridge University Press, Cambridge

Wise, L R and Tschirhart, M (2000) Examining empirical evidence on diversity effects: how useful is diversity research for public sector managers?, *Public Administration Review*, **60** (5), pp 386–394

Woodman, R W, Sawyer, J E and Griffin, R W (1993) Toward a theory of organizational creativity, *Academy of Management Review*, **18** (2), pp 293–321

Woods, P A (2004), Democratic leadership: Drawing distinctions with distributed leadership, *International Journal of Leadership in Education*, **7** (6), pp 3–26

Wrench, J (2005) Diversity management can be bad for you, *Race and Class*, **46** (3), pp 73–84

Wright, P M, Dunford, B B and Snell, S A (2001) Human resources and the resource based view of the firm, *Journal of Management*, **27** (6), pp 701–721

Wright, P M, McMahan, G C and McWilliams, A (1994) Human resources and sustained competitive advantage: a resource-based perspective, *International Journal of Human Resource Management*, **5** (2), pp 301–326

Wright, P and Snell, S (1998) Toward a unifying framework for exploring fit and flexibility in strategic human resource management, *Academy of Management Review*, **23** (4), pp 756–772

INDEX

NB: page numbers in *italic* indicate figures or tables